D0549454

STA'   RD LOAN
rthy Tyd OCCUPATIONAL HEALTH
AND SAFETY LAW

OCCUPATIONAL HEALTH AND SAFETY LAW

Third Edition

Brenda Barrett

Professor of Law
Middlesex University

Richard Howells

Emeritus Professor of Law
University of Westminster

London · Hong Kong · Johannesburg · Melbourne · Singapore · Washington DC

Pitman Publishing
128 Long Acre, London WC2E 9AN
Tel: 0171 447 2000   Fax: 0171 240 5771
A Division of Pearson Professional Limited

First published as *Health and Safety Law* in 1993
Second edition published as *Occupational Health and Safety Law* in 1995
Third edition 1997

© Pearson Professional Limited 1997

The right of Brenda Barrett and Richard Howells to be identified as authors
of this work has been asserted by them in accordance with the Copyright,
Designs and Patents Act 1988.

British Library Cataloguing in Publication Data
A CIP catalogue record for this book can be obtained from the British Library.

ISBN 0 7121 1067 4

10 9 8 7 6 5 4 3 2 1

Typeset by WestKey Limited, Falmouth, Cornwall

Transferred to digital print on demand 2001

Printed and bound in Great Britain by Antony Rowe Ltd, Eastbourne

CONTENTS

Part three
COMPENSATION FOR INDUSTRIAL ACCIDENTS

PREFACE

The first edition of this book was prepared in 1992 and its Preface suggested that the impact, which was then being experienced, of European Directives on British health and safety law made it appropriate to present a book at that time. The enthusiasm with which the Community was at that time utilising Article 118A of the Treaty of Rome as the basis for Directives was then about to impact on domestic occupational health and safety law and the authors' objective was to present a book which took account of the new laws which were then about to be brought into effect. They recognised, however, and expressly acknowledged in their Preface, that their book might need revision once the new laws were in place. In 1993 six important sets of Regulations (now colloquially referred to as the 'Six Pack') became part of British law; in the view of the authors it quickly became necessary to recognise, more fully than the first edition was able to do, the impact of these Regulations on the system which has been in operation since the enactment of The Health and Safety at Work Act 1974. Therefore the second edition was published in 1995. However the law has continued to develop both through new regulations and through judicial interpretation and it is now appropriate to produce a third edition to incorporate these developments and reflect their impact on the remaining law.

The intention of this book remains that of catering for persons who have a special interest in occupational health and safety although they may not have studied law in depth. It will be useful to students undertaking HND or undergraduate courses in areas such as business studies, environmental studies or engineering. It should be particularly valuable to students undertaking postgraduate or post-experience vocationally oriented studies, such as in safety management, occupational health, personnel management or business management. It may also be of value to students studying more general topics such as employment law.

The authors believe it is so structured that it may be of assistance to managers who have special responsibilities for occupational health and safety. It may, for example, provide a good foundation for practitioners undertaking NVQs in occupational health and safety.

Finally, students may find it helpful to supplement their use of this book by reference to a companion volume, *Cases and Materials in Occupational Health and Safety*, which the authors published in 1995, through Cavendish Publishing Limited. The latter is intended as a reference book for those who do not have ready access to law reports and statutory materials, to enable them to go directly to the materials upon which the authors have drawn when writing this book.

September 1996
BB
RH

TABLE OF CASES

TABLE OF STATUTES

TABLE OF STATUTORY INSTRUMENTS

OFFICIAL REPORTS

EC DIRECTIVES

EC REGULATIONS

1

INTRODUCTION

1. General

Every year the Health and Safety Commission publishes a report which includes official statistics both as to the number of people killed or injured in connection with work and as to the activities of the Health and Safety Commission and Executive in striving to improve the safety record of British industry. The Annual Report for 1994/95 recorded that in 1993/94 (the most recent year for which full statistics were available) while the number of reported injuries fell for the fourth successive year there had nevertheless been 151,900 injuries to employees, of which 245 were fatal. Moreover for a variety of reasons these figures may give less than a full picture: there may be under-reporting, the system of reporting does not take account of injuries suffered by members of the public, and the only injuries which are recorded are those which have caused three or more days absence from work.

The rate of major injuries has fallen greatly in recent years and is expected to have fallen to its lowest ever in 1994/95: it is likely to be as low as one per 100,000 employees. Similarly fatal accidents are less than a quarter of those at the beginning of the 1960s and less than half of those in the 1970s. This improvement is due to changes in employment away from the heavy industries. Changes in work demands have, on the other hand, led to new forms of health risk, in many cases related to stress, both physical and mental. Physical strain injuries alone cause 5.5 million working days to be lost every year and the 1990s have witnessed the first litigation by employees against their employers for compensation for ill-health arising out of mental stress suffered at work.

A recent study by the Health and Safety Executive showed that the overall cost of work-related ill-health, accidents and safety-related incidents amounts to between £11 billion and £16 billion per annum. This is between 1 and 3% of the Gross Domestic Product; put another way the cost is equal to over 5% of the annual trading profits of UK industrial companies, over £170 for each person employed. The cost to individual workers and their families is estimated to be almost £5 billion a year even after making allowances for social security payments and common law damages.

These statistics bear testimony to the importance of maintaining efforts to achieve health and safety at the workplace.

HISTORICAL BACKGROUND

2. Legal responsibility for accidents

The practice of attributing legal responsibility for work-related injuries and ill-health is essentially a characteristic of industrial societies. Although people must always be prone to suffer injury when working in the home or in the fields, the need to attribute blame for such injuries does not seem to arise until society reaches the point of industrial development at which small-scale work activity at home is replaced by larger-scale activity carried out in special workplaces. England reached this stage of industrialisation in the nineteenth century and it was then that questions of occupational health and safety first came before Parliament and the law courts.

3. Early compensation law

Today, everyone agrees that it is preferable to prevent injuries rather than to mitigate their consequences. In the *laissez-faire* climate of earlier times, however, there was a belief that if employers had to pay compensation to workers for the injuries they suffered as a result of work this would be sufficient to motivate them to minimise the opportunity for injury. However, although it was acknowledged, after the case of *Priestley* v. *Fowler* (1837), that someone who suffered an injury at the workplace might claim damages from the wrongdoer who had caused the injury, in practice it was very difficult for any industrial accident victim to bring a claim in the common law courts, and few obtained compensation.

Even today, it is sometimes argued that in a free market economic forces should be sufficient to ensure safety at the workplace. Those who use this argument maintain that any organisation having such a disregard for safe systems of operation that it failed to manage its activities so as to protect its plant, equipment and workers from being damaged or destroyed in the course of production would incur such heavy replacement and compensation costs that it would be bankrupt. The argument is highly questionable and Western society is unwilling to put the theory to the test!

4. Employer's liability insurance

Unfortunately, the free market theory fails to ensure that those who are injured are adequately compensated. It can be small comfort for the victim to know that the accident has put the organisation out of business; moreover, the bankrupt organisation may not be able to compensate the victims of its unsafe practices. Before the end of the nineteenth century it was realised that it was more important to compensate the victim than to punish the wrongdoer by inflicting the cost of compensation on the wrongdoer personally. The argument that safety might be achieved through making wrongdoers pay personally for the injuries they had caused was seriously weakened by the introduction of employer's liability insurance.

5. Growth of health and safety legislation

Towards the middle of the nineteenth century Parliament intervened to specify minimum standards for certain workplaces, and to empower the making of detailed regulations to cover particular hazards in those workplaces because economic forces were not operating to ensure healthy and safe working environments, particularly in factories and mines. It was, however, only 150 years later, with the passing of the Health and Safety at Work Act 1974, that there was legislation for general application in relation to health and safety in every workplace in Great Britain. The Health and Safety (Northern Ireland) Order 1978 brought similar provisions into effect in that part of the United Kingdom.

THEMES IN MODERN LAW

6. Prevention of injury

The era which opened with the Health and Safety at Work Act finally shifted the emphasis from compensation of the injured to prevention of injury. Legislation nowadays demands the installation and maintenance of safe systems intended to ensure that accidents do not occur and health is not endangered. The decline of the 'smoke stack industries', and the introduction of advanced technology, has now shifted the concerns over safety away from the traditional problems of a dirty working environment and dangerous machinery. The law now acknowledges the principles of ergonomics; its emphasis is upon providing the worker with not only safe plant and equipment, but also with a safe working environment and safe systems of work. British legislation is also concerned to protect persons other than persons at work from exposure to hazards created by persons at work.

Twentieth-century legislation stipulates safety standards, provides for inspectors to monitor that these standards are observed, and provides, in the last instance, for criminal sanctions on those who do not observe the legislative requirements.

7. Continuing importance of compensation

The opening paragraphs of this chapter provide dramatic evidence that in spite of sophisticated safety laws, and sincere efforts to observe them, accidents still do occur and working conditions still do cause ill-health. The necessity remains, therefore, for mechanisms to compensate the victims of work-related injuries. Much income maintenance is now provided through statutory sick pay and social security, but the common law action for damages remains important.

8. Risk management

In recent years it has been fashionable to think of successful entrepreneurial activity as a matter of risk management and that concept has now found its way into considerations of occupational health and safety. Arguably it has always been there but recently it has been more openly acknowledged. Given that absolute health and safety is not achievable, the questions which have to be answered include: What level of risk is acceptable? Who should have responsibility for determining when that level has been identified? To what extent should this responsibility be shared by, or allocated between, government, employers and the workforce?

On the one hand the Chair of the Health and Safety Commission stated, when launching a recent Annual Report:

> No-one can be in any doubt that the public expenditure is tight and getting tighter ...in the face of any further pressures we will have to look carefully at our priorities.

By this the Chair presumably inferred that the role of the enforcement agency might need to be reviewed. At the same time, within that Report, the Commission's own *Review of Regulation* (May 1994) was constantly referred to, especially as identifying the need to pay 'due regard to cost as well as benefits' of regulation. This suggests legislation may be repealed if the evidence is that it is not cost effective. On the other hand the Management of Health and Safety at Work Regulations 1992 impose on employers an onerous reponsibility in the form of a broad general duty to identify and set up systems to respond to risks associated with the conduct of their enterprises. Finally the European Framwork Directive on which these Regulations are based envisages a greater role for a trained workforce to work in partnership with employers in achieving safety. These developments indicate some change in the roles of, and balance of responsibilites between, government, employers and workforce.

SCOPE OF THIS TEXT

9. Focus on English law

The United Kingdom is generally regarded as a single state, and indeed it is so regarded by the EU, but, as its name suggests, there is more than one component. There are three jurisdictions in the UK, namely England and Wales, Scotland, and Northern Ireland, and the laws of these three jurisdictions are not necessarily the same.

The occupational health and safety law of each of the three jurisdictions is very similar but this book will focus on English law and endeavour to explain how it operates today in relation to both the prevention of workplace accidents and the compensation of accident victims. The text in places indicates specifically the application of particular aspects of the law within the separate jurisdictions.

10. Relationship with the European Union

There are few areas of English law which can be considered nowadays without reference to the role of the European Community in the development of that law in recent years. Occupational health and safety law is certainly no exception and there is every indication that, post Maastricht, the European Union will remain actively concerned with working conditions in Member States. The United Kingdom has, in the area of preventative legislation, endeavoured to paste Community requirements into the framework established by the Health and Safety at Work Act 1974 and the text will address how this has been done. At the present time the European Union has had no impact on accident compensation within the United Kingdom.

11. Health and safety law in context

In order to explain the law, it must be put into context, and to achieve this it is necessary to consider the following matters:

(a) the legal system within which occupational health and safety laws are enforced
(b) the historical context from which current law has developed
(c) other similar systems of regulatory control to which occupational health and safety laws relate – such as environmental protection, road traffic and employment protection laws.

5

Part One

OCCUPATIONAL HEALTH AND SAFETY LAW IN CONTEXT

2

OCCUPATIONAL HEALTH AND SAFETY IN THE ENGLISH LEGAL SYSTEM

1. Introduction

Laws have been formulated to provide systems and standards for workplaces; when these laws are not observed, or if someone suffers personal injury at the workplace, the law may be invoked and there may be a trial in a court. Most of this book will be concerned with English occupational health and safety laws; it may therefore be helpful to begin by outlining the ways in which laws are made in England, with some explanation as to how the European Union impacts on the development of English law. This chapter will also describe, in equally broad outline, the system of courts in which health and safety disputes are heard. The chapter will conclude with a short discussion of principles of liability.

2. Sources of law

There are, in the English legal system, two principal sources of law: decided cases and Acts of Parliament.

CASE LAW

3. Common law system

The English legal system is a common law system. In any legal system it is the task of the judge to identify and apply the relevant rules of law. When the English common law system first began, at least 500 years ago, judges made their decisions by reference to what people normally did – thus elevating custom into law. There have now been so many judicial decisions that judges do not often have to investigate custom to find rules of law; they look instead to the decisions of other judges.

4. Law reports

For hundreds of years there has been a system of recording the details of cases and the judgments given in them. For over a hundred years these reports have been of a very high standard. While law reporting remains largely in the hands of commercial publishing houses, it is now common practice for the publishers to use typescripts supplied to them by judges themselves.

In recent years law reports have become readily accessible, for example in university law libraries, and through special 'on-line' and other data retrieval systems. The most authoritative printed law reports are those produced by the Incorporated Council of Law Reporting. These publishers produce *The Law Reports*, a series including Appeal Cases (cited as AC) and Queen's/King's Bench Division (QBD/KBD), and the Weekly Law Reports (WLR). Other major series are All England Reports (All ER), Industrial Case Reports (ICR) and, in employment law, Industrial Relations Law Reports (IRLR). To facilitate reference, libraries shelve reports by series and, within a series, in chronological order. Cases are cited thus: name of case, year of decision, series reference and page within the volume. For example, the famous product liability case about the snail in the ginger beer bottle is *Donoghue* v. *Stevenson* [1932] AC 562.

5. Use of case law

Lawyers usually have little difficulty in finding several cases sufficiently like that before the court for them to be able to refer the judge to them and invite him to follow these earlier decisions. The judge then has to decide whether any of these earlier cases is a *binding precedent* which must be followed.

Whether an earlier case must be followed depends both on the similarity of the two cases and the authority of the court in which the earlier case was decided. Broadly courts are bound by decisions reached in courts which are of senior status and within the same jurisdiction. A judge may avoid following the earlier case if there are significant differences (usually relating to the facts) between the two cases.

Subject to the hierarchy of the courts, statements made by judges in the course of delivering their judgements will be of binding authority when they are central to the reasoning of the decision (*ratio* of the case – short for *ratio decidendi*) whereas propositions made in passing (*obiter* – short for *obiter dicta*) are only of persuasive authority; statements made in courts in other jurisdictions are normally also of only *persuasive* authority. However, if an *obiter* statement is made by a senior judge in an appeal court it is likely to be treated with almost as much respect as if it were a binding authority.

6. Strengths and weaknesses of case law

The system of developing the law through decided cases has both strengths and weaknesses. Its main strength is that it enables law to be built on practical experience. Its weaknesses are firstly that until judges have considered an issue, the law is uncertain, and secondly that outdated rulings may remain in the law long after changes in society have made them inappropriate.

ACTS OF PARLIAMENT

7. Regulatory legislation

Today society is largely shaped by 'regulatory legislation'. Parliament enacts statutes to redirect the common law, or to provide for matters which have never been addressed by case law. The system of regulating society through Acts of Parliament had its origins in the nineteenth century, as industrialisation made fundamental changes in the way in which people lived and worked, and indeed in the way in which industrial activity was financed and managed. Acts of Parliament, and the detailed regulations made under their authority, are very useful tools for laying down minimum standards of behaviour, to protect the health and safety of people at work, and the public generally. Today we have major regulatory Acts of Parliament, and subordinate regulations, on a number of topics such as occupational health and safety, road safety, consumer safety, public health and environmental protection.

Parliament is empowered to legislate for the whole of the UK; when studying any particular statute care must be taken to note whether Parliament has so legislated or whether the statute has a narrower application.

8. Framework safety legislation

The principal statute for occupational health and safety today is the Health and Safety at Work Act 1974. It is an 'enabling' (or framework) Act: it sets up a system for dealing with the problems of occupational health and safety but creates only broad rules for the workplace. An important aspect of the legislation is that it enables the making of regulations to provide detailed standards for particular work situations. Regulations made in accordance with the procedures set out in, and for the purposes allowed by, an Act of Parliament have the same authority, and may carry the same or similar penalties as any rules written into the parent Act itself.

9. Interpretation of statutes

It is a feature of the common law system that while Parliament can, by statute, alter the common law, it falls to judges to interpret the words of Parliament. The role of the judges is very powerful, especially if Parliament has failed to express itself clearly within the text of the legislation. Judicial interpretations of Parliament's words can, if they do not accord with the legislator's intentions, result in amending legislation to re-state Parliament's intention and overrule the judicial interpretation of the original Act.

However, in most instances, judicial interpretations become an important addition to the body of law on the subject. The work of the judiciary in sympathetic interpretation of occupational health and safety legislation has played a vital part in the development of this area of the law. For example, the words 'reasonably practicable' often appear in health and safety legislation and, as will be explained more fully later in the book, the accepted interpretation of them is that provided by Asquith LJ in *Edwards* v. *National Coal Board* [1949].

THE EC AS A SOURCE OF LAW

10. The European Community

The European Communities Act 1972 took the UK into membership of the European Community in 1973 and committed the UK to the Treaty of Rome and other Community treaties. The original purpose of the European Economic Community was to establish a common market between the Member States and the Treaty of Rome had that objective.

Some Articles of the Treaty of Rome are directly enforceable but the Member States can also authorise additional Community legislation to achieve the objectives of the Community. Such legislation is usually by means of Directives. The procedure is that once the content of a Directive has been agreed by all, or, as the case may be, a sufficient number of the Member States, it is adopted by the European Council of Ministers. After the Directive has been adopted Member States have to ensure that, within the time scale stipulated in the Directive, the intentions of that Directive are reflected in their national legislation. Therefore, since becoming a Member State within the Community the UK has had to recognise the EC as a source of UK law and take appropriate measures to ensure that EC provisions are incorporated into UK law.

A common market requires harmonisation of the trading standards of Member States but as the Community has developed it has become apparent that if states are to trade on equal terms there must be similar living and working conditions throughout the Community; otherwise one state might gain an unfair advantage over another by reason of its lower labour standards. Since the Single European Act 1986, the Community has had a considerable interest in harmonising living and working conditions. At that time additional Articles were added to the Treaty of Rome with the intention of strengthening the Community; significantly new Articles provided for their implementation through Directives which had the support of a 'qualified majority vote' of the Member States (i.e. the voting power of a Member State depends on it size). Occupational health and safety is central to labour standards, and in 1986, in special recognition of this, Article 118A was introduced to enable Directives to be made on this subject by qualified majority vote.

11. The EC and product standards

Articles 100 and 100A of the Treaty, concerned with the 'approximation of laws', are important to health and safety in that they enable harmonisation of standards in relation to the working environment, including standards for plant and equipment and personal protective clothing. In due course plant and equipment, including personal protective equipment used at the workplace in Member States of the EC, will have to meet relevant European standards, i.e. those of the Comité Européen de Normalisation (CEN) and, for electrical goods, of the Committee for Electrotechnical Standardisation (CENELEC), rather than British (BSI) standards. Equipment complying with these standards is likely to be marked by the manufacturer with the Community Mark. The UK's Health and Safety Commission is committed to making a major contribution to the development of standards at the national, European and international levels. (*See Policy Statement on Standards* (1991).)

12. The EC and workplace safety

The Community had, by the mid-1980s, already made stipulations on matters, such as dangerous substances used at work, classification, packaging and labelling of substances, and the control of installations which created a major hazard. After Article 118A had been added to the Treaty of Rome the Community's efforts in this area were substantially increased. Article 118A provides:

1. Member States shall pay particular attention to encouraging improvements, especially in the working environment, as regards the health and safety of workers, and shall set as their objective the harmonisation of conditions in this area, while maintaining the improvements made.

2. In order to help achieve the objectives laid down in the first paragraph, the Council acting by a qualified majority on a proposal from the Commission, in cooperation with the European Parliament and after consulting with the Economic and Social Committee, shall adopt, by means of Directives, minimum requirements for gradual implementation, having regard to the conditions and technical rules obtaining in each of the Member States.

In June 1989 Article 118A was used to enable the adoption of a Framework Directive on the introduction of measures to encourage improvements in the safety and health of workers at work and this was soon followed by a number of individual Directives.

13. The Social Charter

Perhaps because Directives made under Article 118A might be adopted on a qualified majority (i.e. without the unanimous agreement of all the Member States) the Community proposed a heavy programme of work stemming from the so-called Commission's Community Charter of Fundamental Social Rights which was drawn up in 1989 shortly before the Treaty of European Union was negotiated at Maastricht. Although the UK was not committed to the Charter, the Commission published a first programme of work to implement it. Proposals for Directives related to safety featured largely in this programme: it might, however, be argued that some of the programme went beyond Article 118A, or indeed the Treaty of Rome itself, even as amended at Maastricht.

14. UK compliance with EC Directives

The UK implements Directives by Acts of Parliament or by Regulations made under an existing Act of Parliament. Directives made under Article 118A are normally implemented by Regulations made under the Health and Safety at Work Act 1974.

15. Current status of Article 118A

The Treaty of European Union signed at Maastricht in 1992 included a Protocol on Social Policy, and an Agreement between other Member States was annexed to the Protocol. This was a response to the UK's objection to the Social Chapter. The Protocol noted that the other Member States wished to continue along the path laid down in the 1989 Social Charter and had adopted the Agreement to that end. The UK still did not accept commitment to the Social Policy. But it did agree to the Protocol allowing the other states to proceed with their Agreement. The Agreement re-drafted those of the Articles of the Treaty of Rome which concerned social policy. Thus in the Agreement Article 118A ceased to exist in the form in which it was introduced in the 1980s, and under the Agreement a general commitment to the improvement of the working environment to protect workers' health and safety became one of a list of items within the completely re-drafted Articles.

In practice occupational health and safety Directives continue to be proposed under Article 118A, though in the case of the Directive on Adaptation of Working Time, adopted under Article 118A (Directive 93/104) without the UK's agreement, the UK challenged whether matters such as introducing a maximum of 48 hours for the working week were sufficiently related to health and safety as to warrant the Directive being based on Article 118A.

CRIMINAL AND CIVIL LAW IN ENGLAND

16. Criminal and civil law distinguished

There are two branches of the law: the criminal law and the civil law. Behaviour which falls short of the standard required for the protection of society is criminal behaviour and is punished by the state. Claims between individuals for the settlement of grievances by awards of compensation (such as damages) are civil claims. The division between criminal and civil law is reflected in the system of courts: criminal cases are heard in criminal courts and civil cases are heard in civil courts.

In both accident prevention law and accident compensation law, however, going to court is the last resort. Whenever possible steps will be taken to get hazards removed without laying criminal charges and in many instances accident victims are able to settle their claims without litigation.

17. Criminal prosecutions

Almost all criminal prosecutions on safety issues are for breaches of the special health and safety legislation which will be the main subject of this book, but it is possible, where unsafe conduct has caused death, for the ordinary law of homicide, which is almost entirely case law, to be invoked. The charge most usually brought is manslaughter. Catastrophies, such as the capsizing of the *Herald of Free Enterprise*, and the King's Cross fire, have made it a matter of some controversy whether homicide charges ought to be laid against industrial organisations, managers or other employees whose acts, or omissions, cause death.

Such charges can be, and indeed have been, brought against both individuals and organisations, but where the corporate entity is large it can be difficult to identify precisely where within the organisation the fault lies. English law has, up to the present time, refused to aggregate the fault of a number of people and attribute the sum of these relatively minor lapses to the corporate employer. The successful prosecutions have been where the corporation is small and has a simple management structure. It is then possible to attribute fault to a particular manager and, on at least one occasion, deem that manager to be 'the deciding mind of the company' and thus secure a conviction against the corporate entity.

18. Civil law and compensation

The civil law relating to compensation for personal injuries is largely the product of decided cases; based for the most part either in contract (where the parties have a legally binding agreement), or, where they do not rely on a contract, in tort (delict in Scotland). Sometimes where statutory provisions which are intended by Parliament primarily to ensure safety have not been followed and personal injury has occurred, the victim may rely on the breach of that statutory duty in a civil court to claim damages.

CRIMINAL COURTS

19. Magistrates' courts and the Crown Court

All criminal prosecutions in England start in a magistrates' court. There are three categories of criminal offence. The most serious (indictable) offences have to be tried upon indictment; that is to say when the magistrates have decided that there is a charge to answer a bill of indictment is framed and the case is sent for trial in the Crown Court. At the other extreme the least serious offences, which are termed summary offences, have to be dealt with in the magistrates' court, which is otherwise known as a court of summary jurisdiction. There is a third category of offences of some severity, known as 'either way offences', which, as their name suggests, can be tried either summarily or upon indictment.

20. Procedure in the magistrates' court

When the accused appears before magistrates, therefore, the first task of the magistrates is to consider which way the case is to be tried. If the charge is of an either way offence the magistrates have to make a choice, but there is an overriding right for the accused to elect to be tried by jury. Homicide offences are always tried upon indictment. Traditionally occupational health and safety offences have been created by statute as summary offences. Since the Health and Safety at Work Act 1974, however, many health and safety offences have been either way offences, though in practice the great majority of cases are still tried summarily.

When magistrates decide whether either way offences are to be tried summarily or upon indictment they take into account the apparent severity of the offence: magistrates have not normally been empowered to award fines of over £2,000 for any one offence, but this general limit is now raised, by s. 17 of the Criminal Justice Act 1991, to £5,000 for 'level 5' and 'either way' offences, and even higher in relation to some offences governed by environmental pollution legislation. Additionally, some health and safety offences committed after March 1992 carry penalties of up to £20,000 or six months' imprisonment (Offshore Safety Act 1992, s. 4). There is no upper limit to the powers of the Crown Court when imposing fines for offences under the 1974 Act. In some instances the Crown Court may impose up to two years' imprisonment. Even though most occupational safety cases are tried summarily, having the power to set serious cases down for trial in the Crown Court may lead magistrates to make use of the higher range of their summary powers.

If the case is intended for trial upon indictment the magistrates conduct a preliminary enquiry, taking statements (called depositions) from the prosecution witnesses to make sure that there is some evidence to support the charge. If the magistrates are not satisfied that there is a case to be tried, they terminate the proceedings. In most cases, however, they will arrange for the case to be tried in the Crown Court.

A major part of the trial court's task will be to receive the evidence in order to establish the facts. Once the evidence has been heard the magistrates, or, in the Crown Court, the jury, decide where the truth lies as between the prosecution's and the accused's stories. In the Crown Court the judge has first to sum up, informing the jury as to the significance in terms of presence or absence of guilt of the various possible interpretations of factual evidence with which they have been presented.

Courts in which cases are first heard, and the evidence is evaluated, are known as courts of first instance; the magistrates' courts and the Crown Court are both courts of first instance.

21. Appeal procedure from the magistrates' court

It is generally possible for the accused to appeal to the Crown Court against a magistrates' court's verdict of guilty. Such an appeal takes the form of a re-trial. Sometimes appeal may be by way of case stated. That is, either the accused or the prosecution may ask the magistrates to state a case for the opinion of a divisional court of the Queen's Bench Division: this is a valuable route by which the prosecution may appeal against an acquittal.

Appeal by way of case stated is a technical procedure which only lies where some irregularity in the trial is alleged such as that the magistrates exceeded their jurisdiction or wrongly interpreted the law. In the past when statutory provisions were narrowly defined this procedure was often invoked to challenge a decision by magistrates. – for example, it might be contended that they had applied the provisions of the Factories Act 1961 to circumstances to which they were not applicable (e.g. *Bolton Metropolitan B.C.* v. *Malrod Insulations Ltd* [1993]).

Appeal against a decision of the divisional court is to the Appellate Committee of the House of Lords.

22. Appeal procedure from the Crown Court

Appeals from the Crown Court, on the other hand, go first to the Court of Appeal Criminal Division; from that court there is a right of final appeal to the House of Lords. Most appeals are about points of law rather than matters of fact, i.e. generally about the application of the law to the facts determined in the trial court. It may be necessary to get permission to appeal; it will always be necessary to get leave to appeal to the House of Lords from the Court of Appeal and this leave will not be granted unless a point of public importance is involved.

In practice it is unusual for health and safety cases to reach the Court of Appeal. Indeed the majority of these cases do not go beyond the magistrates' courts; this means that few of the cases which are prosecuted are reported in the law reports because the decisions of magistrates cannot create precedents. Even Crown Court decisions are of little precedential value and are rarely reported.

CIVIL COURTS

23. County courts and the High Court

Compensation cases will go to trial, according to the size of the claim and the complexity of the issues, in either the county court or the High Court.

The county court system was established in England in the nineteenth century as a system of local courts where small claims might be dealt with swiftly and relatively cheaply and informally. Its jurisdiction is still governed by statute, but it has failed to achieve all the original objectives, to the extent that it has proved necessary to make further provision for small claims. Since the implementation of the Law Courts and Legal Services Act 1990 district judges have been attached to the small claims courts, which now underpin the county court system, and they are empowered to deal with personal injury cases where less than £5,000 is claimed.

Technically there are financial limits to County Court jurisdiction. In practice the cost of litigation and the work load of the High Court has meant in recent years that most personal injury claims have been started in the local county court, or referred back there by the High Court. The High Court and County Courts Jurisdiction Order 1991 abolished many of the limits on the county court's jurisdiction with effect from 1 July 1991. Cases are now allocated for trial according to substance, importance and complexity. All personal injury claims for less than £50,000 are nowadays started in a county court. Very large claims or complicated ones are heard at first instance in the Queen's Bench Division of the High Court.

24. Appeal procedure

Appeal lies from both the county courts and the High Court to the Court of Appeal and there is a further and final appeal to the House of Lords. The decisions of county courts do not create precedents and therefore they are not published in the law reports.

TRIBUNALS

25. Tribunals in general

There are, within the English legal system, institutions known as tribunals which have many of the attributes of law courts, and perform a function similar to courts, in that they hear and resolve disputes. Many of these tribunals are created by, and take their jurisdiction from, statute. For example, there are tribunals to determine disputes over social security claims and these may be referred to by persons who, having suffered an industrial injury, seek one of the various forms of income maintenance which the social security system provides for persons who are physically incapacitated.

26. Industrial tribunals

Industrial tribunals were created by statute in the 1960s and, by further statutes, many of which date from the 1970s, they have acquired a wide and complex jurisdiction. Most of their work is the hearing of complaints by employees that their employers have dismissed them unfairly or for redundancy, or failed to award them the floor of rights to which statute entitles them during the contract of employment. The majority of this employment protection law is contained in the Employment Rights Act 1996. Some aspects of this legislation, and the work of industrial tribunals more widely, is relevant to safety. For example, industrial tribunals have jurisdiction to hear employers' appeals against notices served on them by health and safety inspectors. It has recently been decided that Industrial Tribunals are inferior courts and therefore subject to the general rules relating to contempt of court (*Peach Grey & Co.* v. *Sommers* [1995]).

27. Appeal from industrial tribunals

Appeal lies on a point of law from an industrial tribunal, in employment protection cases, to the Employment Appeal Tribunal (a special body of High Court status) and thence to the Court of Appeal. Appeal lies from decisions concerning safety notices to a specially constituted High Court. In both instances appeal may ultimately be to the House of Lords.

THE EUROPEAN COURT OF JUSTICE

28. The European Court of Justice

A Member State may implement a Directive by whatever legislative techniques are appropriate to its legal system, but if it fails to implement it at all, or implements it imperfectly, that state will be in breach of its Treaty obligations and may be subject to proceedings in the European Court of Justice by the Commission (Article 169) or another Member State (Article 170). A Member State may also challenge the validity of a Directive; indeed it has already been noted that the UK has challenged the legal basis of the Working Time Directive. Moreover, in some instances, a citizen of the State in question may bring an action if that citizen is being deprived of personal rights as a result of the State's breach of Treaty obligation.

Article 177 makes provision for the European Court of Justice to give preliminary rulings on the interpretation of the Treaty itself or of acts of the institutions of the Community: this empowers the court to interpret Directives. Article 177 requires when these matters are in dispute in the courts of Member States that when the final court of appeal in a Member State needs clarification of Community provisions in order to make a decision on the case before it, it must make a reference to the European Court. As long ago as *Macarthys* v. *Smith* [1979] the Court of Appeal was prepared to find for a plaintiff when, as a result of a reference under Article 177, it appeared that English law, which was unfavourable to her case, was in fact contrary to an EC provision. Subsequently, and somewhat controversially, in order to avoid the time and expense of reference to the European Court of Justice, English courts have presumed to read the intention of the Community and interpret UK statutes 'purposively' to make them comply with the Community's intention (e.g. *Pickstone* v. *Freemans plc* [1988]). The European Court has now decided that even statutes which pre-date a relevant EC Directive must be purposively interpreted (*SA Marleasing* v. *La Commercial Internacional de Alimentacion* [1990]). Thus, in the situation where there was a conflict between the Health and Safety at Work Act 1974 and the EC Framework Directive of 1989, the 1974 Act would have to be interpreted to give effect to the Directive. It has been held that even an industrial tribunal is empowered to hear a claim based solely on EC law (*Secretary of State for Scotland and Greater Glasgow Health Board* v. *Wright and Hannah* [1991]).

Nevertheless it is not always easy for a lawyer trained in common law to relate to Directives and other statements emanating from the Community. There is frequently a generality and lack of precision in them which it is difficult for the common lawyer to understand.

Again the legal significance of EC statements of policy is by no means clear though these might be expected to be less than mandatory. It would seem, however, that UK law may be subordinated even to policy statements; EC case law appears to have laid down that UK judges ought not to enforce UK statutes which are not in harmony with EC intentions. (*See R* v. *Secretary of State for Transport, ex parte Factortame Ltd* [1991].)

STRICT AND FAULT LIABILITY

29. Liability in general

There are two fundamental principles of liability in the English legal system: no person shall be liable unless he has personally brought about a wrongful state of affairs, and no person shall be liable except that his state of mind in relation to the wrongful conduct has been to some extent reprehensible. Neither of these principles is without exception and indeed they are not necessarily suitable principles on which to base liability in the circumstances in which society functions today.

30. Criminal liability

General rules

The basic principles of criminal liability are that persons shall not be found guilty of crimes unless the prosecution can establish both that they have by their acts or omissions brought about a prescribed state of affairs (the *actus reus* of the crime) and that they have brought about this state of affairs when in a wrongful state of mind, i.e. showing the necessary *criminal* intent (*mens rea*).

It is never easy for the prosecution to establish the wrongful intent of an accused person. That task is much more difficult when the wrongful situation has occurred in an organisational context.

Status and responsibility

Much regulatory legislation places duties on the organisation itself often by virtue of its status, for example as an employer, a manufacturer, or as the occupier of premises. If a person is, for example, the occupier of premises where many people are present, when a wrongful situation occurs, it certainly may not be the occupier who has personally brought this about. The legislature has often dealt with such situations by creating strict duties making the person on whom the duty is imposed liable if the statutory standard is not achieved without proof of how the situation arose, much less that the accused had a guilty mind. Thus s. 14 of the Factories Act 1961, a provision of fundamental importance in factory law for many years, imposed a duty of strict liability on the occupier of premises providing that the occupier would be liable if dangerous machinery were found there without secure guarding.

Recently a similarly strict interpretation has been placed on those statutory provisions, such as the general duties in the 1974 Act, which are based on the concept of reasonable practicability.

31. Corporate and personal liability

Regulatory duties of this description can be used to attach liability not only to human persons but also to corporate entities. While the law deems a corporation to be a person capable of incurring legal rights and duties, there are – offences of strict liability apart – nevertheless problems of attaching criminal liability to a corporate body, since there are practical and conceptual problems in attributing the necessary *mens rea* to anything other than human persons.

If Parliament has not expressly required proof of *mens rea* the courts will be willing to accept that duties are strict, provided that the offence is a summary one. On the other hand, if Parliament has created an offence, which is triable upon indictment, without stipulating that it is a *mens rea* offence, there is a presumption that the common law principle applies, and the prosecution must prove the defendant had a guilty mind. (*See Sweet* v. *Parsley* [1969].)

Many regulatory statutes contain a clause providing that where it can be established that a corporation has been caused to commit an offence because of the 'neglect' of a director, secretary or senior manager, or with the 'consent or connivance' of one of these senior persons, the human wrongdoer may be prosecuted, as well as or in place of the company. (*See* s. 37 of the Health and Safety at Work Act.)

There remain problems, however, as to whether the company may itself be liable where the *mens rea* is that of a director or other person employed by the company. While in principle the courts are prepared to regard senior personnel as the 'brains' of the company and hold the company liable for their wrongful behaviour, this will only be so where the wrongdoer is at least a senior manager. (*See Tesco Supermarkets Ltd* v. *Nattras* [1971].) It remains unclear whether a series of, what may individually be minor, lapses by individual employees or managers may be totted up, and, in sum, attributed to the company, to give it the necessary state of mind required for an offence. This uncertainty is at the heart of the debate as to whether or not there can be corporate manslaughter when death has resulted from the cumulative effects of a series of lapses in the systems operating within an organisation.

32. Civil liability

Liability for negligence

Actions for compensation for personal injury are usually founded in negligence: thus the plaintiff (the victim) must, in order to win the case, prove that the defendant's conduct was negligent. There are two major exceptions to this general rule.

33. Strict liability

First, the plaintiff may found the claim on the breach of a strict statutory duty. For example, the plaintiff might have injured his hands while working at an unguarded machine in a factory. In the past he might then have claimed damages for breach of s. 14 of the Factories Act, If the accident occurred after 1 January 1993, the situation may be governed by Regulation 11 of the Provision and Use of Work Equipment Regulations 1992. To win the claim he would have to show that the statutory duty had been broken. But as this particular duty is a strict one he would not have to show the defendant's conduct had been negligent in order to prove the breach.

Secondly, where the plaintiff's injury has been caused by the unlawful behaviour of an employee in the course of employment, the plaintiff may elect to sue the wrongdoer's employer rather than, or jointly with, the actual wrongdoer himself. In these circumstances the employer can be held vicariously liable, and have to pay damages to compensate the plaintiff. The principle of vicarious liability enables an accident victim to obtain damages from an employer without proving the employer to be personally at fault.

These themes of strict and fault liability are fundamental to an understanding of the law on health and safety at work. They will be continually referred to, expanded, and applied in this book.

Progress test 2

1. By what law making technique may the European Community bring about improvements in working conditions?

2. What is meant by founding a claim for damages upon a breach of statutory duty?

3. What is meant by *mens rea*?

4. In which court will most civil actions for damages for personal injuries suffered at the workplace be brought?

5. Which court will serve as a court of first instance in criminal cases in England?

6. What is meant by a reference under Article 177?

7. Why is it difficult to succeed in a prosecution for corporate manslaughter?

3

HISTORY OF OCCUPATIONAL HEALTH AND SAFETY LAW

1. Introduction

English law is, in general, difficult to understand without some insight into its historical development: occupational health and safety law is no exception. This chapter will, therefore, outline the development of occupational health and safety law to explain the context of the present law. Occupational health and safety law had its beginnings in the Industrial Revolution. That is where this outline begins.

EVOLUTION OF EMPLOYMENT RELATIONSHIPS

2. 'Master' and 'servant'

The terms 'master' and 'servant' are very ancient, but originally they applied mainly to the relationships between farmers and farm workers, and householders and domestic workers. Other workers progressed through apprenticeship to be journeymen and then master craftsmen.

The Industrial Revolution led to a different working environment where workers frequently worked with machinery rather than hand tools or animals in manufacturing or transportation. Often the persons who worked in these new tasks had a fairly permanent relationship with their employers, a relationship in which they provided only their labour, which might sometimes be skilled, to operate their employers' plant and equipment. The terms master and servant were extended to cover these new working relationships.

3. Intervention of the courts

In time the master and servant relationship came to be treated as a status relationship. Thereafter courts often had to classify working relationships in order to identify the rules governing them.

The first recorded case is *Yewens* v. *Noakes* (1880), in which Bramwell LJ said:

> A servant is a person subject to the command of his master as to the manner in which he shall do his work.

Before long, 'command' was modified to 'control'.

4. 'Employer', 'employee' and the contract of employment

The words 'master' and 'servant' have now given way to 'employer' and 'employee', but the courts still find it necessary to distinguish the contract of employment from other forms of relationship whether or not based on contract. Control over the worker by the employer remains a central feature of the contract of employment.

It was necessary to explain here the contract of employment, and the parties to it, because the nature of the employment relationship has always been an important factor in determining the rights and duties of the persons concerned with both accident compensation and accident prevention. Rights and duties are usually pitched higher where there is a contract of employment.

COMPENSATION FOR PERSONAL INJURY: BARRIERS TO COMPENSATION

5. The doctrine of common employment

Priestley v. *Fowler* (1837) was the first personal injury claim in which importance was attached to the employment relationship. The old law report makes strange reading. However, the facts were broadly that a master butcher employed two servants and had a van in which he carried goods; one servant loaded the van, the other (the plaintiff) suffered injury in the course of a journey in the loaded van. The report fails to make clear whether the accident occurred because the van was defective or because it had been overloaded. At the trial the plaintiff was awarded damages, but that decision was reversed on appeal.

The judgment of the appeal court has been much analysed and severely criticised. Lord Abinger CB made the positive statement that the master '. . . is no doubt, bound to provide for the safety of his servant in the course of his employment . . .', but this was quite overshadowed by the suggestion that: 'If the master be liable to the servant in this action, the principle of that liability will be found to carry us to an alarming extent.' In his Lordship's view finding for the plaintiff would mean that a householder would be liable for accidents caused by faulty goods provided to him by shopkeepers and for injuries suffered by houseguests as a result of the negligence of housemaids. His Lordship apparently failed to recognise that some of his illustrations were unrelated to the employment relationship. More significant, however, was that he attached importance to the lack of evidence that the employer had any knowledge of the events which led to the accident, whereas the victim was able to evaluate the situation. His Lordship concluded:

> . . . to allow this sort of action to prevail would be an encouragement to the servant to omit that diligence and caution which he is in duty bound to exercise on the

behalf of his master, to protect him against the misconduct or negligence of others who serve him . . .

To this judgment was attributed the notorious doctrine of common employment under which a master was not liable for injury suffered by a servant as a result of the wrongdoing of another of that master's servants.

6. Application of the doctrine

The development of employers' liability was much restricted by the doctrine of common employment. There may have been justification for the doctrine in cases where there was little social difference between the employing master craftsman and the servant who was injured. Where the undertaking was larger, and more able than the victim to bear the cost of the accident, the rule became clearly unjust. In *Wilson* v. *Merry* (1868) it was used to defeat the claim where a coal miner had been killed by an explosion resulting from a temporary obstruction of air circulation by the employer's manager: the manager was held to be in common employment with the victim. Some of the worst aspects of the doctrine were mitigated by the Employers' Liability Act 1880 which protected the worker's claim where injury resulted from the negligence of a senior person or one whose orders the workman had to obey.

In the twentieth century the doctrine created difficulties for judges no longer in sympathy with it. In *Wilsons & Clyde Coal Company Ltd* v. *English* [1937] the House of Lords wanted to find for an underground worker injured by a system of work negligently operated by the qualified manager to whom the employers were required, by the provisions of the Coal Mines Act 1911, to delegate responsibility for running the mine. Their Lordships held that the employers owed a non-delegable duty, which overrode the doctrine of common employment, to provide for the safety of their employees. Lord Wright said:

> The whole course of authority consistently recognises a duty which rests on the employer, and which is personal to the employer, to take reasonable care for the safety of his workmen, whether the employer be an individual, a firm or a company, and whether or not the employer takes any share in the conduct of the operations.

Lord Wright's analysis has survived the demise of common employment and *Wilsons Case* is generally regarded as the foundation of the modern law of employer's liability.

7. Abolition of the doctrine

The doctrine of common employment remained until it was abolished by the Law Reform (Personal Injuries) Act 1948, s. 1(1) of which provided:

> It shall not be a defence to an employer who is sued in respect of personal injuries caused by the negligence of a person employed by him, that that person was at the time the injuries were caused in common employment with the person injured.

8. Assumption of risk

One explanation of the doctrine of common employment was that the servant had agreed to accept the risk of injury by another of his master's servants. The concept of acceptance of risk was extended so that the servant was deemed to have accepted the dangers of the workplace. The employer could totally avoid liability by the defence of assumption of risk, known technically as *volenti non fit injuria*. No allowance was made for the fact that workers could not afford to terminate their contracts and lose the source of income on which their survival depended. The House of Lords considered the defence in *Smith* v. *Baker* [1891].

The plaintiff, who was a railway navvy, was working in a cutting while a crane on top of the embankment was removing stones from the cutting. The workman had made several complaints. When stones fell on him he claimed damages. The House found for him; for although he knew of the danger and still continued to do his work, there was no evidence that he had voluntarily undertaken to run the risk of injury.

After this courts have rarely found that an employee has accepted the risk of injury at work.

9. No negligence

The common law of employer's liability was, and still is, fault liability. In order to obtain compensation the plaintiff has to show that the defendant's conduct was negligent and that this negligence caused the plaintiff's injury. The criterion of negligent conduct remains broadly the same now as in the nineteenth century, but courts were then less inclined to find that accidents were caused by an employer's negligence. Society may then have been more cavalier and less safety conscious, but it must also be remembered that there was less technical and scientific knowledge than today, and much less industrial experience, so there was understandably less reason to foresee danger.

DEVELOPMENT OF CONCEPTS OF LIABILITY

10. Negligent system

Today if an accident occurred in circumstances where there was a fault in an organisation's system of work, the courts would find the organisation to be negligent. In the nineteenth century, if the employee knew of the defect in the system and failed to take account of it, then the courts might attribute negligence to the employee rather than the employer.

For example, where a railway disaster was primarily attributable to a known inadequate braking system on the train, it might be argued that the real fault lay with the driver for not operating within the capacity of the faulty brakes!

11. Fatal accidents

At common law rights to compensation did not survive death. This harsh rule was mitigated by the Fatal Accidents Act 1846 which established a principle which remains part of the law today. It enabled a claim to be made on behalf of a widow and certain other dependent relatives to claim against a person who had unlawfully killed the breadwinner.

It had to be established both that it was the defendant's wrongdoing which caused the death and that each claimant was dependant on the deceased for financial support. The court would then award a sum sufficient to provide income maintenance, at the rate the deceased might have provided, given his employment prospects for the remainder of his natural working life.

12. Obstacles to litigation

It is somewhat surprising, given the difficulty of winning an industrial injury claim and that there was little in the way of what has since become legal aid to defray the costs of litigation, that there was any litigation at all.

After *Smith* v. *Baker*, the common law might have developed more favourably to those who suffered injury at work. Whether this would have been so is mere speculation, because the Workmen's Compensation Act 1897 gave employees some entitlement to income maintenance independently of the common law.

13. Workmen's Compensation Act 1897

This legislation imposed upon the employer a duty to provide income maintenance to an employee who suffered injury in an accident 'arising out of and in the course of employment'. The Act was later extended to allow claims to be made where the victim had contracted one of the 'prescribed' industrial diseases. The periodical payments which the employer had to make were modest, being only a proportion of the pre-accident weekly wage of the victim, but they could be claimed without establishing that the injury was caused by the employer's negligence; liability was based entirely on the requirement that the injury arose out of and in the course of employment. The scheme remained in force until after the end of the Second World War and during its operation employee victims had to elect between claiming compensation under the statutory provisions and claiming damages at common law. Between 1896 and 1948 many victims of industrial injury claimed the relatively modest income maintenance which the legislation provided rather than undertake the arduous task of pursuing a common-law claim for negligence.

14. Contract and status

The early rules of liability outlined above were largely applicable to the contract of employment. A parallel relationship, often created independently of contract, was, and continues to be, the relationship between occupier of, and visitor to, premises. After the case of *Indermaur* v. *Dames* (1866) the occupier had a considerable responsibility for the safety of visitors to his premises.

The liabilities of a person (probably an employer of servants!) having the status of occupier of premises to another (probably a workman) having the status of visitor to the premises were different from those which applied as between master and servant and in many respects favourable to the visitor (for example, the doctrine of common employment would not defeat a visitor's claim where the visitor was injured through the fault of the occupier's servant). On the other hand, the defence of *volenti* could defeat an invitee's claim long after that defence had ceased to be significant in the master and servant relationship. (See *London Graving Dock Co Ltd* v. *Horton* [1951].)

It does not appear to have been usual for injured workers to claim damages for personal injury from defendants who were neither their master nor the occupier of premises at which they were working at the time of the injury. *Heaven* v. *Pender* was an exception, and created an important precedent.

In *Heaven* v. *Pender* [1883] the plaintiff was employed as a painter. His employer agreed with a shipowner, whose vessel was in the defendant's dock, to paint the outside of the ship. The defendant supplied, under a contract with the shipowner, the staging to be slung alongside the ship so she could be painted. The ropes from which the staging was slung were unsound and the plaintiff was injured when they broke. There was no contract of employment between the injured party and the defendant, nor was the defendant the occupier of the premises where the accident occurred. Nevertheless, in finding for the plaintiff, Brett MR stated:

> Whenever one person is by circumstances placed in such a position with regard to another that every one of ordinary sense who did think would at once recognise that if he did not use ordinary care and skill in his own conduct with regard to those circumstances he would cause danger of injury to the person or property of the other, a duty arises to use ordinary care and skill to avoid such danger.

LIABILITY FOR NEGLIGENCE

15. The tort of negligence

Principles of liability for personal injury had by the 1930s developed so that it was recognised that a defendant would be liable to compensate another if he owed a duty to that other to take care not to cause him injury and broke that duty by negligent conduct. There was, however, a lack of certainty about the situations in which a duty to take care arose. Indeed, apart from occupiers' liability and transport accidents there were few areas in which duty situations were recognised unless the plaintiff and defendant were in a contractual relationship: in contracts, of which the contract of employment was an important, but not the only, example, it could be said that there was an implied duty to take care for the personal safety of the other party to the contract. Thus in employment the master's duty to take reasonable care for the safety of the servant was deemed to be an implied term of the contract of service and one factor which distinguished servants from other persons who had contracts to supply labour. Similarly a seller of goods might well be in breach of contract if the purchaser suffered personal injury from the goods.

In *Donoghue* v. *Stevenson* [1932] the appellant had suffered personal injury when she drank ginger beer in which there were the remains of a snail. The drink had been manufactured by the respondent, and supplied to a retailer from whom it was bought for the appellant by her friend. The plaintiff had not entered into contract with either the manufacturer or the retailer, and could not therefore bring an action for breach of contract. The majority of the House of Lords nevertheless found that the appellant (consumer) was owed a duty of care by the respondent (manufacturer) and would be able to claim damages from him if she could show that it was by his negligent conduct that the snail had contaminated the ginger beer. Lord Atkin built on the words of Brett MR in *Heaven* v. *Pender* to provide a most important statement as to the criterion for liability in negligence:

> The rule that you are to love your neighbour becomes, in law, you must not injure your neighbour, and the lawyer's question, Who is my neighbour? receives a restricted reply. You must take reasonable care to avoid acts or omissions which you can reasonably foresee would be likely to injure your neighbour. Who, then, in law is my neighbour? The answer seems to be – persons who are so closely and directly affected by my act that I ought reasonably to have them in contemplation as being so affected when I am directing my mind to the acts or omissions which are called in question.

Barely two years later Lord Wright stated in the industrial injury case, *Lochgelly Iron and Coal Co.* v. *M'Mullan* [1934]:

> In strict legal analysis, negligence means more than heedless or careless conduct, whether in omission or commission; it properly connotes the complex concept of duty, breach and damage thereby suffered by the person to whom the duty was owing.

The recognition of a tort of negligence, based on a duty of care arising where plaintiff and defendant were in sufficiently close proximity for them to be deemed neighbours, provided a framework within which the existing duty situations could be housed. It also enabled new categories of duty situations to be recognised.

16. The foundations of modern law

Donoghue v. *Stevenson*, by giving recognition to the tort of negligence, and *Wilsons & Clyde Coal Company Ltd* v. *English*, by spelling out the nature of employers' liability, laid the foundations of modern employers' liability law.

The development of this law was assured by postwar legislation. A new income maintenance scheme was introduced in 1948 by the National Insurance (Industrial Injuries) Act 1946, which, in s. 89(1), repealed the Workmen's Compensation Acts. While the national insurance scheme retained the principle of income maintenance for the victims of industrial accidents in similar language to the earlier legislation, the new statutory entitlement was not lost by those who claimed damages. Indeed the new statutory scheme was administered by the state and the insured victim claimed through the social security system. However, the Law Reform (Personal Injuries) Act 1948 provided that one half of the value of the new industrial injury benefit should be offset against any common law damages awarded as the result of the same accident (s. 2(1)).

The offset of part of the statutory entitlement against a common law claim of which the claim for loss of wages was usually but a small element was no deterrent to a litigant pursuing a substantial claim.

The system of providing compensation for those who accidentally suffered personal injury was subjected to close scrutiny in the 1970s by the Pearson Commission. While the Royal Commission made a number of recommendations for changes within the system, they were of the view that the common law system of fault-based liability should be retained in addition to the social security system. They rejected the suggestion that it would be more satisfactory to make provision for personal injury solely through the social security system. However, the Social Security Act 1989 so increased the power of the State to 'snatch back' from damages, sums which had been paid as social security benefits, that the common law claim has ceased to be attractive in the case of minor injuries.

PREVENTION OF PERSONAL INJURY

17. General historical background

The protection of workers from dangerous and unhealthy working conditions has, in the United Kingdom, come to be regarded, after nearly two centuries of experience of industrialisation, as a matter for Parliament. This approach entered a new phase in 1974 when Parliament, through the Health and Safety at Work Act, adopted a radically new approach to health and safety legislation. However, the appropriateness of relying on legislation with, in the last resort, criminal sanctions was never in dispute when reform was undertaken.

It is possible to trace protective legislation to an Act of 1802 'for the health and morals of apprentices and others', but the real foundations of regulatory control were laid in the 1830s and 1840s following a number of official inquiries. The most important of these enquiries concerned the employment of children in factories, accidents in mines and the working conditions of railway construction workers. However the prevailing doctrine of *laissez-faire* ensured that little was done to regulate the employment conditions of men (except in coal mines) until nearly the end of the century: early legislation focused on the protection of women and children in factories and the prohibition of their employment in mines. Government inspectors were appointed for the first time under the Factories Act 1833.

Early Victorian legislation set a pattern which was to be followed up until the Health and Safety at Work Act 1974. Narrow regulatory standards were formulated for particular categories of person in relation to particular hazards in specific industries, notably factories and mines.

30

Writing at the beginning of the twentieth century, B.L. Hutchins and A. Harrison could fairly suggest:

> This century of experiment in factory legislation affords a typical example of English practical empiricism. We begin with no abstract theory of social justice or the rights of man. We seem always to have been incapable even of taking a general view of the subject we were legislating upon. Each successive statute aimed at remedying a single ascertained evil. (*A History of Factory Legislation*)

Until the Health and Safety at Work Act 1974, the same comments might have been made, perhaps even more forceably about mining legislation.

At the time of the enactment of the Health and Safety at Work Act 1974 the principal factory legislation was the Factories Act 1961. The principal mining legislation was the Mines and Quarries Act 1954, but by the 1970s the declining importance of the mining industry, the reduction of the underground work-force, and greater mechanisation had greatly reduced the importance of this legislation.

18. Other regulatory legislation

The empirical approach led to a number of other statutory codes each providing safety standards for a particular group of the workforce. In addition, the principal Acts each supported a number of detailed sets of regulations. By the 1970s there were over 30 statutes and 500 sets of regulations. Apart from factories and mines other areas of employment covered were agriculture, railways, offices, shops and railway premises, offshore installations and nuclear installations. The Offices, Shops and Railway Premises Act 1963 covered almost as many employees as the Factories Act – 8 million; on the other hand, the Mineral Workings (Offshore Installations) Act 1971 and the Nuclear Installations Act 1965 covered two of the most hazardous operations. It was nevertheless believed that before the Health and Safety at Work Act 1974 there were at least 5 million employees who worked where there were no statutory safety standards; in this group were many employees in premises to which the public were invited such as hospitals, hotels, leisure complexes and educational premises. With hindsight 5 million is believed to be a conservative estimate.

CIVIL ACTIONS FOR BREACH OF STATUTORY DUTY

19. Primary purpose of safety legislation

The primary purpose of legislation such as that which has just been discussed is to set standards to remove or reduce the hazards which may result in personal injury. Normally these laws are enforced through the criminal courts. However, in *Groves* v. *Lord Wimborne* [1898] the civil Court of Appeal allowed a plaintiff to rely on the breach of a statutory provision to support a claim for damages.

The defendant employer had failed to comply with a statutory duty to guard certain dangerous machinery where the plaintiff was employed and as a result the plaintiff was seriously injured. The statute provided that in the event of a breach of this duty a fine not in excess of £100 could be imposed and, at the discretion of the Secretary of State, the whole or any part of this could be applied for the benefit of the injured person or his family. The provision clearly envisaged that the compensation award would become payable upon a conviction in the criminal courts. Nevertheless, the Court of Appeal relied on the statutory provisions to find for the plaintiff in civil litigation and awarded £150. A.L. Smith LJ, in giving judgment, stated:

> ... unless it can be found from the whole purview of the Act that the legislature intended that the only remedy for a breach of the duty created by the Act should be the infliction of a fine upon the master, it seems clear to me that upon proof of such a breach of duty and of injury done to the workman, a cause of action is given to the workman against the master ...

The Court of Appeal was apparently influenced by the difficulty which common employment created for the employee seeking damages from his employer. The doctrine was not a defence against liability for breach of statutory duty, where the obligation was imposed on the employer personally.

The possibility of using the criminal law in this manner, once admitted, was frequently tested. Judges allowed many of the provisions of the statutory codes to be used in this way, though they were somewhat reluctant to allow health and welfare, as opposed to safety provisions, to be invoked. In the twentieth century regulatory legislation usually states whether civil actions will lie.

Civil litigation on the statutory codes has provided the principal source of statutory interpretation of the words used in the codes.

THE HEALTH AND SAFETY AT WORK ACT 1974

20. The Robens Committee

In May 1970 the then Secretary of State for Employment appointed a select committee with the following terms of reference:

> To review the provision made for the safety and health of persons in the course of their employment ... and to consider whether any changes are needed in:
>
> (1) the scope and nature of the major relevant enactments, or
>
> (2) the nature and extent of voluntary action concerned with these matters ...

This, the Robens Committee, reported in June 1972. Its succinct report found much wrong with the system and proposed a new approach to the regulatory control of occupational health and safety.

While most of the Report is concerned with making proposals for change, the first chapter, entitled 'What is Wrong with the System?', identified a number of problems which prompted the Committee to consider that the time was ripe for change.

The report noted that every year about 1,000 people were killed at their work in Great Britain and about half a million suffered injuries causing 23 million work days to be lost. Moreover, annual reports from the inspectorates showed that accidents continued to rise. Evidence suggested that new methods of production, including the greater use of chemical substances, might lead to substantial further increases in accidents and ill-health in the relatively near future.

21. Problems in the system of safety legislation

In the Committee's view the most important single reason for accidents at work was apathy. They noted:

> . . . safety is mainly a matter of the day-to-day attitudes and reactions of the individual, . . . if individual experience is not in the normal course conducive to safety awareness, then safety awareness must be deliberately fostered . . .

In looking at the pattern of existing safety legislation, the Committee identified the following matters as militating against safety awareness – many of these defects being caused by the piecemeal development of the system:

(a) *There was too much law.* People thought of safety legislation as detailed provisions imposed by external agencies: they failed to appreciate that the primary responsibility for doing something about work-related accidents and ill-health lay with those who created the risks and those who worked with them.

(b) *The law was defective.* It was badly structured and had an unsatisfactory complexity.

(c) *The law was primarily concerned with physical circumstances,* such as the safeguarding of machinery. It paid too little attention to attitudes and the organisational systems within which people worked.

(d) *The fragmentation of administrative jurisdictions.* Law enforcement was divided between five government departments – in addition there was extensive participation by local authorities.

22. Solutions to the problems

Propositions emerging in the body of the report were:

(a) The criminal process ought to be reserved for cases where there had been a wilful or reckless disregard for safety.

(b) Legislation should impose duties upon employers for the protection of employees and other workers and the general public.

(c) Workers should know of the hazards of their workplace and be consulted about the introduction of and monitoring of safe systems.

(d) The civil action for breach of statutory duty did not assist with accident prevention: fear of civil liability inhibited employers in post-accident investigation and subsequent updating of systems.

(e) Despite its weight and complexity, the law neither gave protection to all employed persons, nor covered all hazardous situations within workplaces which were within the ambit of the regulatory codes.

The committee concluded its survey of what was wrong with the system with the following statement:

> The most fundamental conclusion to which our investigations have led us is this. There are severe practical limits on the extent to which progressively better standards of safety and health at work can be brought about through negative regulation by external agencies. We need a more effectively self-regulating system.

The new approach, of a broad legislative framework of general duties, imposing more positive responsibility on those at the workplace to devise safe systems of work, was to be known as the 'Robens Philosophy'. The publication of the Report was soon followed by the Health and Safety at Work Act 1974, which largely adopted the Robens philosophy.

DEVELOPMENTS AFTER 1974

23. Intentions of the Act

The Health and Safety at Work Act 1974 was intended as framework legislation on which future regulatory control could be based. A number of Regulations were introduced to repeal some of the piecemeal provisions of the earlier legislation and replace them with provisions applying to all persons at work.

24. Impact of EC

The Act now also provides a vehicle through which European Community initiatives are incorporated into UK law.

On 1 January 1993 the European Community's Framework Directive and five subsidiary Directives were implemented in Great Britain by six new sets of Regulations (known colloquially as 'The Six Pack'). While these Regulations were implemented as subordinate to the 1974 Act, they have brought about changes in the law almost as radical as the 1974 Act itself. On the implementation of the six pack the opportunity was taken to repeal most of the then remaining provisions of legislation pre-dating the 1974 Act, notably provisions of the Factories Act 1961.

25. Civil liability for breach of statutory duty in the 1990s

The phasing-out of the older legislation, especially the Factories Act and Mines and Quarries Act, on which so many of these civil actions were based, together with the development of the tort of negligence, has seemingly reduced the importance of this aspect of civil litigation. Many of the recent regulations are actionable in the civil courts, but the law reports provide little evidence that they have been tested in civil litigation. However the old legislation has a strange after-life in that many of the much litigated phrases (for example 'reasonably practicable') have been utilised in current legislation; thus judicial interpretations given in relation to laws now repealed continue to be very persuasive authorities.

Progress test 3

1. Explain the importance of the following cases:
    (a) *Smith* v. *Baker*
    (b) *Wilsons & Clyde Coal Company Ltd* v. *English*
    (c) *Groves* v. *Wimborne*.

2. When, and in what context, were the first government inspectors appointed?

3. Why was the development of health and safety legislation described as 'empirical'?

4. What major faults did the Robens Committee find with the regulatory system which had developed by 1970?

5. What did the Robens Committee consider to be the major cause of accidents?

6. What did the Robens Committee consider to be the solution to the problem?

7. What developments provided the impetus for repealing most of the pre-1974 legislation which had survived into the 1990s?

8. How does the pre-1974 legislation continue to influence the interpretation of health and safety legislation?

9. What is meant by 'The Six Pack'?

Part Two

FRAMEWORK FOR OCCUPATIONAL HEALTH AND SAFETY LAW

4

FRAMEWORK LEGISLATION FOR OCCUPATIONAL HEALTH AND SAFETY

1. Introduction

This chapter will describe the purposes of the Health and Safety at Work etc. Act 1974 and outline its provisions. It will also describe the relationship between it and other relevant statutory provisions. Finally it will outline the provisions of the EC's Framework Directive, and some of the Directives which are subsidiary to this Directive. It will also outline the UK response to these Directives.

The general duties, regulation-making powers and enforcement provisions of the 1974 Act will be dealt with in greater detail in subsequent chapters. These provisions will then also be related to the regulations introduced to achieve compliance with the Framework and selected subsidiary Directives.

2. Background to UK framework legislation

The Robens Report and After

A principal recommendation of the Robens Committee was that:

> There should be a new, comprehensive Act dealing with safety and health at work. The Act should contain a clear statement of the general principles of responsibility for safety and health, but otherwise should be mainly enabling in character.

The Committee reported in June 1972; the Health and Safety at Work Act 1974 (hereafter called the 1974 Act), which received the Royal Assent on 31 July 1974, was passed to implement that recommendation.

The Act was intended, in the Robens philosophy, to be a framework, or enabling Act, i.e. it introduced a broad and general system for the provision of regulatory control of the workplace, while enabling further detailed arrangements to be made as, with the passage of time, changing circumstances might require.

THE HEALTH AND SAFETY AT WORK ACT 1974

3. The purposes of the legislation

In its long title the 1974 Act is described as:

> An Act to make further provision for securing the health, safety and welfare of persons at work, for protecting others against risks to health or safety in connection with the activities of persons at work, for controlling the keeping and use and preventing the unlawful acquisition, possession and use of dangerous substances, and for controlling certain emissions into the atmosphere; . . .

4. The arrangement of the Act

In order to achieve its purposes the Act is divided into four Parts but this book will mainly be concerned with Part I. Indeed Part III (ss. 61–76) which makes provision for building regulations is only marginally related to occupational health and safety and may explain the inclusion of the word 'etc.' in the short title of the Act. Part II (ss. 55–60) is entirely concerned with the functions and responsibilities of the Employment Medical Advisory Service and Part IV (ss. 77–85) provides for amendment of certain earlier statutes and the extent, application and commencement of the Act itself.

Part I is entitled 'Health, Safety and Welfare in Connection with Work, and Control of Dangerous Substances and Certain Emissions into the Atmosphere'. Within this Part the following matters are covered:

ss. 2– 9 General duties
ss. 10–14 The Health and Safety Commission and the Health and Safety Executive
ss. 15–26 Health and safety regulations, approved codes of practice and appointment and powers of inspectors
ss. 27–28 Obtaining and disclosure of information
ss. 29–32 Special provisions relating to agriculture
ss. 33–42 Provisions as to offences
ss. 43–54 Financial provisions, application to the Crown and interpretation provisions

The Act contains a number of Schedules some of which relate to matters covered in Part I: of particular importance are Schedule 1 (Existing Enactments which are Relevant Statutory Provisions) and Schedule 3 (Subject-Matter of Health and Safety Regulations).

5. Objectives of Part I

The first (preliminary) section of the 1974 Act sets out the purposes that Part I is intended to fulfil giving helpful guidance to all those who have to implement the Act – from Secretary of State to employers – as to the meaning of its provisions. Section 1 states:

(1) The provisions of this Part shall have effect with a view to –

(a) securing the health, safety and welfare of persons at work
(b) protecting persons other than persons at work against risks to health or safety arising out of or in connection with the activities of persons at work
(c) controlling the keeping and use of explosive or highly flammable or otherwise dangerous substances, and generally preventing the unlawful acquisition, possession and use of such substances; and
(d) controlling the emission into the atmosphere of noxious or offensive substances from premises of any class prescribed for the purposes of this paragraph.

The Offshore Safety Act 1992, ss. 1 and 2 added to these purposes matters relating to safety on offshore installations and offshore and onshore pipelines.

Thus, while the primary focus of the Act is upon the health and safety of employees, the Act has wider purposes, aiming also to protect both workers who are not employees and the public.

6. Health, safety and welfare

Rather surprisingly, the concepts, health, safety and welfare, which are central to the purpose of the 1974 Act, are not defined within the Act. Putting the words health and safety in the context of the purposes of the Act the words may reasonably be supposed to mean without risk of personal injury. Since, however, the purpose of the legislation is the prevention of personal injury, a person may well be found liable for creating or permitting a dangerous situation which might foreseeably cause injury, even though injury has not in fact been suffered: the breach of the law is in creating the risk of injury, or failing to protect against an existing risk, rather than in causing injury.

Welfare is not emphasised in the 1974 Act: it is merely one aspect of the employers' duty to their employees (*see* s. 2).

7. Relevant statutory provisions

The expression 'relevant statutory provisions' is used in the 1974 Act to delimit the jurisdiction of the administrative, enforcement and regulation-making powers provided in the Act. The expression is interpreted in s. 53 of the Act. Relevant statutory provisions are:

(a) The provisions (particularly the general duties) contained in Part I of the 1974 Act.

(b) Any health and safety regulations and agricultural health and safety regulations made under Part I of the 1974 Act.

(c) The existing statutory provisions listed in Schedule 1 of the Act.

Section 53 is in Part I of the 1974 Act and the relevant statutory provisions are either contained within, created under, or brought into the system by, Part I of the Act.

8. The general duties

Sections 2–9 of the 1974 Act impose general duties on persons for the protection of others, as broadly outlined below:

s. 2   on employers for the protection of employees;

s. 3   on employers for the protection of persons who are not their employees and on the self-employed for the protection of themselves and others;

s. 4   on controllers of non-domestic premises for the protection of those who are not their employees but use the premises as a place of work or as a place where they may use plant or substances provided for their use there;

s. 5   on the person having control of certain premises to prevent emissions from those premises into the atmosphere;

s. 6   on suppliers of articles and substances for use by people at work;

s. 7   on employees for their own safety and for the safety of others;

s. 8   prohibits any person from interfering with anything provided in the interests of health and safety;

s. 9   prohibits an employer from charging an employee for anything done or provided in pursuance of any specific legal requirement concerning safety.

9. The strictness of the duties

The general duties do not impose absolute liability: thus they do not require persons upon whom duties are imposed to *ensure* safety without qualification. In fact most of the above duties require the persons upon whom they are imposed only to do what is *reasonably practicable* to ensure health and safety. For example, s. 2(1) requires an employer:

> ... to ensure, so far as is *reasonably practicable*, the health, safety and welfare at work of all his employees.

Section 5 – now repealed – required the use of the *best practicable means* to prevent emissions.

Section 40 provides that once it has been shown that a duty or requirement has not been complied with, it is for the defendant to satisfy the court that it was not reasonably practicable, or practicable, as the case may be, to have done more to satisfy the duty or requirement. The effect of qualifying the general duties by concepts such as reasonable practicability is that the duties are pitched at strict liability subject to the defence provided by s. 40. Section 40 is particularly significant because there are no other defence provisions within the 1974 Act.

10. What categories of persons are protected?

Broadly the Act is intended to provide for the health and safety of all employees, all self-employed persons and the public, but there are exceptions to this general statement, as explained below.

(a) Employed and self-employed

The 1974 Act applies to both the employed and the self-employed but individual provisions of the Act may well apply to one category rather than the other. Thus s. 2 is concerned with the duties imposed on employers for the protection of their employees while s. 3 includes the imposition of duties on the self-employed.

(b) Other categories of workers

The Act does not necessarily impose duties on, or for the protection of, workers who are neither employees or self-employed persons. For example, charity 'workers' giving voluntary service would not be protected by ss. 2 or 6, but might be covered by ss. 3 and 4.

(c) The general public

The duty which s. 3 imposes on an employer 'to conduct his undertaking in such a way as to ensure, so far as is reasonably practicable, that persons not in his employment who may be affected thereby are not exposed to risks to their health or safety' is wide enough to cover public safety, including 'neighbourhood risks', and some regulations made under the Act, such as the Control of Industrial Major Accident Hazards Regulations 1984, are particularly focused on public safety issues.

Section 4 imposes a duty on controllers of premises to provide for the safety of persons who use those premises as a place where they may use plant or substances provided for their use there. It is essentially an 'occupier's' duty, designed to protect persons who have no legal relationship, other than as visitors, with the 'controller' of the premises. This provision appears broad enough to provide protection not only to visiting workers but also, in some circumstances, to the general public; for example, to shoppers using supermarket trolleys or customers using washing machines in laundrettes.

The fact that s. 2 of the Act applies to many premises to which the public resort, for example hospitals, schools, theatres or sports facilities, gives wide protection to the general public over and above the specific protections given by ss. 3 and 4 because these premises will in any event have to be maintained to a high standard by the employer for the protection of his workforce. If an employer maintains a workplace to the standards required by s. 2 it follows that it will be relatively free from hazards which might endanger any visitors of whatever status.

11. What classes of persons owe duties?

The general duties not only indicate the scope of responsibilities, they also indicate the categories of persons upon whom these responsibilities are imposed.

Duties are imposed on:

(i) *Employers* – ss. 2–3 and, in practice, ss. 4,5 and 6, because these latter sections impose obligations on enterprises which will also be employers

(ii) *Controllers* (occupiers) of premises – s. 4

(iii) *Designers, manufacturers, importers and suppliers* of articles and substances – s. 6

(iv) *Self-employed* – s. 3(2)

(v) *Employees* – s. 7 unless they are in one of the categories of employment, e.g. domestic service or working overseas, to whom the Act does not extend.

(vi) *The parties to a service contract* – a contract between two employing organisations under which one organisation is to supply labour to, or provide a service for, or work in cooperation with, the other organisation is within the ambit of s. 3 of the 1974 Act, which makes provision for one employer to have regard for the health and safety of the other employer's employees. This incidentally is one of the most important sections of the 1974 Act given the importance of ensuring cooperation between employing organisations if safe systems are to be identified, introduced and maintained. It is a concept which has been further developed in the Management of Health and Safety at Work Regulations 1992, Regulation 9 of which deals with circumstances where two employers share a workplace.

(vii) *'Any person'* – s. 8 prohibits any person from intentionally or recklessly interfering with or misusing anything provided in the interests of health, safety or welfare 'in pursuance of any of the relevant statutory provisions'. Not only does this provision protect members of the public as well as persons at work but the public are not exempted from the duty imposed by it.

12. General application of the Act

Section 84(1) of the 1974 Act states that Part I of the Act applies to Great Britain, i.e. England, Wales and Scotland. However, s. 84(3) provides that Her Majesty may by Order in Council make provision for the Act (or parts of it) to apply in 'relation to persons, premises, work, articles, substances and other matters outside Great Britain'. Orders in Council have from time to time been made to extend the Act to offshore installations on the Continental Shelf in the North Sea (currently The Health and Safety at Work etc. Act 1974 (Application outside Great Britain) Order 1995) and another to provide for a comparable regulatory system in Northern Ireland (The Health and Safety (Northern Ireland) Order).

The jurisdictional limits to the application of the Act mean that unless there has been an Order in Council made under s. 84(3) it will not be possible to invoke the protection of the Act for persons employed to work outside Great Britain, even though such persons may be employed by organisations operating from Great Britain and have contracts of employment made in Britain and governed by British laws. A major practical reason for the exclusion of such workers from the protection of the Act is that inspectors appointed under the Act have no authority to inspect and institute enforcement proceedings outside the jurisdiction.

Inspectors might visit the employers' operational base in Great Britain and take action there against the employers for operating systems which endangered employees overseas; for example, faults might be found in the employer's systems of training and kitting out personnel to be sent abroad. The circumstances in which this course of action would be available would seem to be fairly limited.

13. Specific situations

Specific situations in which the Act does or does not apply are detailed further below.

(a) *Domestic employment*

Section 51 provides that nothing in Part I of the 1974 Act 'shall apply in relation to a person by reason only that he employs another, or is himself employed, as a domestic servant in a private household'.

This section does not prevent inspectors from enforcing the Act in domestic premises. It might be enforced in relation to non-domestic work carried out on such premises, and indeed the Act might be invoked following accidents caused by faulty workmanship connected with provision of public services, such as gas or electricity, to private dwellings. In other words the Act applies to construction and maintenance work performed on domestic premises by commercial organisations; but does not apply to the DIY activities of the residents. Even in this instance, however, the householder might be liable if the work were being undertaken as a commercial activity, e.g. converting an old house into tenements; there might also be other regulatory provisions governing the situation, e.g. in the case of an unqualified person (i.e. someone not a 'CORGI') installing a gas boiler.

(b) *Merchant shipping*

Merchant sailors do not enjoy the protection of the 1974 Act. They are given statutory protection through the Merchant Shipping Acts. The 1974 Act will apply to certain operations on or round shipping in harbours, e.g. unloading or loading cargo, and will apply to work undertaken on ships in dry dock.

(c) *Crown premises*

The inspectorate may enter Crown premises where persons are at work, but they cannot bring proceedings to enforce the Act against the Crown (s. 48), although the Crown is under an obligation to observe the law. The inspectorate has adopted the practice of serving a 'Crown Notice' on the Crown to record circumstances where the law is not being observed in their premises.

In some situations the activity undertaken in the premises may necessitate a careful balancing of safety against security, e.g. it may be difficult to maintain the security needed in military areas or prisons while providing adequate means of escape in emergency situations. These considerations, though not confined to operations conducted by or on behalf of the Crown, are likely to be particularly relevant to the operations of the Crown. With the increase in contracting out of work (e.g. catering services) not all those employed on Crown premises will necessarily be Crown servants.

(d) Transport

The Act applies to transport of all descriptions. It will certainly be enforced in relation to transport of articles and substances (*see* s. 2(2)(b)) and in premises, such as railway stations, used in connection with the provision of transport services. Passenger transportation (and carriage of goods) by ship or aircraft largely takes place outside the jurisdiction and is in any case specifically covered by other legislation. Similarly there is special legislation dealing with safety on the railways and the roads. Responsibility for enforcement of safety standards in transport by rail has since 1990 been transferred to inspectors appointed under the 1974 Act, and the Clapham Junction rail catastrophe of 12 December 1988 resulted in a successful prosecution, leading to the imposition of a very heavy fine on British Rail under that Act. On the other hand, the 1974 Act is not really appropriate for dealing with unsafe driving on the public highway: it has, however, been used to deal with unsafe driving on private premises covered by the 1974 Act (e.g. factory premises) and it might be used in relation to drivers' conditions of employment (e.g. an unsafe system for loading or unloading vehicles). The occupational safety inspectorate has responsibility for monitoring and enforcing regulations concerned with the carriage of dangerous substances by road (e.g. The Road Traffic (Carriage of Dangerous Substances in Road Tankers and Tank Containers) Regulations 1992).

(e) Food safety

Food safety is covered by special legislation but the premises where food is manufactured, or where it is supplied to the public, are also covered by the 1974 Act.

(f) The police force and other public services

It is questionable whether the 1974 Act applies to protect police constables, since they are neither employees nor self-employed persons. Civilians, who nowadays play an increasingly important role in supporting constables in the operation of police services, are undoubtedly within the protection of the 1974 Act. The Consultative Document on the implementation of the EC Directive on manual handling of loads recognises that to secure full implementation of the Directive special consideration would have to be given to provision of protection for the police. In the event they do not appear to be covered by the Manual Handling Operations Regulations 1992.

Similar arguments apply in relation to the armed services: in proposals to implement EC Directives provision was made for the Secretary of State for Defence to exempt military forces from the regulations in the interests of national security; and this has been done (e.g. Regulation 6 of the Manual Handling Operations Regulations 1992).

Other public emergency services, such as those provided by firemen and ambulance crews, are within the ambit of the 1974 Act but the inherently dangerous nature of their work, not least the emphasis on public rather than personal safety, present particular problems in the application of the Act.

(g) *Agriculture*

When the Bill which became the 1974 Act was debated in Parliament there was controversy as to whether agriculture should be included: it is in fact within the Act. It presents its own particular problems not least because of the hazards to which children are exposed on farms both at play and when working with other members of their family.

(h) *Factories, mines, etc.*

There were many workplaces and work-related situations, of which factories and mines are but two examples, which were within the ambit of protective legislation before the 1974 Act. This earlier legislation was not immediately repealed by the enactment of the 1974 Act. On the coming into force of that Act it remained in force and the establishments and situations covered became subject to two sets of regulatory legislation, that is both the detailed standards of the old law and the general duties within the new law.

The earlier legislation which was to be embraced by the system established by the 1974 Act was identified in Schedule 1 of the Act as 'Existing Enactments which are Relevant Statutory Provisions'. Within this schedule are listed some 30 Acts of Parliament. In the years after 1974 change occurred, and there were partial repeals of much of this legislation. The Alkali etc. Works Regulation Act 1906, for example, was virtually repealed and the situations covered by it are now transferred from the jurisdiction of the 1974 Act to The Environment Agency.

However, 20 years after 1974 some of the standards contained in the earlier legislation were still applicable, though the penalties and the enforcement procedures were, in respect of both old and new laws, those of the 1974 Act. However, with the passage of time the old laws became of less significance. The revision and phasing out of earlier legislation was, from the 1980s, conducted in the context of UK responses to EC Directives. The implementation of the six pack on 1 January 1993 provided the opportunity for repealing much of the legislation pre-dating the 1974 Act which was still in force at that time.

14. System of updating

Section 1(2) of the 1974 Act stated that it was a specific intention of the new law to enable the older laws to be progressively replaced by a system of regulations and approved codes of practice to operate in association with the provisions of the 1974 Act itself. New laws made under s. 1(2) had to be drafted to maintain or improve the standards established under the earlier Acts.

Section 1(2) made no provision for the repeal of old laws without replacement. The Deregulation and Contracting Out Act s. 37 gives the Secretary of State power to repeal obsolete pre-1974 safety legislation without enactment of comparable modern provisions. Section 1(2) is not repealed; so there is some uncertainty as to how the new system for updating the law will relate to the system under s. 1(2) of the 1974 Act.

15. Interpretation

Like most contemporary statutes, the 1974 Act contains interpretation sections; in this instance they are mainly located at the end of, and refer to, Part I. They are supplemented by other interpretative provisions within other parts of the statute. All of these, together with provisions within other statutes as well as case law, give guidance as to the meaning of the words used within the Act.

Among the more important interpretation provisions are those discussed below.

(A) 'Work' and 'at work'

Section 52(1), giving meaning to 'work' and 'at work', provides:

(a) 'work' means work as an employee or as a self-employed person;
(b) an employee is at work throughout the time when he is in the course of his employment, but not otherwise; and
(c) a self-employed person is at work throughout such time as he devotes to work as a self-employed person.

Section 52(2) enables the meaning of 'work' and 'at work' to be extended by regulations. Regulation 16(2) of the Management of Health and Safety at Work Regulations 1992 has extended it for certain limited purposes:

For the purposes of Part I of the 1974 Act, the meaning of 'at work' shall be extended so that an employee or a self-employed person shall be treated as being at work throughout the time that he is present at the premises to and in relation to which these Regulations apply.

However s. 52, like many interpretation sections, leaves questions unanswered. Some further guidance is to be found in other sections of the 1974 Act but the full meaning can only be discovered by reference to case law drawn from general employment law.

The Regulations would appear to intend the extended definition to apply only to offshore installations.

(B) 'Employee' and 'self-employed'

Section 53, the general interpretation section for Part I of the 1974 Act, provides the important information that:

'employee' means an individual who works under a contract of employment, and related expressions shall be construed accordingly;

and:

'self-employed person' means an individual who works for gain or reward otherwise than under a contract of employment, whether or not he himself employs others.

These, and other definitions in the interpretation sections and related legislation, are particularly important in governing the scope and width of coverage of the 1974 Act. The Health and Safety (Training for Employment) Regulations 1990 have provided that 'employee' includes trainee.

If a contract for work is not a contract of employment, but is with an individual worker, that worker is likely to be a self-employed person, although there are yet other relationships under which work is performed. For example, some persons work under contracts which make them agents for principals. Others, notably policemen, have a special status as 'office holders'.

16. Administration and inspection

The 1974 Act made radical changes in the arrangements for administration, management, enforcement and development of occupational health and safety law. Section 10 provides for the establishment of two bodies corporate – the Health and Safety Commission (HSC) and the Health and Safety Executive (HSE) – and authorises their powers and functions. The creation of a Commission with responsibility for health and safety, and no other responsibilities, was a major innovation. Previously safety responsibilities had been shared by a number of government departments. Allocating overall responsibility to a specialist commission was calculated to raise the profile of the problem of achieving and maintaining improved working conditions.

The Health and Safety Executive, as its name implies, is the body responsible for putting policy into operation. High in priority among the functions of the Health and Safety Executive are making provision for the appointment of inspectors and monitoring that there is compliance with the provisions of the 1974 Act and other relevant statutory provisions.

17. Regulation-making powers

An important feature of the 1974 Act is the very wide and general powers which it gives to the Secretary of State to make regulations to implement the general duties, or more widely, the general purposes (as set out in s. 1(1)) of Part I of the Act (s. 15). Schedule 3 of the 1974 Act sets out some of the purposes for which regulations may be made, but s. 15(2) in referring to the Schedule makes it clear that it is not an exhaustive list. Section 1(2), expanding on the general purposes of the Act, suggests an intention that in due course the 1974 Act and regulations made subsequent to it should constitute the sole source of occupational health and safety legislation. This intention has rapidly moved towards fulfilment as EC Directives have provided the momentum for reviewing the scope and standards of the older UK laws.

It is clear from s. 15(3) that, although the general duties may be qualified by the words *reasonably practicable*, regulations may be made to stricter standards, and this is so even if they are expressly related to a particular general duty which is so qualified.

18. Codes of practice and other guidance

Regulations should not be confused with approved codes of practice: the HSC is authorised to issue such codes for the purpose of providing practical guidance with respect to the provisions of the general duties (s. 16). In contrast to regulations, compliance with a code is not mandatory so no person may be prosecuted merely for failure to observe a code, but a code may be used in evidence in criminal proceedings for breach of a relevant statutory provision.

The HSE issues guidance on how to comply with the law. Guidance notes do not have any legal significance, but can be of significant practical value and can give insight into the HSE's policy. For example, in connection with their 'Guidance Note: *Training and standards of competence for users of chainsaws in agriculture, aboriculture and forestry*' the HSE expressed the opinion that in order to comply with ss. 2 and 3 of the 1974 Act employers and self-employed persons needed to ensure that chainsaw users had adequate training and a certificate of competency. Often regulations are published with both a supporting code of practice and guidance. For example, the Safety Representatives and Safety Committees Regulations 1977 has an accompanying code of practice and two sets of guidance notes.

19. Sanctions and enforcement

The 1974 Act, like earlier occupational health and safety legislation, is rooted in the criminal law. Section 33 provides that it is an offence to break any of the duties imposed by the Act or regulations made under the Act, and that it is also an offence to contravene any requirement imposed by an inspector, or to obstruct an inspector (or indeed other persons) in the performance of the duties imposed upon them by the Act or regulations made under it. The 1974 Act differs from earlier occupational health and safety legislation in two respects: first it creates 'either way' offences under which prosecutions may lead to trial upon indictment in the Crown Court. Secondly, it empowers inspectors to serve notices rather than invoke the criminal law. Notices may be served on persons, who, in the inspector's judgment, are either breaking a duty expressly imposed upon them or are otherwise responsible for a situation entailing a risk of serious personal injury. Notices have proved a useful means by which inspectors can improve workplace health and safety without resorting to prosecution.

20. Worker participation

The Robens Committee was firmly of the view that higher safety standards could only be achieved by cooperation between employers and employees. The legislation authorised the making of regulations to set up a system for the introduction of employee safety representatives with whom the employer would be required to consult on safety matters. The Safety Representatives and Safety Committees Regulations 1977 empowered recognised trade unions to appoint safety representatives. This limited provision for worker participation undoubtedly fell short of the broad requirements of the Framework Directive for all workers to be involved and additional Regulations now extend representation to workplaces which are not unionised.

21. Relationship of the Act with other UK legislation

The 1974 Act from its inception embraced that substantial portion of the then existing occupational health and safety legislation which was identified by Schedule 1 of the Act for treatment as 'relevant statutory provisions', and the HSE have more recently been given further responsibilities in relation to industry (e.g. the offshore petroleum industry) and transport (e.g. railways) in situations where the 1974 Act was not originally the principal legislation.

Nevertheless there remain many matters which impinge upon occupational health and safety, such as public health and road safety, where the principal legislation is not within the list of relevant statutory provisions, and the legislation caters for situations where the HSE has no real authority. In some of these situations, for example shops (including those which sell food), the process of inspection and enforcement is simplified because authority has been granted to inspectors, other than those directly employed by the Health and Safety Executive, to enforce both the relevant statutory provisions and other legislation, such as the Public Health Acts. Thus Environmental Health Officers employed by local government authorities play a major part in enforcing the 1974 Act. Other legislation, like the Road Traffic Acts, is part of the general criminal law, monitored and enforced by the police, and offences – certainly those committed on the highway – will not be investigated by the HSE.

However, the boundaries between areas of responsibility may sometimes be blurred. The HSE may, for example, have to investigate motor vehicle accidents which occur on factory premises. Similarly the boundaries between environmental protection and occupational health and safety are particularly unclear in situations where workplace activities may endanger public health.

EC FRAMEWORK DIRECTIVE

22. Relationship between the UK approach and EC initiatives

On 12 June 1989 the Council of the European Community adopted a Framework Directive on the introduction of measures to encourage improvements in the safety and health of workers at work. This Directive stipulated implementation of its provisions in Member States of the Community not later than 31 December 1992.

The intent of the Directive was broadly similar to that of the 1974 Act. Indeed it might have been argued that the 1974 Act implicitly covered the matters dealt with in the Directive. Nevertheless, in the autumn of 1991, a consultative document was published proposing the Health and Safety (General Provisions) Regulations, and an accompanying approved code of practice, to spell out explicitly the general provisions of the 1974 Act in such a way that it could not be doubted that the UK was honouring the Directive.

In due course the Regulations were finalised as the Management of Health and Safety at Work Regulations 1992, and they and five other sets of Regulations (one set to implement each of the five subsidiary Directives) became law in Great Britain on 1 January 1993. The other five sets of Regulations are:

The Workplace (Health, Safety and Welfare) Regulations 1992
The Provision and Use of Work Equipment Regulations 1992
The Personal Protective Equipment at Work Regulations 1992
The Manual Handling Operations Regulations 1992
The Display Screen Equipment Regulations 1992.

Since 1974 the UK system has been one in which a very broad statutory framework was supplemented by detailed regulations to provide for specific problems, albeit problems common to most work situations. The Management Regulations sit uneasily between these two familiar levels of provision, giving some flesh to the general provisions of the Act itself, while falling short of prescribing standards for control of particular hazards.

The other sets of regulations listed above have the general application of the British 'at Work' Regulations introduced between 1974 and 1992 (e.g. the Control of Lead at Work Regulations 1980); they apply to particular workplace hazards, but apply to all workplaces without regard to the class of industry or the type of premises. They lack the clear standards of the traditional Factories Act style of legislation.

The new British regulations incorporate the concept of 'reasonable practicability' and there is some debate as to whether the EC Directives allow this qualification of liability.

23. General provisions of the Framework Directive

The provisions of the Directive concern general principles for the identification and control of occupational risks, the protection of safety and health, the informing, consulting (with balanced participation in accordance with national laws and/or practices) and training of workers and their representatives. The Directive is intended to set minimum standards and is said to be without prejudice to existing or future national and Community provisions which are more favourable to protection of the safety and health of workers (Article 1). The Directive applies to both public and private sectors of activity (Article 2).

Article 3 defines employer and worker: the latter is any person employed by an employer (thus 'worker' is not necessarily synonymous with UK 'employee').

24. General obligations of the employer under the Framework Directive

The general obligations of the employer are identified as including the prevention of occupational risks and the provision of information and training. The employer's strategy should include avoiding risks wherever possible; evaluating those which cannot be avoided; combating risks at source; adapting the work to the individual; adapting to technical progress; giving collective protective measures priority over individual protection and giving appropriate instructions to workers (Articles 5 and 6). The employer must designate one or more workers to carry out activities related to safety matters; where there are no persons within the organisation competent to do this task, the employer must enlist competent external services (Article 7).

Employers must ensure that workers and/or their representatives are provided with adequate information concerning the safety and health risks at their workplace (Article 10). Employers must consult with workers and/or their representatives on all questions relating to safety, including forward planning (Article 11). Article 12 requires employers to ensure that each worker receives adequate safety and health training.

25. General obligations of the worker under the Framework Directive

Article 13 imposes obligations on workers including the duty to inform their employer immediately of dangers.

26. Comparison between the two frameworks

The EC Directive seeks only to identify minimum standards so it does not invalidate national standards which are higher. With this proviso the following are areas in which there are similarities or differences between the Directive and what is expressly required by the 1974 Act:

(a) Both frameworks are of general application, covering almost every type of employment.

(b) The Directive seemingly makes less distinction between employees and other kinds of workers – the employing organisation has responsibilities to both.

(c) The Directive makes more explicit the employer's duty to train the worker, setting out the occasions when training is needed.

(d) The Directive requires the employer to rate 'collective' safety more highly than the safety of specific employees. If this means providing a safe working environment rather than individual protective clothing etc., it reflects the UK approach.

(e) The Directive requires employers to appoint competent persons to carry out safety management functions.

(f) The Directive envisages a greater degree of worker involvement in consultation with the employer.

(g) The 1974 Act does not expressly require the employer to assess all risks and respond to the assessment. However, regulations made under the Act, e.g. the Control of Substances Hazardous to Health Regulations 1994, do.

It might have been arguable that any slight mismatch between the 1974 Act and the Directive was not particularly important in view of the practice now adopted by the House of Lords (see Pickstone v. Freemans plc [1988]) and followed by other lower courts of interpreting UK law purposively, i.e. in such a way as to reflect the intentions of the EC in cases where there is apparent conflict between domestic and EC legislation.

The major mismatch, to which it would have been difficult to apply a purposive interpretation, was in relation to worker participation, where the Directive seemed to envisage a wider worker involvement than had currently been required by UK law where statutory support for worker representation was confined to consultation with appointed representatives of recognised trade unions. The fact that the Directive permits consultation in accordance with national laws and practices might infer recognition of the principle of subsidiarity, which allows Member States to adopt their own practices rather than follow that prescribed in the EC model. On this basis the UK's somewhat narrow approach to worker involvement might lawfully have survived the implementation of the Framework Directive, though it is doubtful whether the EC requirement for balanced participation would be met. New safety consultation Regulations resolve the dilemma.

Further a decision of the European Court of Justice has ruled that the British statutory provisions for consultation with recognised trade unions concerning proposed redundancies does not meet the worker involvement requirements of the EC's Acquired Rights Directive. This decision strongly suggests that the then current British provisions for involvement in occupational safety would similarly fall short of EC requirements for worker participation (*Commission* v. *UK* (*Collective Redundancies*) (1994).

UK RESPONSE TO THE EC FRAMEWORK DIRECTIVE

27. Management of Health and Safety at Work Regulations 1992

The Health and Safety Commission's most direct response to the Directive was to propose the Management of Health and Safety Regulations which came into effect on 1 January 1993. The main thrust of these regulations is to impose obligations on employers, supplementary to the general duties in the 1974 Act. In broad outline these Regulations (which are considered more fully in a later chapter) stipulate that every employer must:

(*i*) assess the risks to which employees and other persons are exposed

(*ii*) make, and give effect to, such arrangements as are appropriate for the necessary protective and preventive measures

(*iii*) ensure that the health of its employees is monitored in such way as is appropriate

(*iv*) appoint competent persons to assist in setting up a safe system

(*v*) set in place procedures for responding to serious and imminent dangers

(*vi*) provide its employees with information about the risks to health and safety identified by the assessment

(*vii*) where a workplace is shared co-operate to produce a safe system

(*viii*) take into account the capabilities of their employees as regards health and safety and also ensure that they are provided with adequate safety training.

Employees must use machinery, etc. in accordance with any training or instruction which has been provided, and inform the employer of any unsafe situation of which they are aware.

Progress test 4

1. What is 'enabling legislation'?

2. On whom are the general duties of the 1974 Act imposed?

3. What sections of the 1974 Act protect:
   (a) the self-employed
   (b) the general public?

4. Are there any workers not covered by s. 2?

5. What are the principal functions of:
   (a) the Health and Safety Commission
   (b) the Health and Safety Executive?

6. What is meant by 'relevant statutory provisions'?

7. What are the principal employer obligations identified by the Framework Directive?

8. How has the UK complied with the Framework Directive?

9. Do the Management of Health and Safety at Work Regulations fully address the EC objective for worker participation.

5

THE GENERAL DUTIES AND GENERAL PRINCIPLES OF LIABILITY

1. Introduction

The Health and Safety at Work Act appears to contain little substantive law: this impression is deceptive. The Act was novel in that it contained no detailed regulatory standards: instead it contained very broad and general duties, which covered virtually every contingency relating to health and safety at the workplace. There was in 1974 no British precedent for this broad approach to regulation, and many doubted whether the Act could succeed in its objectives. It is interesting, however, that this regulatory technique has now been followed in other legislation, e.g. the Consumer Protection Act.

This chapter will describe the general duties and analyse the general principles of liability under the 1974 Act. A later chapter will suggest how the Management of Health and Safety at Work Regulations 1992, which are intended to ensure compliance with many aspects of the Framework Directive, relate to the individual general duties in Part I of the 1974 Act. In the two subsequent chapters the particular general duties in the Act will be considered in greater depth. There is relatively little case law interpreting these duties. This is not unusual, for regulatory legislation which is largely enforced in magistrates courts and (apart from the Road Traffic Acts!) is rarely the subject of appeal.

THE RANGE OF GENERAL DUTIES

2. Under the 1974 Act

The general duties in the 1974 Act, in accordance with the purposes of the Act (s. 1(1)), relate to all persons at work and the protection of others who might be injured by the activities of persons at work. They also aim to ensure that all persons, whatever their status, who are associated with the workplace, and the activities carried out and the articles and substances used there, bear some responsibility for health and safety in relation to that workplace. It is as if the legislature regarded the workplace as a stage and ensured that each person who walked on stage had some role to perform. Alternatively, perhaps the legislature modelled these duties on the civil law of negligence in which a general duty to take reasonable care rests on persons who are in sufficient proximity to each other for them to be deemed to be 'neighbours'.

THE EMPLOYER'S GENERAL DUTIES

3. The duty of employers to employees

The 1974 Act emphasises that employers have great responsibilities for the health and safety of their employees. Thus s. 2(1) of the Act imposes a general duty on the employer:

> to ensure, so far as is reasonably practicable, the health, safety and welfare at work of all his employees.

This is the core provision of the Act, placed early in the order of arrangement of the duties, and in s. 2(2) spelt out in considerably more detail than any of the other duties. The priority given to the employers' duty to protect their employees is in the traditional pattern of occupational health and safety legislation. It also reflects the legislature's statement of intent in s. 1(1)(a) of the Act, where the first and foremost of the intentions of the Act is said to be 'securing the health, safety and welfare of persons at work'.

The breadth and generality of the duty distinguishes it from earlier statutes which had narrow standards. Moreover, in contrast to earlier legislation, this duty, as expanded in s. 2(2), is at least as much concerned with human behaviour as with the physical environment in which persons are employed.

4. Duties of the employer to non-employees

Section 3 of the Act also imposes a general duty on employers, but in this case the duty is imposed in respect of the conduct of their undertakings for the protection of persons other than their employees. The general duty in s. 3(1) requires the employer:

> to conduct his undertaking in such a way as to ensure so far as is reasonably practicable, that persons not in his employment who may be affected thereby are not thereby exposed to risks to their health or safety.

This duty aims to protect at least two categories of persons. First, it serves to protect workers, such as the employees of another employer, or the self-employed; the duty is particularly significant where two or more organisations are working in proximity on the same or related projects, e.g. on a construction site. Secondly, it requires the employer to have regard for the safety of members of the public.

5. Duty of the employer not to charge for safety measures

Section 9 is barely a general duty, but is contained in that part of the Act which sets out the general duties. It prohibits the employer from:

> levying or permitting to be levied on any employee of his any charge in respect of anything done or provided in pursuance of any specific requirement of the relevant statutory provisions.

This clearly prohibits any charge being made, for example for personal protective equipment, such as safety boots, glasses or hard hat which is specifically required by statute. It is not self-evident that it actually prohibits making a charge for any other safety measure which the employer regards as a practical requirement if a safe system of work is to be achieved; for example, the employer might wish to make it a work rule that safety glasses must be worn not only by persons working on the production process but also by any person passing through the production area. Whatever the extent of s. 9, if the employer's assessment that the protection is necessary to the operation of a safe system is correct, it seems unlikely that the employer would be deemed to have done all that was reasonably practicable to achieve that system by issuing a ruling that protective equipment must be worn while expecting individual employees to provide it for themselves.

GENERAL DUTIES OF OTHER PERSONS

6. Duties of those in control of premises

Section 4 imposes duties upon the controller (in effect the occupier) of premises. Since the duty does not apply to domestic premises, it is in practice normally imposed on a corporate body. The section recognises that control of premises may be shared and provides that any one controller is only to be liable in relation to those matters which are within its control. This duty, while primarily an occupiers' duty, may well fall upon a body which is also an employer. The duty is a complex one. It is a duty to do 'what it is *reasonable* for a person in his position to do to ensure, so far as is *reasonably practicable*, that the premises, all means of access thereto or egress therefrom and any plant or substance in the premises, or provided for use there, is safe and without risks to health'.

The duty is owed to persons who are not employed by the controller but who go to the premises as a place of work or to use plant or substances provided for their use there. The duty applies equally to persons other than employers, for example a landlord, who has some right of control over the premises without employing anyone there, such as the occupiers of an exhibition hall, let out to exhibitors with cleaning and catering services provided by sub-contractors.

7. Duties with regard to emissions into the atmosphere

Section 5 imposes a general duty on persons in control of certain premises in relation to harmful emissions into the atmosphere. This section straddles the boundary between occupational safety and environmental protection: the Environmental Protection Act 1990 acknowledged this and made arrangements for its substance to be put more firmly into legislation whose primary purpose is protection of the environment. The Environment Act 1995 provided, *inter alia*, for all the control of pollution responsibilities contained in Part I of the 1974 Act to be transferred to the Environment Agency established under that Act, as from 1 April 1996. The duty in s. 5 requires the controller of premises to use the best practicable means to prevent emissions into the atmosphere of harmful substances.

8. Duties of those supplying goods

Section 6 imposes duties on those supplying goods to the workplace. Section 6 predated, but now marches with, consumer safety legislation: it imposes duties upon designers, manufacturers, importers or suppliers of articles for use at work and is matched by similar duties on persons manufacturing, importing or supplying substances. Broadly it is the duty of these persons to ensure, so far as is reasonably practicable, that the articles or substances supplied are as safe as is reasonably practicable for use at the workplace. The Consumer Protection Act 1987 aimed to place a similar duty on sellers of dangerous goods, and, on the enactment of the latter legislation, the opportunity was taken to amend s. 6, in order to bring consumer safety and this aspect of occupational safety broadly into line, while updating occupational safety law in the light of experience.

PERSONAL DUTIES

9. General

While the main thrust of the 1974 Act is against the corporate entity in one or other of its capacities (i.e. employer, occupier of premises, manufacturer and/or trader) it also imposes duties upon individuals. These are discussed in more detail in paragraphs **10–16**.

10. Employee's duty to take reasonable care

Section 7 of the 1974 Act imposes a duty upon each individual employee to take reasonable care while at work for the health and safety of himself and other persons. This is a much wider duty on employed persons than any found in earlier legislation which has either proscribed wilful wrongdoing or imposed relatively narrow duties on certain persons with particular qualifications and/or responsibilities.

11. Duties of the self-employed

While s. 3 is a duty imposed primarily upon employers it recognises that there are some business organisations which consist only of the self-employed proprietor. It therefore imposes on the self-employed person the same duty to ensure the safety of others, so far as is reasonably practicable, as is imposed on the employer (s. 3(2)). The self-employed are also required by s. 3 to take care for themselves.

12. Duty not to interfere with safety precautions

Section 8 imposes a duty on all persons not intentionally or recklessly to interfere with or misuse anything provided in the interests of health, safety or welfare in pursuance of any of the relevant statutory provisions. This duty could be invoked against members of the public as well as persons at work, e.g. against a student who took a guard off a machine in a training workshop, a hospital patient who interfered with some electrical equipment, or a customer in a department store who removed an emergency exit sign. The limitation on the scope of the provision is not on the classes of person who might be liable but on the conduct which is proscribed, i.e. liability is only for reckless or intentional interference. This leaves questions as to whether there could be liability for well-motivated but dangerous interference, e.g. switching off a fire alarm believed to be too sensitive to be reliable.

Liability is only for interference with something which has been provided specifically to comply with safety legislation. Thus not every dangerous practical joke (e.g. putting a mouse trap in the drawer of an office desk) or theft of valuable equipment (e.g. a word processor) would necessarily create liability under this section. However the practical joker, if an employee, might arguably incur liability under s. 7.

13. The actual offender

The 1974 Act contains complex provisions such as are commonly found in regulatory legislation to enable an actual wrongdoer to be brought to justice where a duty has been placed upon one person, but the breach in law has been caused by another. Paragraphs 14 and 15 below give further details.

14. Offences caused by others

Section 36 provides that where the commission by any person of an offence under any of the relevant statutory provisions is due to the act or default of another person that other person may be charged with and convicted of the offence whether or not proceedings are taken against the other person. For example, if an employee (or the student in the example given above in relation to s. 8) took a guard off a machine, the presence of the unguarded machine could render the employer in breach of s. 2 and/or s. 3 of the 1974 Act. The person who had removed the guard might be personally prosecuted by virtue of s. 36, but this prosecution would not preclude the employer from being prosecuted also, and convictions might be secured against both person and organisation if the circumstances were such as to show they were both at fault – the individual for doing the wrongful act, the organisation for failing to identify and rectify the situation.

15. Directors' liability

Section 37, a 'directors' liability' provision, enables liability to be imposed upon board-level managers where the corporate body is in breach of its duties. The section may only be invoked against the most senior management, persons who, as it were, represent the *alter ego* (the very brain) of the corporation. Whereas s. 36 is aimed primarily at the person who by *positive action* brings about an unsafe situation, s. 37 is particularly appropriate for situations where senior managers have *omitted* to set up a safe system or to curb unlawful behaviour – allowing wrongs to go unchecked through connivance or ignorance based on neglect.

Section 37(1) provides:

Where an offence under any of the relevant statutory provisions committed by a body corporate is proved to have been committed with the consent or connivance of, or to have been attributable to any neglect on the part of, any director, manager, secretary or other similar officer of the body corporate or a person who was purporting to act in any such capacity, he as well as the body corporate shall be guilty of that offence and shall be liable to be proceeded against and punished accordingly.

A person may be liable under this section even though he does not in fact have the management position he holds himself out as having. Also the section assumes a conviction under this section will be in addition to, rather than an alternative to, a conviction against the corporation.

Section 37(2) provides that if the affairs of a corporation are managed by its members such members may be prosecuted as if they were directors.

Liability under both ss. 36 and 37 lies in relation not only to breaches of the general duties under the 1974 Act itself but also in relation to breaches of duties in other relevant statutory provisions.

16. Personal and corporate liability

It will be apparent that the 1974 Act, like certain other regulatory legislation (e.g. seat-belt provisions of road traffic legislation), does not allow a person to escape the burden of compliance where no other person is at risk. Section 3(2) and s. 7 are especially relevant in this respect.

In the case of the 1974 Act, however, it is comparatively rare for the individual person to be solely liable: it is likely, though not inevitable, that if an individual person is creating a hazard, there will be an organisation – either an employer or a contractor – who is at fault for tolerating the presence of this hazard. If this is so, that organisation may also face prosecution. For example, if a worker is not using plant and equipment according to proper safety routines, then the organisation is likely to be at fault for permitting this misuse. The most common exception to the general position is director's liability under s. 37 (discussed above) especially in the case of small companies. It is relatively common for criminal liability to be imposed upon the managing director of a small company.

APPLICATION OF THE LAW

17. Criteria for prosecution

It is now necessary to consider what the prosecution has to prove to establish that the accused is guilty of an offence, and what the defendant has to establish in order to escape liability. This is partly a matter of determining the relevance of the defendant's attitude (or state of mind – see paragraphs **21–28** below), and partly a question of identifying the standard of performance the law requires.

18. Standard of performance required

The majority of the duties under the 1974 Act – i.e. ss. 2, 3, 4, 6 – require the person upon whom they are imposed to ensure health and safety at the workplace to the extent that is *reasonably practicable*. However, s. 4 is complicated by the further qualification that a controller of premises has to take such measures as are *reasonable for a person in his position* to ensure the premises are as safe as is *reasonably practicable*. Section 5 requires *the best practicable means* to be taken by the controller of premises to prevent emission into the atmosphere of noxious or offensive substances. Section 7 requires the employee to take *reasonable care*. Section 8 imposes liability only on the person who *intentionally or recklessly* interferes. Section 9 imposes on the employer an *absolute prohibition* on raising levies to pay for safety measures.

DEFENDANT'S STATE OF MIND

19. Common law criteria

The common law rule is *actus non facit reum nisi mens sit rea*, i.e. a wrongful act does not make a person guilty unless their mind is also blameworthy. Thus the common law imposes on the prosecution the burden of proving both *the wrongful state of affairs (actus reus)* and the state of mind in which the wrong was committed (*mens rea*) in order to establish that a defendant has committed an offence. If both elements of the offence cannot be proved then the prosecution has not made out a case. The following paragraphs explore this aspect further.

20. Mens rea in statutes

Section 8 of the 1974 Act, which states that liability depends on proof that the accused had intentionally or recklessly interfered with something provided in the interests of health, safety or welfare, is, at least as far as the word intentionally is concerned, in the tradition of the common law *mens rea* offences, requiring the prosecution to establish that the accused actually intended to interfere. The courts have interpreted 'intention' as being synonomous with 'aim'. In *R* v. *Mohan* [1976], the Court of Appeal defined intention as:

> a decision to bring about, insofar as it lies within the accused's power, [a particular consequence], no matter whether the accused desired that consequence of his act or not.

21. Reckless

The meaning of the word reckless is more problematic. It has been considered by the courts on a number of occasions in the context of a number of statutes, and it is not easy to reconcile the various judicial statements. It is clear that a person is reckless when taking an unjustifiable risk. The doubt is whether the test of what is unjustifiable is an objective or a subjective test. That is to say, is it unjustifiable because reasonable people would think it unjustifiable (the objective test), or is it unjustifiable because the defendant personally foresaw that he was taking a risk (the subjective test). For example, applying the subjective test might exonerate someone of limited intelligence who took what to normal people might appear an unjustifiable risk.

To some extent the case law varies according to the statute under consideration. It is arguable that s. 8 of the 1974 Act has much the same purpose as s. 1 of the Criminal Damage Act 1971 which makes it a criminal offence for someone intentionally or recklessly to destroy property belonging to another. In relation to this section the courts have in recent years applied the subjective test, using what is now known as the *Caldwell* test.

In *R* v. *Caldwell* [1982] Caldwell set fire to a hotel, when he was drunk, in pursuit of a grievance he had against the owner. Caldwell claimed that he was so drunk that he did not know what he was doing. While disallowing a defence of being drunk, the House of Lords nevertheless chose to give an explanation of the meaning of recklessness as used in s. 1(1) of that Act. Lord Diplock, with whom two other of their Lordships agreed, said:

> In my opinion, a person charged with an offence under s. 1(1) of the 1971 Act is 'reckless as to whether or not property would be destroyed or damaged' if (1) he does an act which in fact creates an obvious risk that property will be destroyed or damaged and (2) when he does the act he either has not given any thought to the possibility of there being any such risk or has recognised that there was some risk involved and has none the less gone on to do it.

In *R* v. *Savage* (1991), the House of Lords considered *Caldwell* in the context of s. 20 of the Offences Against the Person Act 1861. They held that under s. 20 the prosecution had to prove either the defendant intended, or that he actually foresaw, his act would cause harm.

22. Gross negligence in criminal law

In *R* v. *Holloway* [1993], in which an electrician was charged with the common law offence of manslaughter, after his poor workmanship had led to the death of a householder, the Court of Appeal was inclined to equate recklessness with gross negligence. Lord Taylor stated he considered there to be evidence of gross negligence where there was:

(a) indifference to an obvious risk of injury to health

(b) actual foresight of the risk coupled with the determination nevertheless to run it

(c) an appreciation of the risk coupled with an intention to avoid it but also coupled with such a high degree of negligence in the attempted avoidance as the jury consider justifies conviction

(d) inattention or failure to advert to a serious risk which goes beyond 'mere inadvertence' in respect of an obvious and important matter which the defendant's duty demanded he should address.

23. Ambiguity in statutory provisions

Where the legislature's intentions are less clearly stated, it is necessary to refer to the rule that statutes should be interpreted as narrowly as possible, on the presumption that they do not intend to change the common law. Applying this rule in *Sweet* v. *Parsley* [1969] (a case concerning unlawful possession of drugs) the House of Lords took the view that, even if a statutory provision is silent as to whether the prosecution has to establish the defendant's *mens rea*, the normal rules of statutory interpretation imply the necessity for the defendant to be shown to have had a guilty mind, if the offence is an indictable one with a heavy penalty. It is arguable that the *Sweet* v. *Parsley* ruling should be applied to offences under the 1974 Act when they are tried upon indictment, but it may be that proof of *mens rea* is only required if the offence is one which carries imprisonment.

24. Strict liability

Traditionally, regulatory legislation dealing with matters such as occupational health and safety has deviated from the common law rules by imposing strict liability, i.e. the prosecution has been required only to show that the accused's act or omission was wrongful in order to discharge the burden of proving an offence has been committed.

The Factories Act 1961 had within it a number of duties which were of strict liability, the best known of which, s. 14(1), provided: 'Every dangerous part of any machinery . . . shall be securely fenced . . .'.

Courts to some extent reduced the duty by finding that the machinery was not dangerous and therefore did not require a fence. Cases like *Hindle* v. *Birtwhistle* [1897] established that for the purposes of s. 14(1) machinery was only to be regarded as dangerous if it were a reasonably foreseeable cause of injury to anybody acting in a way in which a human being may be reasonably expected to act in circumstances which may be reasonably expected to occur. Thus what might otherwise have been regarded as an offence of little less than absolute liability was reduced to one of strict liability, by making reasonable foresight of danger a criterion of liability.

25. Absolute liability

Offences of absolute liability are rarely found in English law. An offence is in theory of absolute liability if it is one in which the defence has no answer once the prosecution has made out a prime facie case. Arguably s. 9 of the 1974 Act is in this category. However, it is noteworthy that senior judges have lately suggested that general duties to do what is reasonably practicable create absolute liability subject only to the defence of reasonable practicability. (*See* e.g. *R* v. *British Steel plc* [1995] per Steyn LJ.)

26. Defences

Sometimes the legislation expressly gives certain defences to offences of strict liability: these can be invoked by a defendant to answer the prosecution case. For example, s. 161 of the Factories Act 1961 enabled a person charged with an offence to lay information alleging that someone else was the actual offender; then, if the offence was established against the person charged, that person might escape liability if he could prove to the satisfaction of the court:

(a) that he has used all due diligence to enforce the execution of this Act . . . ; and

(b) that the said other person had committed the offence in question without his consent, connivance, or wilful default.

Defence sections containing the phrases 'used all due diligence' and 'without his consent, connivance, or wilful default' were often written into regulatory statutes, and are still found in regulations. There is no such defence provision in the 1974 Act.

27. State of mind and general duties

The fact that all the general duties are qualified by expressions such as *reasonably practicable* suggests they are not pitched at a standard of strict liability. But it has been held that these duties are strict – indeed some judges have said absolute – subject only to the s. 40 defence that it was not reasonably practicable to achieve absolute safety (*Mailer* v. *Austin Rover Group plc* [1989] below). It must follow that the prosecution can make out a case without reference to the defendant's state of mind, but, possibly, the defendant could rebut a prima facie case of liability by showing a lack of intent – the reverse of the normal rule of criminal law. However, a defendant would not succeed by establishing lack of intent if, in the view of the court, his conduct had, objectively considered, been negligent or lacking in foresight.

STANDARD OF DEFENDANT'S CONDUCT

28. Reasonably practicable

This expression, which is used so frequently to qualify the standard of performance required by the duties under the 1974 Act, was previously used to qualify some of the duties in the Factories Acts and Mines and Quarries Acts. Judicial statements as to the meaning of the expression were given in civil cases for damages for breach of statutory duty. Thus in *Nimmo* v. *Alexander Cowan & Sons Ltd* [1968], a case on the interpretation of s. 29(1) of the Factories Act 1961 (safe means of access to, and safe place of, employment), the House of Lords held that, once the hazard had been established, the onus of proving that it was not *reasonably practicable* to remove it in order to comply with a statutory obligation lay on the defendant. This judicial interpretation of the onus of proof, given in a civil court, has now been placed firmly in the criminal law by s. 40 of the 1974 Act. Section 40, which also applies to duties where the qualifying words are *practicable* or a duty requires the use of *the best practical* means, provides:

> In any proceedings for an offence under any of the relevant statutory provisions consisting of a failure to comply with a duty or requirement to do something so far as is practicable or so far as is reasonably practicable, or to use the best practicable means to do something, it shall be for the accused to prove (as the case may be) that it was not practicable or not reasonably practicable to do more than was in fact done to satisfy the duty or requirement, or that there was no better practicable means than was in fact used to satisfy the duty or requirement.

The Act is unclear as to what the prosecution has to establish before the burden of proof passes to the defendant. At first sight the duties are strict duties comparable to the strict duties of the earlier legislation such as the Factories Act 1961 – the comparison seems the more appropriate because the defence of 'reasonably practicable' appeared in that legislation. The matter was considered by Lord Goff in *Mailer* v. *Austin Rover Group plc* [1989], a case concerned with the liability of controllers of premises under s. 4 of the 1974 Act. In considering the meaning of 'safe and without risks to health' as used in s. 4(2), Lord Goff stated:

> Counsel for the respondents submitted that, for present purposes, premises should be regarded as 'safe and without risks to health' if they are in such condition as to be unlikely to be the cause of injury, harm or risk to health to persons who are, or who may reasonably be expected to be, in them . . .
> This proposition I am, however, unable to accept. To me the words 'safe and without risks to health' mean, prima facie, what they say, though no doubt they have to be related to the use for which the relevant premises are made available. Take the example of premises which, owing to an unknown and indeed unforeseeable defect, are in fact unsafe for such use . . . I do not for my part see how the unforeseeable nature of the defect . . . can nevertheless mean that the premises . . . are safe . . . It may be that if the danger in question is not foreseeable, the defendant

will not be held to be in breach of his duty; but if so, that will not be because, in the examples I have given, the premises . . . are to be regarded as safe, but because the qualified nature of the duty may not give rise to any liability in the particular circumstances.

Thus his Lordship was arguing that the duties are absolute rather than strict duties, and unforseeability relates to the defence of reasonably practicable rather than to the standard of the initial duty.

Lord Goff's analysis was not expressly adopted by the remainder of the House, but as indicated above, Steyn LJ adopted the same approach in *R* v. *British Steel* [1995].

29. What the defendant has to establish

Lord Goff's proposal that the defendant could escape liability by pleading that the risk was not foreseeable – presumably that it was not objectively foreseeable, rather than that the defendant personally did not foresee it – raised a previously unconsidered interpretation of the defence allowed by s. 40. The usual interpretation is that the task of evaluating what is *reasonably practicable* is a cost-benefit exercise, a matter of weighing the cost of removing or controlling the hazard against the probability of injury and the likely severity of that injury. The words of Asquith LJ in *Edwards* v. *National Coal Board* [1949], spoken in the context of a civil action for breach of the duty imposed by s. 102 of the Coal Mines Act 1911, are usually adopted as expressing that criterion of liability:

'Reasonably practicable' is a narrower term than 'physically possible', and implies that a computation must be made in which the *quantum* of risk is placed in one scale and the sacrifice involved in the measures necessary for averting the risk (whether in money, time or trouble) is placed in the other, and that, if it be shown that there is a gross disproportion between them – the risk being insignificant in relation to the sacrifice – the defendants discharge the onus upon them. Moreover, this computation falls to be made by the owner (i.e. defendant) at a point of time anterior to the accident.

The question of what was *reasonably practicable* in relation to general duties under the 1974 Act was considered in *West Bromwich Building Society Ltd* v. *Townsend* [1983]. The building society had an improvement notice served on it requiring it to install bandit screens. The case was of considerable importance because it had implications for all banking premises. On appeal the High Court allowed the appeal of the building society. The Court made the point that the risk had to be weighed against the cost, which would be onerous, and suggested that the industrial tribunal had considered only whether it was physically and financially possible to erect the screens, rather than whether it was reasonably practicable to do so.

In another, unreported, appeal, heard in an industrial tribunal against a prohibition notice, the tribunal again had to consider the cost in relation to the risk. A prohibition notice was served upon a hotel proprietor requiring certain improvements to a swimming pool. The owner complied with all but one term of the notice – a term which required that there be constant lifeguard supervision while there were bathers in the pool. The proprietor stated that the cost of full-time supervision would be in the region of £30,000 p.a. and alleged that this type of expenditure was not *reasonably practicable* in view of the small number of local users who would continue to use the pool in the off-peak season. The tribunal agreed that, when a computation was made between the degree of risk and the amount of money which would have to be spent, the term was not a reasonable one and should be removed from the notice.

30. No defence of limited means

An organisation is not able to argue that its own limited means make it impracticable for it to comply with the terms of either an improvement or a prohibition notice: the cost-benefit analysis is in relation to the risk, not the profitability, or indeed the viability, of the enterprise (*Belhaven Brewery Company Ltd* v. *McLean* [1975]).

31. Cost-benefit vs. foresight?

The cost-benefit and the foresight tests are not necessarily mutually exclusive. It is not inconceivable that a relatively cheap safety measure might be ignored because the need for it was not foreseen. For example, a poisonous fluid can easily be coloured at small cost: it would not appear necessary to do this if not even experts had known that the particular fluid could be poisonous.

32. Practicable and best practicable means

Practicable and *best practicable means* are expressions not commonly found in current health and safety legislation. *Best practicable means* is used only in s. 5 of the 1974 Act, but *practicable* has been used in earlier statutory provisions, such as s. 157 (impracticable) of the Mines and Quarries Act 1954.

It is agreed that *practicable* means something other than physically possible: to be *practicable* a measure must be possible in the light of current knowledge and invention (per Parker J in *Adsett* v. *K & L Steelfounders and Engineers Ltd* [1953]). In *Jayne* v. *National Coal Board* [1963] Veale J held that 'impracticability' was a concept different from that of 'impossibility'. He said:

> ... the latter is absolute, the former introduces at all events some degree of reason and involves at all events some regard for practice.

33. Reasonable care

The employee is required to take reasonable care for the safety of himself and of other persons while at work. The concept of *reasonable care* is more commonly associated with the civil law of negligence than with the criminal law. In civil law the term is applied to evaluate the defendant's conduct objectively: it is a matter of what other reasonable people think about the defendant's behaviour and it is immaterial what the defendant himself believed or intended. It seems that when used in the context of s. 7 of the 1974 Act it is used as a yardstick of the defendant's conduct rather than in relation to the guilty intention of the defendant.

COMPETENT PERSONS

34. Lack of legislative definition

The term has not hitherto been interpreted in primary legislation, though a Home Secretary expressed the opinion that in relation to the examination of machinery or plant the person should have such practical and theoretical knowledge and actual experience of the type of machinery or plant which he had to examine as would enable him to detect defects or weaknesses which it was the purpose of the examination to discover.

There is some case law on the meaning of competency because it has been included in earlier legislation. Indeed, it has been used fairly frequently in the Factories Acts and the Mines and Quarries Acts, and associated subordinate legislation, to describe the attributes of a person entitled to carry out periodic statutory examinations on pressure vessels, lifting machinery and the like, or, in some circumstances, to supervise safe working conditions. It is also to be found in regulations made under the 1974 Act (e.g. the Electricity at Work Regulations 1989 and the Control of Substances Hazardous to Health Regulations 1988).

Winn J considered the concept in *Brazier* v. *Skipton Rock Company* [1962], a case arising under the Quarries (General) Regulations 1956, Regulation 41 of which required the manager '. . . to make and ensure the efficient carrying out of arrangements to secure that every inspection . . . to be carried out or done by a competent person appointed by him is assigned to a competent person so appointed.' His Lordship expressed the opinion that experience might be as important as academic qualifications. The case was a compensation claim in which the plaintiff, a one-eyed man (appointed as the competent person), had failed to observe a hazard and had in consequence suffered personal injury. His Lordship stated, dismissing the claim:

> It sometimes seems to me that when, in courts of law, we consider the practical workings of industrial and other organisations, we tend to become somewhat academic and overlook the fact, the truth, that experience is so often of much greater value than book learning or certificates, and that a man who has been at the job for the best part of 25 years day by day watching the indications of peril to himself and his mates is at least as likely to be competent as a young man who has just come from a mining technical college.

In effect the organisation which had to appoint a competent person had to exercise its judgment as to whether a particular person was suitable for the appointment. In the event that an obvious hazard was discovered, or an accident occurred which was related to the appointment, then the appointing organisation could be put on enquiry to as whether they had discharged their duty.

'Competence' is now defined in Regulation 6 (5) of the Management of Health and Safety at Work Regulations 1992 for the purposes, at least, of those Regulations.

35. Competency under the 1974 Act

The general duties under the 1974 Act do not expressly require the appointment of competent persons, though it is arguable that if the employer is to set up the safe systems which the Act undoubtedly requires, then competent persons must be appointed.

THE SIGNIFICANCE OF THE GENERAL DUTIES

36. Common attributes

The following attributes are shared by all the general duties:

(a) They are enforceable in their own right. The contrary argument was made, and rejected, in the Court of Appeal, criminal division, in relation to s. 3(1) in *R v. Swan Hunter Shipbuilders Ltd* [1981].

(b) The general duties may be used to support regulations, but regulations may be made under s. 15 for the general purposes of the Act without relying on a general duty.

(c) Regulations may stipulate minimum standards in relation to general duties.

(d) Regulations, and indeed particularisation of duties within the Act itself, will not exhaust the general duty. For example, s. 2(2) following on from the statement made in s. 2(1) of the employers' general duty to his employees, begins:

Without prejudice to the generality of the employer's duty under the preceding subsection . . .

and then proceeds to list matters to which the general duty extends – but the preamble clearly intends that the following paragraphs (a) to (e) do not exhaust the duty in s. 2(1).

(e) The duties are enforceable to ensure the control of hazards; thus liability can arise even though there has been no incident, accident or injury.

(f) The duties carry criminal sanctions, but their interpretation frequently falls to be made in appeals arising out of improvement or prohibition notices, proceedings which are not, in themselves, criminal.

(g) The duties are not intended to secure environmental protection though they may incidentally assist this in that some environmental pollution is hazardous to health; however this may be less relevant now that the Environment Act 1995 has expressly defined the boundaries between environmental protection and occupational health and safety.

(h) The general duties may not be used to support a civil action for compensation (s. 47(1)(a)).

(i) The provisions of the Act, including the general duties, are not enforceable against the Crown (s. 48), though Crown premises are not generally exempt from inspection.

(j) The similarity between the general duties and the civil law invites reference to compensation claims based on negligence to provide guidance in their interpretation. This invitation was accepted by Dunn LJ in giving judgment in the *Swan Hunter* case:

> Mr Potts, for the Crown, submitted that there was nothing revolutionary or novel in the duties imposed by ss. 2 and 3 of the 1974 Act. He pointed out that before 1974 there was a duty on the main contractor to co-ordinate the operations at a place of work so as to ensure the safety not only of his own employees, but also the employees of sub-contractors. He referred us to *McArdle* v. *Andmac Roofing Co and Others* [1967] . . .

His Lordship then went on to quote at some length from the judgment of Edmund Davies LJ in the civil case.

Progress test 5

1. Name the categories of persons on whom general duties are imposed.

2. What provision is there in the 1974 Act for ensuring that actual wrongdoers do not escape liability?

3. What is meant in this context by 'directors' liability?'

4. Which of the duties are not at the standard of what is 'reasonably practicable'?

5. What is meant by:
   (a) strict liability
   (b) absolute liability
   (c) *mens rea*?

6. Does The Health and Safety at Work Act 1974 impose liability for 'gross negligence'?

7. Outline the meanings which judges have given to the expression 'reasonably practicable'.

8. Are the general duties enforceable:
   (a) in their own right
   (b) against the Crown?

6

RESPONSIBILITIES OF EMPLOYERS AND EMPLOYEES

1. Introduction

This chapter will provide more detail about the general duties which, under the 1974 Act, regulate the relationship between employers and their own employees (s. 2) and employers' relationships with other persons (s. 3). It will then consider the duties of controllers of premises (s. 4). The duties which employees owe to themselves and to others will also be analysed (s. 7).

2. Duties owed in respect of employees

The paramount duty of employers under the 1974 Act, as under earlier statutory provisions, is to provide safe working conditions for their own employees. Section 2 of the Act, which sets out this duty, covers the following matters:

(a) The general duty (s. 2(1))

(b) Particular matters related to the general duty (s. 2(2))

(c) Safety policy (s. 2(3))

(d) Worker participation (ss. 2(4),(6) and (7)).

The following paragraphs generally follow this analysis.

THE EMPLOYERS' GENERAL DUTY

3. Summary of s. 2(1)

The general duty set out in s. 2(1) has already been identified in the previous chapters. It is therefore only necessary now to make a few brief points:

(a) The duty is owed by the employer in respect of his employees, so it cannot be imposed upon an enterprise in situations where it has no employees.

(b) Persons other than employees may incidentally benefit or suffer according to whether the duty is observed or not, e.g. visitors to a safe workplace will not be placed at undue risk.

(c) The duty is in respect of health, safety and *welfare*. The concept of welfare is rarely invoked in the 1974 Act. Most of the matters which would formerly have been classified as welfare issues are now likely to be considered as health matters.

(d) The duty normally applies only so long as the employee is 'at work' as defined in s. 52(1) of the Act. However *Bolton Metropolitan Borough Council* v. *Malrod Installations Ltd* [1993] held that there could be criminal liability for failure to observe safety legislation even though at the time in question no worker was present or at risk (see below)

The duty, being a public duty, rather than a duty owed to particular workers, has to be complied with to ensure that the workplace, its plant and equipment are safe at all times regardless of whether employees are actually present.

A breach will occur when unsafe plant and equipment is made available for use. The law requires that the workplace is prepared and maintained in such a way as to 'protect the employee who comes to work to-morrow' (per Tudor LJ sitting in the Queens's Bench Divisional court in *Bolton Metropolitan Borough Council* v. *Malrod Installations Ltd* [1993]). Thus the law will be broken if unsafe equipment is at a workplace in circumstances where it might be used, even though no-one is using, or has used, it at the time it was identified as unsafe.

(e) The duty is owed in respect of employees, rather than to employees: it is not enforceable by employees but by the Health and Safety Executive or their agents.

(f) There is some doubt as to the circumstances in which enforcement can be based on breaches of s. 2(1). On the one hand an improvement notice based on a breach of s. 2(1), standing alone, was upheld in *Chrysler UK Ltd* v. *McCarthy* [1978]; on the other hand McNeill J in the *West Bromwich Building Society* case said:

> It is not easy to visualise the factual situation in which a breach of s. 2(1) could be charged and my impression is that it is really a parliamentary 'safety net' designed to catch any, if there be any, alleged breaches of obligations other than the obligations in s. 2(2) to (7) inclusive . . .

Nevertheless the Court of Appeal upheld a conviction under both s. 2(1), and the comparable s. 3(1), in the leading case of *Swan Hunter*.

PARTICULAR MATTERS RELATED TO THE GENERAL DUTY

4. General

Section 2(2)(a) to (e) itemises particular aspects of the employers' duty to their employees in very general terms. The emphasis is throughout on *systems* rather than *standards* and in every paragraph the requirements are qualified by the words *reasonably practicable*.

While s. 2(2), paragraphs (a) to (e), are very general, they apply to every workplace within Great Britain whereas earlier legislation and regulations made under it applied only to specified categories of premises or situations and the

1974 Act in no way extended the ambit of these earlier laws. Nevertheless earlier regulatory standards accepted by industry in the particular situations to which they applied might, since 1974, in the absence of specific regulations, have been evidence of what it was reasonably practicable for all employers to do in compliance with the more general requirements of s. 2(2)(a) to (e). For example, the standards set for the heating and lighting of factories under ss. 3 and 5 of the 1961 Factories Act might well have been indicative of the standards which it was reasonably practicable to achieve in workplaces which are not covered by detailed regulatory standards.

Indeed, even after the repeal of the Factories Act 1961 many of the Factory Act standards are still to some extent cited in codes of practice and guidance issued supplemental to newer provisions of more general application, but less specific content. This is particularly true of the Workplace (Health, Safety and Welfare) Regulations 1992. Nevertheless the value of these older regulatory standards has decreased, because the standards themselves have been overtaken by advancing technical knowledge.

4(i). Section 2(2)(a): machinery

Section 2(2)(a) requires:

> the provision and maintenance of plant and systems of work that are, so far as is reasonably practicable, safe and without risks to health.

Giving first priority to safety of machinery at the workplace follows in the tradition of earlier legislation which laid considerable emphasis on this aspect of workplace safety. There are, however, at least two ways in which s. 2(2)(a) enables progress beyond the point of the detailed provisions of the earlier legislation and the regulations made under it:

(a) It requires not only the installation of safe plant, it also requires it to be maintained and used according to a safe system, e.g. not overloaded or used for purposes other than that for which it was intended.

(b) It requires the plant and systems to be such as not to endanger health, e.g. plant in itself safe, in that it was securely guarded, might nevertheless be in contravention of this provision if it were set at such a speed as to cause the user to suffer repetitive strain injury.

4(ii). Section 2(2)(b): handling, storage and transport

Section 2(2)(b) requires:

> arrangements for ensuring, so far as is reasonably practicable, safety and absence of risks to health in connection with the use, handling, storage and transport of articles and substances.

This paragraph takes the 1974 Act beyond the Robens Report for transport which was expressly excluded from that Committee's terms of reference. However, s. 2(2)(b) relates only to transport of goods, not to the transport of persons.

(Transport of employees might possibly be covered by s. 2(2) (d) (below) which requires provision of a safe means of access to work.)

Transport and handling of goods at the workplace is clearly an important aspect of workplace safety. Hoists and lifts and lifting tackle have long been subject to regulatory control (*see* ss. 23–27 of the Factories Act 1961).

Section 2(2)(b), imposing duties on employers in respect of the handling of goods, relates to s. 6, and regulations such as the Chemicals (Hazard Information and Packaging) Regulations 1994, made under it. The duties under s. 6 are imposed primarily on persons such as the supplier of these substances, but clearly s. 2(2)(b) imposes a duty on the employer to ensure that the information supplied by the supplier is taken into account at the workplace.

In the same manner compliance with the requirements of the Control of Substances Hazardous to Health Regulations 1994, and the duties they impose on the employer to assess substances before they are used at the workplace and ensure that they are used safely, serves to discharge the obligations imposed by s. 2(2)(b).

The Health and Safety Executive have introduced training systems for fork-lift truck drivers.

4(iii). Section 2(2)(c): information, instruction, training, supervision

Section 2(2)(c) requires of the employer:

> the provision of such information, instruction, training and supervision as is necessary to ensure, so far as is reasonably practicable, the health and safety at work of his employees.

This paragraph is at the very core of the legislation. It provides the element which distinguishes it from earlier statutes which placed their emphasis on the working environment rather than on the behaviour of people at the workplace.

Section 2(2)(c) is strengthened by the duty imposed on the inspector under s. 28(8) to communicate to employees factual information obtained by him during an inspection of premises about matters which affect their health, safety or welfare. The employer additionally has a quite separate duty to consult with authorised safety representatives (s. 2(6)). The duty under s. 2(2)(c) is, however, owed to each employee individually, not to safety representatives.

The requirement for the provision of instruction, training and supervision stresses the need for employers to introduce and maintain systems of work. Before new systems are introduced those whom they will affect should be instructed as to their purposes, trained as to their implementation and thereafter monitored to ensure that the systems put in place are actually employed in practice.

4(iv). Meaning of 'instruction'

There is judicial authority for the proposition that 'instruction' has two meanings: it means both to teach and to order (*Boyle* v. *Kodak Ltd* [1969]), and the employer who is to discharge his duties must be prepared in the last instance to invoke disciplinary measures against an employee who does not follow the systems put in place for reasons of safety. In practice it is unlikely that an inspector will prosecute a worker who is not following the employer's system of work without also bringing a parallel prosecution against the employer for failure to do all that is reasonably practicable to ensure that the system is actually implemented and maintained.

4(v). Wider implications of s. 2(2)(c)

The discussion about s. 2(2)(c) has, to this point, focused on its operation in the context of the contract of employment, and there is no doubt that a duty imposed for the protection of employees will not be complied with if it is not implemented in the relationship between an employer and its own employees. However, a careful reading of s. 2(2)(c) reveals that it does not merely require the employer to provide information, instruction, training and supervision solely to employees so that they may protect themselves. It also requires the dissemination of information, the provision of instruction and training to, and the supervision of, whomsoever might otherwise by their conduct endanger employees. This was confirmed by the Court of Appeal in:

> R v. *Swan Hunter Shipbuilders Ltd* [1981]: There was a fire on HMS *Glasgow* which was under construction in Swan Hunter's yard: eight men were killed. The fire started during welding operations by contractors. The fire, which started in a confined space in the well of the ship, was particularly intense because the atmosphere was oxygen enriched. The dangers of using oxygen in poorly ventilated spaces were well known to Swan Hunter and their Safety Officer had drawn up a 'Blue Book' of instructions for users of fuel and oxygen. Copies of this book were distributed to Swan Hunter's own employees but not to employees of other companies working alongside Swan Hunter's own men. At the trial Swan Hunter were found guilty of failing to provide information to Telemeter employees. They appealed against this conviction.

The Court considered the application of s. 2(2)(c) to these facts. Swan Hunter had, at trial, submitted that no duty lay on them under s. 2(2)(c) to provide information or instruction to any workers other than their own employees. The trial judge had ruled against this submission and the main ground of the appeal was that, as a matter of law, the judge was wrong. It was submitted for Swan Hunter that an employer had no right to instruct those employed by others and that therefore the duty to provide information, instruction and training could not extend to those employed by other undertakings. The Court of Appeal nevertheless upheld the ruling of the trial judge that there was a strict duty to provide a safe system of work for an employers' own employees, and if fulfilling that duty involved information and instruction being given to persons other than the employer's own employees, then the employer was under a duty to provide such information and instruction. The employers's protection was contained in the words 'so far as is reasonably practicable': the onus of proving, on a balance of probabilities, that it was not reasonably practicable in the particular circumstances of the case lay on the employer. If another employer obstructed the giving of the necessary information and instruction, then that employer would himself be guilty of an offence under s. 36 of the Act.

4(vi). Section 2(2)(d): place of work

Section 2(2)(d) requires:

> so far as is reasonably practicable as regards any place of work under the employer's control, the maintenance of it in a condition that is safe and without risks to health and the provision and maintenance of means of access to and egress from it that are safe and without risks.

This provision virtually replicated s. 29 of the Factories Act 1961, but unlike s. 29 it applies to all workplaces. This difference is compensated by the qualification in s. 2(2)(d) that the employer's duty extends only to any place of work which is under the employer's control. Significantly, s. 29 of the Factories Act was repealed by Regulation 27 and Schedule 2 of the Workplace (Health, Safety and Welfare) Regulations 1992 and there is no comparable replacement provision within these new regulations.

4(vii). Section 2(2)(e): working environment

Section 2(2)(e) requires from the employer:

> the provision and maintenance of a working environment for his employees that is, so far as is reasonably practicable, safe, without risks to health, and adequate as regards facilities and arrangements for their welfare at work.

This provision does not seem necessary in relation to the physical working environment since this is provided for in earlier paragraphs, especially in s. 2(2)(d). It is arguable that it applies to job satisfaction, and in particular to stress engendered by poor working arrangements.

SAFETY POLICY

5(i). Requirements of s. 2(3)

A novel and important feature of the 1974 Act was the requirement in s. 2(3) that an employer write a safety policy. Section 2(3) is not particularly well phrased and needs careful analysis in order to understand its full import. It reads:

> Except in such cases as may be prescribed, it shall be the duty of every employer to prepare and as often as may be appropriate revise a written statement of his general policy with respect to the health and safety at work of his employees and the organisation and arrangements for the time being in force for carrying out that policy, and to bring the statement and any revision of it to the notice of all of his employees.

The subsection in fact requires three matters to be addressed:

(a) the organisation's statement of policy

(b) an identification of personnel with safety responsibilities

(c) a statement of arrangements for dealing with particular hazards.

Organisations have found it difficult to determine what s. 2(3) requires and have been puzzled why the Health and Safety Commission does not provide more detailed guidance. For the Commission to have provided a model document would have completely defeated the purpose of the section. The intention is that the organisation shall spend time identifying the relationship between the actual management structure and system of operation and its safety needs. The requirements of s. 2(3) will be considered in more detail in a subsequent chapter.

5(ii). Exception to s. 2(3)

All but the smallest organisations have to have safety policies: the Employers' Health and Safety Policy Statements (Exceptions) Regulations 1975 exempted organisations where less than five people were employed in the undertaking.

In *Osborne* v. *Bill Taylor of Huyton Ltd* [1982] the defendant company were served with an improvement notice under s. 2(3) requiring them to prepare a written safety policy. Subsequently when they were charged with the criminal offence of ignoring the notice, they argued that they were within the exception regulations. The company owned and controlled 31 betting shops but at the shop which was the subject of the notice they employed only two full-time, and one part-time, member of staff. The justices accepted that the betting shop was a distinct place of work; it was the undertaking for the purposes of the Regulation and the exception regulations applied. On appeal by the prosecution by way of case stated it was held by the Divisional Court that the justices had correctly interpreted the regulations in that the test was not how many employees were on the 'payroll' but how many were at work at any one time; provided no more than five worked at one time an undertaking was exempt.

In *J Armour* v. *Skeen* [1977] there was a controversial conviction of the director of roads for Strathclyde under s. 37 of the 1974 Act following a fatal accident in which a workman had fallen to his death. Mr Armour's prosecution under s. 37(1) was in relation to his 'neglect' in fulfilling the responsibilities for health and safety placed on him by the council, including having a sound safety policy for his department, informing employees of the implications and requirements of the Act, and training and instructing them in safe working practices. Mr Armour appealed against the decision of the Sheriff Court on the grounds that he personally was not under a statutory duty to provide a safe system of work and therefore the accident could not be attributable to any neglect of such a duty. In addition, he claimed that he could not be personally prosecuted as he did not fall within the ambit of s. 37(1).

The High Court of Judiciary upheld the conviction. The neglect on the part of a person charged under s. 37(1) need not be a neglect only in relation to a duty which the legislation had placed on that person; s. 37 referred to *any* neglect. In the present case the council's safety policy placed responsibility for ensuring safe conditions of work on directors and the appellant's duty was to prepare a written general safety policy in relation to the work of his department. His failure to do so constituted neglect within the meaning of s. 37(1). Moreover, while the appellant was not a 'director' as that word was used in s. 37(1), having regard to his position in the organisation of the council, and the duty which was imposed on him in connection with the safety policy, he was within the class of person referred to in s. 37.

WORKER PARTICIPATION

6. Section 2

The remaining provisions of s. 2, while imposing duties on employers, are somewhat different in emphasis from the earlier subsections of s. 2, being concerned with procedures for worker involvement in safety at the workplace. These provisions were a response to the Robens Committee's concern that accidents were caused by apathy arising from workers' failure to associate themselves with maintaining safe systems at the workplace. The detail and implications of these provisions will be discussed in the chapter on worker involvement.

EMPLOYERS' DUTIES TO WORKERS NOT THEIR EMPLOYEES

7. General

Section 3 of the 1974 Act imposes upon employers duties in respect of persons who are not their employees. Section 4, while imposing its obligations upon controllers of premises, in practice may often be imposing duties on employers in respect of workers visiting their premises: such certainly was the situation in *Mailer* v. *Austin Rover Group plc* [1989]. Neither s. 3 nor s. 4 is exclusively concerned with the protection of employed persons; indeed, both sections are wide enough to provide protection for persons other than workers. It has been held that an organisation may owe duties under s. 4 even though there are no persons employed to work at the premises concerned (*Westminster City Council* v. *Select Managements Ltd* [1985]). In this chapter ss. 3 and 4 will only be considered in the context of the protection of workers.

7(i). Duties imposed by s. 3(1)

Section 3(1) imposes a general duty in the following words:

> It shall be the duty of every employer to conduct his undertaking in such a way as to ensure, so far as is reasonably practicable, that persons not in his employment who may be affected thereby are not thereby exposed to risks to their health or safety.

This duty has proved to be most important, making a very substantial contribution to the establishing and maintaining of safe systems of work where two or more undertakings are working in close proximity. Section 3(1) is particularly suited to the situation, such as commonly occurs on building sites, where a head contractor (who may possibly have his own employees on site) subcontracts to one or more other organisations to carry out specialist work on site. There is, in these circumstances, a need for each group of workers to have regard for the other group(s) when planning their work and there may on occasion be a need for the head contractor to inform the subcontractors of hazards, e.g. asbestos, which may be encountered in the course of the work. The importance of the section has increased because of the tendency in permanent workplaces to reduce the size of the directly employed work units, with the consequence that employers contract-out services such as catering and cleaning. At mobile work sites, as are found in construction work, there has been a considerable growth of small specialised employers.

The requirements of s. 3(1) were considered by the Appeal Court in the *Swan Hunter* case (*see* above). Swan Hunter argued that s. 3(1), though directed to the protection of persons like the visiting employees of the subcontractors, imposed no duty on them because it required nothing specific. They pointed out that s. 3(3) enabled regulations to be made identifying circumstances in which employers had to provide information to persons not in their employment and argued that the only cases in which there would be a duty on employers like themselves would be if there had been regulations made under s. 3(3) specifying that particular information had to be imparted. The trial judge dismissed this contention and the Court of Appeal had no hesitation in adopting the words in which he did so as being a correct statement:

> ... subsection (3) does not impinge upon nor does it limit in any way subsection (1) of s. 3. Subsection (3) is dealing with a very limited class and a very limited number, namely the prescribed cases where only prescribed information is to be given. If subsection (1) were to be subject to subsection (3), why then I should expect it to say so, but the words in my judgment in subsection (1) are wide enough to include the giving of information and instruction to employees other than one's own employees ...

The Court of Appeal therefore held that s. 3(1) required the giving of information to the visitors for their own protection.

7(ii). Enforcement of s. 3(1)

Since s. 3(1) is enforceable only by the Health and Safety Executive it is not directly available to employers (or workers) as a tool for establishing and maintaining safe systems.

7(iii). Satisfying the duties imposed by s. 3(1)

Where the safety of two workforces is dependent on co-ordination of the activities of their respective employees, the proper way to achieve the necessary safe system is through contractual arrangements. Where there is a contract between two organisations for the performance of work that contract should almost certainly contain details as to the system to operate for the purposes of ensuring safety. The occupier of premises bringing another employer's workforce on to the premises may well wish to stipulate that the visitors follow the established site procedures. This contractual provision will only be effective if the occupier can be confident that both the visiting employers and their workers are conversant with these procedures. Merely enclosing a copy of the safety policy amongst other contractual documents may not achieve this. It may well be necessary to instruct and supervise the visiting workers directly.

The giving of information contractually to employers of other workers is only relevant in cases where there is a contract between the two employers. It would not be relevant where both employers were subcontractors of the head contractor. In cases such as this the subcontractors are each dependent on their separate contracts with the head contractor.

Where a subcontracting organisation considers its employees are endangered by the working conditions under the contract, that employer owes a duty to its own employees either to ensure that the working arrangements are made safe or the contract is terminated. Putting pressure on the head contractor is likely to be the only practical way in which a subcontractor can respond to hazards created by another subcontractor. The obverse of this proposition is that there is a duty on the head contractor in such circumstances to make certain that the work of the subcontractors is coordinated so that the undertaking, of which their separate undertakings are but part, is in total a safe operation. The Court of Appeal noted this in *Swan Hunter*, quoting from the judgment of Edmund Davies LJ in *McArdle v. Andmac Roofing Co. & Others* [1967], a compensation case arising out of personal injury suffered by a contractor's (Andmac) employee when working together with the employees of another subcontractor (Newton), at a site occupied by the head contractors (Pontins). Of the latter's contract manager his Lordship said:

> He not only engaged the subcontractors but directed all the work that they were to do and when they were to do it, and in some instances gave orders how it was to be done. He conceded that he was the coordinating authority to bring together the various subcontractors at the right time and the right place . . . Safety precautions were never discussed with any subcontractor . . . He simply expected them to make such safety arrangements as they thought fit.

Pontins' failure to set up a safe system rendered them liable to contribute to the compensation of the accident victim. They shared liability with the two subcontractors whose systems were at fault in that they ought also to have foreseen the hazards created by the uncoordinated system of work. Under the 1974 Act all three employers might expect to be found criminally liable under s. 3(1) in a situation such as this.

The Construction (Design and Management) Regulations 1994 now set out the responsibilities of enterprises engaged in major building work; but the cases cited here would not necessarily have fallen within the ambit of these Regulations. In any case the principle of having clear contractual arrangements remains correct.

In *R* v. *Mara* [1987] the Court of Appeal considered the meaning of the phrase *conduct his undertaking* as used in s. 3(1). Mr Mara was the director of a cleaning company under contract with a high-street store. The cleaning work involved the use of certain electrical cleaning machinery, including a polisher/scrubber. To overcome problems of interfering with the clients' work, it was agreed that cleaning of the loading bay should be done by the clients themselves but using the contractor's equipment. The prosecution arose because one of the client's employees was electrocuted by the contractor's defective polisher/scrubber. Mara was convicted under s. 3(1). The question raised on appeal was whether the use of the defective equipment by the employee at the store in the particular circumstances could be said to relate to the conduct of Mara's undertaking, since the accident occurred on a day when Mara had no contractual duty to clean the premises. The Court of Appeal nevertheless upheld the conviction. In their view the employees at the shop were persons who might be affected by the conduct of Mara's undertaking and the court could not accept the argument that the duty in s. 3(1) was only applicable when the undertaking was in the process of actively being carried on.

7(iv). Recent cases on s. 3(1)

A number of important recent cases have addressed the principles first laid down in *Swan Hunter* without necessarily producing greater clarity.

7(v). *RMC Roadstone Products Ltd* v. *Jester* [1994]

This case seemed to limit the implications of *Swan Hunter* for the employer who enters into contract with another organisation with the purpose of the other employer bringing on site a workforce to carry out specialist activities which were unrelated to the business carried out on that site.

The Divisional Court in an appeal by way of case stated provided that an employer's mere capacity or opportunity to exercise some control over the activity of an independent contractor was not enough to bring that activity within the ambit of the employer's conduct of his undertaking for the purposes of s. 3(1).

The appellant, which carried on the business of manufacturing road-making materials, had engaged general repairers to replace some broken asbestos sheets in the side of a tower at the appellant's premises. There was no suggestion that the repairers were not genuine independent contractors. The only equipment provided by the appellant, for the use of the contractors, was a front-loading shovel. The Justices found that the appellant was in a position to give specific directions to the contractors on how the work was to be done but it was implicit in their findings that the contractors were left to do the work in any way they chose. The appellant was under no duty to lay down a safe system of work for them. A contractor fell through a skylight and suffered fatal injuries. The appellants were convicted of an offence under s. 3(1).

On appeal Mrs Justice Smith found that repairing the premises was part of the appellant's undertaking, but the question was whether when putting the repair work in the hands of independent contractors the appellant could still be said to have been conducting its undertaking. The respondent had suggested that where control was shared by both an independent contractor and his principal the activity in question might form part of the conduct of the undertaking of each.

However, to succeed the respondent had to establish not only that complete control was not necessary but also that the mere capacity to exercise some control, where there was no duty under the civil law so to do, brought that activity within the ambit of the conduct of the undertaking. There was apparently no authority for such a proposition and her Ladyship was unable to accept it. In her view it was necessary for the employer either to exercise actual control or to be under a duty to do so. Her conclusion, she noted, appeared to be consistent with the proposition which the Court of Appeal had accepted in *Swan Hunter*, as least so far as s. 2 was concerned, that the criminal law did not impose a wider duty than the civil law.

Even more recently the Court of Appeal has, in *R* v. *Associated Octel Company Ltd* [1994], cast doubt on *Roadstone* by finding an employer liable under s. 3(1) when a visiting contractor caused an accident when failing to follow the permit to work procedure required by the 'safety case' at a major hazard installation, even though the employer's own employees were not on site at the time.

7(vi). *R* v. *Associated Octel Co Ltd* [1994]

This case cast considerable doubt on *Roadstone* without directly overruling it.

An employee (C) of a contractor (RGP) was seriously injured when there was a fire and explosion in the tank where C was working on Octel's premises, carrying out maintenance work which Octel had engaged RGP to undertake during the period when the plant was closed down. Octel's plant was designated a 'major hazard installation' and so Octel had had to lodge a 'safety case' with HSE. The safety case laid down a system for the control of contractors, including that contractors must comply with the 'permit to work' system and operate under Octel's supervisor. When the accident occurred the safety case procedures were not being followed. Octel were convicted under s. 3(1).

When Octel appealed the Court of Appeal noted that it was not usual to find an employer criminally liable for the wrong doing of an independent contractor, but nonetheless considered that the maintenance work by the contractor was being carried out within the conduct of Octel's undertaking. They did not consider that an employer had to be in control of work for it to incur liability under s. 3(1); but the question of control might be relevant to what was reasonably practicable for the employer to do to ensure safety. It was more likely that it would be reasonably practicable for a large organisation to achieve control of a visiting specialist contractor than it would be for a small organisation to do so. Octel was held liable.

Their Lordships spelt out that the ingredients of the s. 3(1) offence are: that the accused is (1) an employer (2) who so conducts his undertaking (3) as to expose to risk to health or safety (4) a person not employed by him (5) who may be affected by such conduct of the accused's undertaking.

7(vii). Can *Octel* and *Roadstone* be distinguished?

It might be considered significant that Octel's plant was a major hazard installation, whereas the Roadstone plant was not. Again a possible distinction is that in Octel's case the contractors were working on the employer's specialist production plant while in Roadstone the work was general building maintenance.

7(viii). *R* v. *British Steel plc* [1995]

The ruling of the Court of Appeal in the *British Steel* case suggests that the strict standard imposed in *Octel* is to be preferred to the more lenient approach in *Roadstone*.

British Steel employed two men on a labour-only basis to re-position a section of steel platform at their plant. The defendant's engineer was deployed to supervise the operation. When the engineer was not present the workmen rendered the platform unstable and it fell on to, and killed, one of them. When charged under s. 3(1) the defendants accepted that re-positioning the platform was inherently dangerous but argued that the accident occurred because the men had not followed the British Steel engineer's instructions and they pleaded that they had done all that was reasonably practicable to ensure the safety of the men. Further they pleaded that if there had been any fault it was that of their engineer and the company should not, in criminal law, be liable for the fault of a relatively junior employee in the discharge of his duties.

In the Court of Appeal Steyn LJ held that s. 3(1) imposed absolute liability subject to the defence of reasonably practicability and a corporate employer could not avoid liability on the basis that the company had taken all reasonable care at senior management level. The employer was liable under s. 3(1) in relation to the acts of even junior employees, where their action exposed non-employees to risk. Accordingly the Court of Appeal upheld British Steel's conviction.

7(ix). Section 3(2): duties imposed on the self-employed

Section 3(2) treats the self-employed person as if he were an employer and places exactly the same obligation upon him in regard to the conduct of his undertaking as s. 3(1) places on the employer. In *Jones* v. *Fishwick* (1989) an industrial tribunal upheld an improvement notice served on a master butcher under s. 3(2), requiring him to wear a chainmail apron to prevent him stabbing himself when boning out meat.

8. Duties imposed by s. 4

The duties which s. 4(1) imposes upon a controller of premises are owed in relation to persons who are not the controller's employees, but who use those (non-domestic) premises as a place of work or as a place where they may use plant or substances provided for their use there. The duty is imposed by virtue of s. 4(2) on each person who has, to any extent, control of premises to which the section applies. It is a duty to take such measures as it is reasonable for a person in the controller's position to take to ensure, so far as is *reasonably practicable*, that the premises are safe and without risks to health. The section suggests that the duty may be confined to making the premises safe for the purpose for which the controller makes them available, but this is not entirely clear; it may be that the controller, having granted access to the premises, is liable for their condition, even if used beyond the purposes for which he intended access. However, the liability in respect of plant or substances is expressly limited to liability for plant and substances provided for the use of the visitors.

The House of Lords considered the implications of this section in relation to visiting workers in *Mailer* v. *Austin Rover Group plc* [1989]. Austin Rover (the respondents) had premises containing a spray painting booth beneath which was a large sump used to collect excess paint and thinners during painting operations. The booth contained a piped supply of highly flammable thinners for use in painting. The respondents employed a contractor to clean the booth at times when there was no production. The contract for the work required that nobody should be in the sump when anyone was working in the booth above, that the contractor's employees should not use the piped supply of thinners but should use their own supplies, that thinners used in the cleaning should not be sent into the sump, and that only a flameproof electric lamp should be taken into the sump. These safety provisions were ignored. There was a flash fire and a man in the sump was killed. The respondents were prosecuted under s. 4(2) for failure to take such measures as were reasonable for them to take to ensure so far as was reasonably practicable that the sump and piped thinners were safe and without risks to health. The House of Lords held that once it was proved in a prosecution under s. 4(2) that premises which had been made available by a controller were unsafe and constituted a risk to health the onus lay on the respondent to show that, weighing the risk to health against the means, including cost, of eliminating the risk, it was not reasonably practicable for him to take these measures. However, if the premises were not a reasonably foreseeable cause of danger to persons using the premises in a manner or in circumstances which might reasonably be expected to occur, it was not reasonable to require any further measures to be taken to guard against unknown and unexpected events which might imperil their safety.

Since it was not reasonable for the respondents to take measures to make the spray painting booth and sump safe against the unanticipated misuses of those premises by the contractor's employees the magistrates had been wrong to convict the respondents.

The reasoning of their Lordships was interesting. They took the view that the starting point was that the premises should be absolutely safe so that if they proved to be unsafe, regardless of the way in which they had been used, the burden shifted to the controller, who might then escape liability by establishing that it was not foreseeable that the premises would be used in the manner in which they had been used and/or it was not incumbent on him to have done more to make the premises safe. In deciding the extent of the duty the court had to bear in mind the double qualification on the controller's duty: s. 4(2) required the controller to do only what was reasonable for someone in his position to do to ensure so far as was reasonably practicable that the premises were safe.

It may be noted that the facts of this case are very similar to those of the *Octel* case but this was brought under s. 4 and *Octel* brought under s. 3.

DUTIES ON THE EMPLOYEE

9(i). Duty to take reasonable care

Section 7(a) imposes on the employee while at work a duty to take reasonable care for the health and safety of himself and of other persons who may be affected by his acts or omissions at work.

While the duty is to take reasonable care, it is owed not merely by ordinary employees, but also by management up to boardroom level. What is required for the discharge of the duty may well vary according to the status of the employee, and the terms of the contract of employment. The unskilled worker is unlikely to be liable for anything short of dangerous horseplay; the senior manager may be liable for failure in professional judgment, if that failure amounted to negligence. Even at management level, however, the employee's conduct will be judged in relation to the training he has been given, the authority he has, and the resources he has been allocated for the performance of his task. There has been a reluctance to invoke s. 7 when the true responsibility lies with the employer. Indeed, even in those cases in which there is actionable conduct on the part of the employee, the organisation may well be prosecuted for tolerating this conduct within its system.

9(ii). Duty to cooperate with employer

Section 7(b) of the 1974 Act imposes on the employee a duty:

> as regards any duty or requirement imposed on his employer or any other person by or under any of the relevant statutory provisions, to cooperate with him so far as is necessary to enable that duty or requirement to be performed or complied with.

This provision may overlap with s. 8 which renders an employee (as any other persons) liable for wilful or reckless interference with anything provided for safety. It may also overlap with s. 36 which enables the actual wrongdoer to be prosecuted rather than the person upon whom the duty is imposed. However, there may be circumstances which neither of these other provisions cover, e.g. where an employee did not interfere with anything and did not actually cause his employer to break a duty imposed on him but merely made it more difficult for that duty to be performed, as by failing to provide the employer with information needed for the performance of his duty. In this connection it is obvious that the more senior the employee in an organisation, the wider will be the area within which his failure to 'cooperate' may render him criminally liable under s. 7(b).

Progress test 6

1. What provisions of the 1974 Act require information to be given to employees or their representatives?

2. What meaning have the courts given to the word 'instruction'?

3. How did the *Swan Hunter* case link the employers' duty to his own employees with that owed to visiting workers?

4. What matters ought a safety policy to cover?

5. What organisations are exempted from the requirement to have a written safety policy?

6. Can an employer be conducting his undertaking though his own employees are not at work?

7. How may employers ensure that safe systems exist where several workforces are working in close proximity?

8. Is it possible that the ambit of s. 3(i) may be less than the *Swan Hunter* case suggests?

9. What has the Court of Appeal found to be the ingredients of the s. 3(1) offence?

7

OTHER GENERAL DUTIES: SAFE INDUSTRIAL ACTIVITY

1. Introduction

In this chapter the general duties will be considered in relation to the safety of goods marketed for the workplace and also in relation to public safety. These are matters which the EC has not addressed in its occupational health and safety Directives since these have been made under Article 118A of the Treaty of Rome which is concerned only with the health and safety of workers. Therefore this chapter is solely concerned with the way in which the 1974 Act approaches these issues.

However, Britain has implemented EC Directives, particularly the Framework Directive, by Regulations which require employers to relate their compliance with EC provisions to compliance with the duties in the 1974 Act and other relevant legislation. Thus in Britain EC standards have to be observed, not only for the protection for workers, but also for the protection of the public.

Some consideration must also be given to the behaviour of the public. Can members of the public be liable if workers are endangered by their activities? Could employers be liable if members of the public placed their employees in danger?

PROTECTION FOR ALL

2. Purposes of the Act

The 1974 Act gave statutory recognition to the dangers to which the public can be exposed as a result of work activity. The general purposes of the 1974 Act set out in s. 1(1) include not only the safety of people at work but also:

> protecting persons other than persons at work against risks . . . arising out of or in connection with the activities of persons at work (s. 1(1)(b)).

The incident that endangers employees may also endanger other workers and the self-employed: the employees of other employers and the self-employed are persons at work and within paragraph (a) of s. 1(1). Paragraph (b) is therefore concerned with protection of the general public. A group of workers treating wood with toxic chemicals may endanger themselves if they are not wearing suitable masks and other protective clothing; for this their employers may be liable under s. 2 and the workers might bear some personal responsibility under s. 7. If the spraying activity endangers other workers engaged nearby in, say, putting in window frames, then the woodtreaters' employers might be in breach of s. 3, using that section in the way that it was discussed in the previous chapter in relation to the protection of workers not in the employment of the employer upon whom the duty is placed. Those put at risk might also include workers employed by another employer who, at the time (as was actually the position in an unreported case), were taking a meal break, sitting eating their sandwiches in the vicinity of the spraying!

If residents in a neighbouring flat were put at risk they would be persons envisaged by the purposes of the Act as set out in s. 1(1)(b) and they would be within the scope of the employer's duty under s. 3(1). Similarly, the employee's duty under s. 7 is not confined to circumstances in which those at risk are persons at work; both sections 3 and 7 can also be invoked where the persons at risk are members of the general public.

3. Position of the self-employed

The duties are the same if the workers are self-employed; s. 3 imposes on them duties for the protection of other persons (both other workers and members of the public). The self-employed are also under a duty to protect themselves.

4. Duties of controllers of premises

Similarly s. 4 imposes duties on controllers of premises both for the protection of the general public and for the protection of workers.

5. Duties with respect to the environment

Section 5 imposes duties upon controllers of 'prescribed premises' to use 'the best practicable means' for preventing the emission of noxious or offensive substances into the atmosphere and for rendering harmless and inoffensive such substances as may be emitted. Since the coming into force of the Environment Act 1995 the enforcement of this duty has been assumed by the Environment Agency.

6. Duties on manufacturers and distributors

Section 6 imposes duties on persons engaged in the production and distribution of articles and substances for use by persons at work. Section 6, while closely related to consumer protection legislation, is in fact directly concerned with the safety of persons at work, albeit not in the employment of, or working in any geographical proximity to, any person upon whom the s. 6 obligations are imposed, i.e. the duty under this section is imposed for the protection of the 'ultimate consumers' of the article or substance, rather than the protection of those engaged in the manufacture or supply of that article or substance.

RELATIONSHIP BETWEEN THE 1974 ACT AND OTHER LEGISLATION

7. General

Many of the problems raised in this chapter are problems which were beyond the scope of earlier occupational safety legislation which focused narrowly on the employers' responsibilities to his own employees; some problems of public safety and health were formerly only dealt with in separate legislation such as environmental protection or transport safety legislation. Experience, since the implementation of the 1974 Act, has been that the boundaries between occupational safety, public safety and environmental protection are extremely difficult to maintain, though environmental protection is a wider concept, covering preservation of amenity as well as safety.

8. Leisure and sports facilities

The 1974 Act brought premises where leisure activities are enjoyed, like theatres and sports arenas, within the ambit of occupational health and safety legislation for the first time. This also blurred the boundaries between public and employee safety. For example, there was a suggestion that the HSE should bear some responsibility for the tragic fire causing the death of spectators at the Bradford football stadium, when it emerged that HSE inspectors had failed to take action which might have prevented the fire when they had noted the debris which had accumulated under the spectator seating – debris which was, with hindsight, found to be a substantial cause of this fire. Prior to the Act such situations would have been without protection under occupational health and safety legislation though they might have been, for some purposes, within the ambit of other legislation, such as the Public Health Act or the Fire Precautions Act.

9. Transport

The general duties in s. 2 clearly extend to protect transport workers, and s. 3 extends to passengers and others who might be affected by the transport undertaking, but the extent to which the 1974 Act ought to be relied on in transport cases remains controversial when more specialised legislation, and, in some cases, a more specialist inspectorate, is involved. However, the tendency is to bring transport within the province of the HSE: the HSE is responsible for enforcing the Road Traffic (Carriage of Dangerous Substances in Road Tankers and Tank Containers) Regulations 1992 and the Road Traffic (Carriage of Dangerous Substances in Packages) Regulations 1992.

Similarly the HSE has recently assumed responsibility for rail transport, using both the 1974 Act and (acting under an agency agreement with the Department of Transport) the older, specialised railway safety legislation; this special legislation is largely concerned with the safety of railway passengers. As a measure to ensure that existing standards of health and safety on railways are maintained, and, where necessary, improved, in preparation for privatisation of the railway system, the Railways (Safety Case) Regulations came into force on 28 February 1994 and the Railways (Safety Critical Work) Regulations came into force on 1 April 1994.

The HSE will also be responsible for enforcing two further sets of Regulations: the Carriage of Dangerous Goods by Road and Rail (Classification, Packaging and Labelling) Regulations 1994 and the Carriage of Dangerous Goods by Rail Regulations 1994.

THE EMPLOYERS' UNDERTAKING AND PUBLIC SAFETY

10. Provisions protecting the public

Sections 3, 4 and 5 are the sections most relevant for protection of persons other than persons at work, though s. 7 might well be invoked against an employer who, through lack of care, endangered the public, e.g. was extremely negligent in maintenance work carried out in domestic premises.

It does not appear that the 1974 Act is intended to protect the public from hazards other than those created by people at work. However the Act might well cover situations where persons, whose work included maintaining protection against natural hazards, failed to do all that was reasonably practicable to achieve that purpose. For example, a local authority might be required to monitor the level of water in a river and set in motion a flood warning system when the water reached a certain level. If the warning system failed there might be liability under the Act.

11. General duties

It has been noted that duties in s. 3(1) (on the employer) and s. 3(2) (on the self-employed) are sufficiently wide to require those upon whom they are imposed to consider the safety of the general public as well as of workers who are not in their direct employment. Both duties are phrased in the very widest possible terms requiring from the employer the 'conduct of his undertaking in such a way as to ensure so far as is reasonably practicable that persons not in his employment who may be affected thereby' are not endangered.

12. Situations in which the Act applies

Now that cases such as *Swan Hunter* have established that s. 3(1) is enforceable in its own right, it is apparent that there are innumerable situations in which an employer needs to consider, if s. 3 is to be complied with, whether his undertaking is endangering the public. For example, construction work undertaken near to the highway must be arranged in such a way as to ensure that building materials do not fall on to pedestrians. In 1991 a construction company were convicted under s. 3(1), and fined £15,000, when falsework fell from the seventh floor of a building under construction and killed a young woman in the street below. Similarly, an employer operating a storage and distribution unit may need to consider whether the movement of his heavy lorries to and from the highway endangers neighbouring residents and road users, and an employer may need to consider whether contaminated work clothing taken home for laundering might endanger those with whom his employees share living accommodation.

In *Regina* v. *Board of Trustees of the Science Museum* [1993] the Health and Safety Executive brought a charge under s. 3(1) when inspectors found that the cooling tower of the Museum's air conditioning plant contained the bacterium which causes legionnaire's disease. The prosecution's allegation was that members of the public in the street outside the building had been exposed to risk of legionnaire's disease as a result of the defendant's inadequate maintenance of the plant. The defendants admitted that bacteria were present in the cooling tower and it was common ground that escape of bacteria *could* expose members of the public to risk. The defendants unsuccessfully submitted that there was no case to answer as *no actual risk had been proved*. In summing up, the judge directed that *it was sufficient if there had been a risk of bacteria being there*. The defendants were convicted and appealed on the grounds that the judge had been wrong to reject their two submissions of no case to answer and that thereafter the judge had misdirected the jury as to the necessary ingredients of the offence charged.

Steyn LJ delivered the judgement of the Court of Appeal. In his Lordship's view the critical question was whether the prosecution had merely to prove that there was a risk that the bacteria *might* emerge from the cooling plant into the atmosphere, or whether they had to go further and show that it *did* so emerge and might then be inhaled. The prosecution had illustrated the problem by the proposition that a loose object was on a roof near to a pavement: this object might **(a)** remain in a position where it *might* fall and hit a pedestrian; **(b)** fall and *expose pedestrians to danger*; **(c)** fall and cause *actual* injury to a pedestrian. The prosecution's argument was that s. 3(1) covered all of these situations. His Lordship agreed. The conviction was therefore upheld.

13. Provision of safety information

Section 3(3) envisages that certain situations might be identified in which regulations might impose detailed requirements on employers and self-employed persons to give information to others. The provision refers throughout to 'prescribed circumstances':

> In such cases as may be prescribed, it shall be the duty of every employer and every self-employed person, in the prescribed circumstances and in the prescribed manner, to give to persons (not being his employees) . . . the prescribed information.

The statutory language is somewhat vague in that it does not indicate how these situations may be 'prescribed'; any doubt is removed by the interpretation section which states that prescribed means prescribed by regulations (s. 53).

14. Subordinate legislation

The Control of Industrial Major Accident Hazards Regulations 1984 provide an example of exactly the sort of subordinate legislation which s. 3(3) seems to expect. These regulations require that the manufacturer operating a site which constitutes a major hazard should provide information to people living or working in the vicinity of the site. In fact these regulations were made under the general regulatory power given by s. 15 of the 1974 Act without reference to s. 3(3).

The regulation-making power under the Act is so wide that it is not necessary, as was the case with older legislation, for particular sections of the Act expressly to empower the making of regulations in relation to matters dealt with in that section. It is interesting, therefore, that specific power is given in relation to this general duty – possibly for clarification given the novelty of the duty itself. Certainly it is noteworthy that the Act is similarly specific in relation to regulation-making powers in the two other areas in which duties, which were at that time novel, were created or proposed, namely safety policy and safety representatives.

15. Employers' general duty to inform the public

In *Swan Hunter* s. 3(1) was read in conjunction with s. 2(2)(c) to require an employer to provide information, instruction and supervision to workers, other than his own employees, in order to protect his own employees from hazards which might otherwise be created by the other workforce. There seems no reason, in principle, why in certain circumstances, employers might not have the same obligations placed upon them to inform and even supervise the conduct of members of the public, even though no specific regulations have been made under s. 3(3) or otherwise. For example, it is common practice for public utilities to place warning notices, such as 'Danger, Keep Away' or 'No Smoking', when persons are working in or near manholes or excavations on the highway. It is arguable that this warning to the public is needed for employers to comply with both their s. 2 and s. 3 duties to persons at work and their s. 3 duty to the public.

If, as seems probable, the employers' duty does require some control of the public in such situations, both for their own safety and for the safety of the workforce, it may be questioned whether merely placing a warning notice, without taking further 'policing' measures to ensure that the notice is obeyed, is doing all that is reasonably practicable to ensure the safety of either the workers or the public.

SAFETY OF PREMISES

16. Safety of premises open to the public

A feature of the 1974 Act was that it brought within occupational health and safety legislation for the first time many premises which were open to the public generally, or in consequence of contractual arrangements between the occupier of the premises and individual members of the public, such as educational establishments, leisure premises from theatres to sports centres, hospitals and hotels.

17. Compliance with ss. 3 and 4

In many cases compliance with s. 3 duties may make adequate provision for the safety of persons visiting such premises; it would certainly be arguable that the employers were not conducting their undertaking to the standard required by s. 3 if their premises were not as safe as it was reasonably practicable for them to be for the persons they invited to come on to them. Section 4 makes special provision for situations in which persons are lawfully on non-domestic premises, otherwise than in the course of employment by the occupier of those premises, in circumstances in which the controller may not be an employer conducting an undertaking. Thus while there are large areas of overlap between ss. 3 and 4 the two sections are not necessarily coterminous.

18. Safety of non-domestic premises

The s. 4 duty is imposed by s. 4(1) on persons controlling non-domestic premises in relation to those (excluding the employees of those on whom the duty is imposed) who use premises:

> made available to them as a place of work or as a place where they may use plant or substances provided for their use there (s. 4(1)(b)).

It has already been noted that this provision was invoked in *Mailer* v. *Austin Rover Group plc* for the protection of visiting workers using premises and plant and equipment on the premises to carry out maintenance work at a time when the controller's own employees were not on the premises.

19. 'Place of work'

Indeed, in so far as the persons protected are required by the first limb of the subsection to be using the premises as a 'place of work' the s. 4(1)(b) duty envisages exactly, and little more than, the circumstances of the *Mailer* v. *Austin Rover Group plc* [1989] case. 'Work' in the expression 'place of work' is subject to the interpretation given in s. 52, i.e. work as an employee or a self-employed person. This limb of s. 4(1) therefore would grant no protection to, for example, undergraduates using a reference library in the course of their studies, albeit they themselves would consider they were 'working' in the library!

20. Other premises

While the student in the example in **19** might not be within the ambit of the first limb of the subsection there are nevertheless situations in which members of the public (possibly including the student) might be within the ambit of the second limb of s. 4(1)(b) as persons who use non-domestic premises as a place where they may use plant or substances provided for their use there. When the 1974 Act was first enacted it was noted that the Robens Report had expressed some concern at the hazards faced by members of the public using machinery such as washing machines in laundrettes, a situation which was not necessarily within the protection of the then existing Offices, Shops and Railway Premises Act 1963. It was therefore suggested that s. 4 was intended to provide safety standards in premises such as laundrettes. Certainly the word 'plant' interpreted in s. 53 to mean 'machinery, equipment or appliance' would seem to include washing machines in laundrettes, facilities in public conveniences, supermarket trolleys, petrol pumps and other garage forecourt equipment, and perhaps furniture in hospital wards or hotel bedrooms, to mention but a few examples.

21. Scope of the provision

Since the duty is only owed in relation to non-domestic premises, there is some doubt whether the provision would apply to blocks of flats. It is true that s. 4 was utilised successfully in relation to a block of flats in *Westminster City Council v. Select Managements Ltd* [1985] but the application was somewhat special, and the Court of Appeal was not unanimous. The case arose because inspectors had required a property management company to carry out work to improve the lift at a block of flats. Although the company did do the repair work, they challenged whether s. 4 of the 1974 Act could be used to require them to do so, since they alleged that the flats were domestic property. In the principal judgment Parker LJ referred to s. 53 and found that it provided that 'domestic premises means premises occupied as a private dwelling'. In his Lordship's view the lifts and other common parts of the premises were not within the definition of domestic property. He also found that the definition of premises included an 'installation' and he considered the lifts to be installations within the definition of premises. The majority held that s. 4 did apply even though there was no evidence that the property company actually employed any person to work on the premises: the purposes of the Act were wide enough to protect the public even where no worker was at risk. Eveleigh LJ dissented, because there was no evidence that any person at work, such as a milkman visiting the premises, would be at risk. In his view s. 4 was only intended to protect persons at work.

None of their Lordships noted that the purposes in s. 1 of the Act are limited to protecting persons from risks arising out of or in connection with the activities of persons at work. If this provision were narrowly interpreted it is doubtful whether the above case would be considered good law, and indeed many of the hypothetical examples listed above might prove to be beyond the scope of the provision, including the laundrettes identified by Lord Robens, unless the washing machines therein had been rendered unsafe by poor maintenance carried out by persons at work!

However, in *Moualem* v. *Carlisle City Council* [1994] the Queens' Bench Divisional Court found that the duty imposed by s. 4 on the controller of premises extended to the provision of equipment and fittings at an indoor play centre; these could be deemed to be unsafe plant provided for the children's use. Again the point was not taken that the children were not endangered by the activities of persons at work.

22. Significance of the benefit

The significance of any benefit given to the public in any case depends entirely on the extent to which the section can be enforced since no civil action for breach of statutory duty may be brought by any person who suffers personal injury because this duty (or indeed any other general duty) has not been observed. Possibly there are fewer opportunities for inspectors to identify risks to the public in breach of s. 4, than there are for identification of hazards in industrial premises.

THE CONTROLLER OF PREMISES

23. Meaning of 'controller of premises'

Section 4(2) imposes the duties under s. 4 on:

> each person who has, to any extent, control of premises . . . or of the means of access thereto or egress therefrom or of any plant or substance in such premises . . .

The provision thus contemplates that more than one person may have some control of any given premises at any given time, and that every person with control has some responsibility under s. 4. It is rather surprising that the statute uses the word 'controller' since both civil and criminal law are more inclined to use the word 'occupier'. However, the argument is circular: the Occupiers' Liability Act 1957 fails to define 'occupier' but states that for the purposes of the civil liability under that Act the 'persons who are to be treated as an occupier . . . are the same as the persons who would at common law be treated as an occupier . . .' (s. 1(2)). The civil case of *Wheat* v. *Lacon & Co Ltd* [1966] (though not necessarily a binding precedent when determining issues of criminal liability under s. 4 of the 1974 Act) may usefully be considered in the present context.

Wheat v. *Lacon & Co Ltd* [1966]: The case concerned premises which were owned by a brewery. The ground floor was run as a public house by a manager employed by the brewery. The manager occupied the upper part as his private dwelling and, in the summer, his wife took in boarding guests for her private profit. Mr Wheat (a guest) fell to his death down the back staircase in the private part of the premises. The trial judge found that there were two causes of the accident: **(a)** that the handrail was too short; and **(b)** that there was no bulb in the light fitting on the stairs. Their Lordships had to determine whether the brewers or their manager were occupiers. Lord Denning deduced:

> In order to be an 'occupier' it is not necessary for a person to have entire control over the premises. He need not have exclusive occupation. Suffice it that he has some degree of control. He may share the control with others. Two or more may be 'occupiers'. And whenever this happens, each is under a duty to use care towards persons coming on to the premises, dependent on his degree of control.

Their Lordships found that both the brewery and the manager were occupiers of the premises. The manager had responsibility for the day-to-day management, including ensuring the presence of a light bulb; the brewery had responsibility for structural matters such as the handrail.

24. Duties when more than one controller

The criminal law, as set out in s. 4 of the 1974 Act, recognises the possibility of dual control of premises, and also spells out that responsibilities may be shared between controllers according to the extent of their control: s. 4(2) provides that it is the duty of each person who has to any extent control of premises to which the section applies 'to take such measures as it is reasonable for a person in his position to take'. Reference to *Wheat* v. *Lacon* may therefore be relevant not only to determine who has the status of occupier but also to provide guidance as to how responsibilities should be allocated where there is more than one occupier.

25. Others on whom the duty is imposed

The duty is specifically imposed on any person who, by reason of a contract or tenancy in relation to premises, has responsibility for maintenance or repair of the premises or for the safety (or absence of risk to health) of plant or substances at the premises (s. 4(3)). The sub-section is not however phrased to provide an exhaustive definition of 'controller': an owner occupier, for example, would clearly also be a controller. The duty under s. 4 applies only to a person who has control of premises in connection with the carrying on by him of a trade, business or other undertaking (whether for profit or not) (s. 4(4)). Arguably, therefore – depending on the interpretation of 'undertaking' – the s. 4 duties might apply to church premises or premises occupied by a charity for a fund-raising event, provided always, however, that there was sufficient association between the hazard and the activities of persons at work for the situation to be within the purposes of s. 1(1)(b) of the Act.

26. Scope of the duty

The duty is complicated because it is not a duty to ensure that the premises are absolutely safe, but only to make them as safe as is reasonably practicable. The duty of individual controllers is to do what is reasonable to achieve what is reasonably practicable! In *Mailer* v. *Austin Rover Group plc* [1989] it was held that a controller had a duty to ensure that the premises were safe for those to whom he had given the right of entry and would be prima facie liable if the premises proved unsafe, even if the defect was unforeseeable, or the visitors (who might have control to some extent) put them to some unexpected use. The controller in such circumstances would, in the view of Lord Goff, only escape liability if it were not reasonably practicable for him to foresee the risk. By stressing that the duty is an absolute one subject to the defence of reasonable practicability his Lordship leaves open the question of the relevance of the word 'reasonable' in relation to the duty; a matter of particular significance where there is more than one controller of the premises. The problem is compounded if, as in *Mailer* v. *Austin Rover Group plc* [1989] itself, the unsafe situation is produced by the behaviour of the visitors or their workers.

27. Control of the general public

It is not impossible that in order to comply with s. 4 controllers of premises might have to exercise some control over members of the public, such as crowd or vehicle control, if, without such control, the premises would not be safe.

NEIGHBOURHOOD RISKS

28. Emission of noxious or offensive substances

It has been noted that s. 3 requires the undertaking to have regard for neighbourhood risks. Section 5 relates to a particular neighbourhood risk: the emission into the environment from the work premises of noxious or offensive substances. The section was expressly related to the purposes of the Act set out in s. 1(1)(d):

> controlling the emission into the atmosphere of noxious or offensive substances from premises of any class prescribed for the purposes of this paragraph.

29. Scope of the provision

Section 5 relates only to premises, and the emission therefrom of noxious and offensive substances where the premises and the prescribed substances have been identified by regulations. The section clearly had in view the situations covered by the earlier Alkali etc. Works Regulation Act 1906, which was a relevant statutory provision. The Health and Safety (Emissions into the Atmosphere) Regulations 1983 prescribed certain classes of premises for the purposes of s. 5 and further provided that premises which the 1906 Act treated as scheduled premises should be deemed to be 'prescribed premises' under the 1974 Act and that the same substances should be deemed to be noxious and offensive for the purposes of both Acts. Enforcement of s. 5 has been transferred to the Department of the Environment by the Control of Industrial Air Pollution (Transfer of Powers of Enforcement) Regulations 1987.

The Environmental Protection Act 1990 envisaged the repeal of both s.1(1)(d) and s. 5 while making complex arrangements for the involvement of the HSE in the identification and resolution of environmental matters which would formerly have been within Part I of the 1974 Act.

The Environment Act 1995 made provision for the creation of an Environment Agency for England and Wales and a Scottish Environment Protection Agency. Since 1 April 1996 these agencies have been responsible for enforcement of the 1906 Act and what was formerly s. 5 of the 1974 Act (Environment Act 1995, ss. 2 and 21). The creation of the new Agencies is a major step towards the implementation of the system of integrated pollution control introduced by the 1990 Act. It remains to be seen whether s. 5 and what remains of the 1906 Act will in due course be repealed and replaced by legislation squarely within the environmental protection regime.

For present purposes further discussion of this section is no longer appropriate. However the *Science Museum* case [1993] (discussed elsewhere) serves as a reminder that risks to public health and safety by emissions into the atmosphere might be prosecuted under s. 3.

THE WORKER AS CONSUMER

30. General

Section 6 of the 1974 Act contained provisions for the worker, as a user of articles and substances, in terms which have since been largely adopted for the protection of consumers generally by virtue of the Consumer Protection Act 1987, Part II. In addition, on the enactment of the 1987 Act, s. 6 of the 1974 Act was revised both to clarify certain phrases originally used within s. 6 and also to bring fairground equipment within the ambit of s. 6 (Consumer Protection Act 1987, s. 36 and Schedule 3). Section 6 is, however, except for the provisions concerning fairground equipment, intended solely for the protection of persons at work.

31. Persons under duty

Section 6 imposes its duties on persons who design, manufacture, import and supply articles for use at work (s. 6(1)) or any article of fairground equipment (s. 6(1A)), and on persons who manufacture, import or supply any substance for use at work (s. 6(4)). Surprisingly, in the revised wording, the duty in regard to articles apparently applies only when goods are intended, i.e. manufactured etc., for use at work, whereas the duty in respect of substances applies when substances are used at work, seemingly whether or not this was the intention of the manufacturer etc. Section 6(3) places duties on persons who erect or install articles for use at work, or who erect or install fairground equipment.

32. Nature of duty

The duties in s. 6 are to do what is *reasonably practicable* to ensure so far as is *reasonably practicable* that the articles, fairground equipment and substances are safe and without risks to health in the circumstances to which the duties relate.

The difference in wording between s. 6(1) and s. 6(4) identified in the previous paragraph may not therefore be very significant: a supplier etc. who does not intend that substances are for use at work may be able to establish that it was not *reasonably practicable* for him to identify the risk of their being so used.

It may be noted that articles and substances not intended for use at work might be intended for supply to the general public and might then be products falling within the ambit of the Consumer Protection Act 1987. However, Part I of that Act (civil liability) provides the producer with certain defences including that 'the person proceeded against did not supply the product to another' (s. 4(1)(b)): clearly articles produced by another manufacturer would fall within this defence and presumably goods stolen from the producer would not be supplied and would also fall within s. 4(1)(b) of the 1987 Act. Under s. 6 of the 1974 Act it might not be reasonably practicable to prevent stolen articles and substances being used at the workplace, but it might further be necessary, in order to escape criminal liability under the 1974 Act, for the defendant manufacturer to show that at the time when stolen they were not *intended* for the workplace.

33. Activities to be protected

(a) An article is required to be safe and without risks to health, so far as reasonably practicable, 'at all times when it is being set, used, cleaned or maintained by a person at work', and that (see below in relation to provision of information) it is safe etc. 'when it is being dismantled or disposed of'.

(b) The obligation in respect of fairground equipment is to ensure its safety 'at all times when it is being used for or in connection with the entertainment of members of the public'.

(c) The obligation in respect of a substance is to ensure its safety 'at all times when it is being used, handled, processed, stored or transported by a person at work or in premises to which s. 4 applies', and that (see below in relation to provision of information) it is safe etc. 'when being disposed of'.

34. Application of the provisions

Broadly the obligations apply to the use of the articles, equipment and substances at work, but it has been deemed necessary to spell out activities in association with their use to ensure that the duty is not evaded by arguing that the activity being conducted was not use at work. For example, if the words 'stored', 'transported', 'cleaned' and 'maintained' had not been expressly included it might be argued that any of these activities, even though possibly associated with use at work, was distinct from that activity and without the scope of a duty which was stated merely to apply to 'use'.

Nevertheless in *McKay* v. *Unwin Pyrotechnics* (1991) the Divisional Court held that there had been no contravention of the duty under s. 6(1)(a) when a person was injured while carrying out the first trial and demonstrations of a dummy mine. It could not be said that the mine was designed for use at work. Thus there was no breach of the provision even though the victim had been injured while at work.

35. Fairground equipment

In the case of fairground equipment the requirement relates to its condition when it is being used for, or in connection with, the entertainment of members of the public. Bringing this provision within the 1974 Act illustrates the concern which has been felt in recent years for matters of public safety.

36. Specific requirements regarding articles

Those bearing duties in respect of articles and fairground equipment are required to ensure that these commodities are safe (and without risks to health) in design and construction. Further to this requirement they are required to carry out, or arrange for the carrying out, of such testing and examination as may be necessary to ensure their safety. However, persons are not required to repeat any testing or examination if the circumstances are such that they may reasonably rely on the results of work which has been undertaken by others.

37. Provision of information

There is a duty, expressed in similar, but not identical terms, in relation to the provision of adequate information about articles and fairground equipment:

> to take such steps as are necessary to secure that persons supplied by that person with the article are provided with adequate information about the use for which the article is designed, or has been tested, and about any conditions necessary to ensure that it will be safe and without risks to health.

The duty in respect of articles applies when they are being set, used, cleaned or maintained by a person at work and when they are being dismantled or disposed of. The duty in respect of fairground equipment applies only when it is being used for, or in connection with, the entertainment of members of the public. This raises the question whether there is any statutory protection for those who are cleaning, maintaining, dismantling, etc., fairground equipment. Presumably it would be argued that when these activities are being carried out by persons at work, and the public is not involved, the general provisions concerning articles would apply to the equipment in question, i.e. that the special provisions in relation to fairground equipment are in addition to, not an alternative to, the general provisions relating to articles.

38. Revision of information provided

In respect of both articles and fairground equipment there is a duty to secure, so far as is reasonably practicable, that persons who have been supplied with information are also provided with any revisions of information which are necessary by reason of it becoming known that anything gives rise to a serious risk to health or safety.

39. Specific requirements regarding substances

The specific duties in respect of substances are very similar to those outlined in respect of articles, though, to take account of the different inherent problems in relation to substances, the duty in respect of provision of information is somewhat differently worded (s. 6(4)(c)):

> to take such steps as are necessary to secure that persons supplied by that person with the substance are provided with adequate information about any risks to health or safety to which the inherent properties of the substance may give rise, about the results of any relevant tests which have been carried out on or in connection with the substance and about any conditions necessary to ensure that the substance will be safe and without risks to health . . .

The duty to carry out tests and research in relation to substances before they are marketed for use at work (s. 6(5)) is especially important given the large number of new chemical substances being brought into use in industry at the present time. The onerous nature of the duties means that it will be unlikely that a manufacturer or supplier of something which emerges as a dangerous substance is able to plead that the risk to persons at work from the use of that substance was not foreseeable.

Moreover the general duty has been underpinned, by the introduction of the Notification of New Substances Regulations 1993 (to implement part of an EC Directive on classification, packaging and labelling of dangerous substances). The basic requirement is that a manufacturer or importer may not supply a new substance in any substantial quantity unless the HSE has been provided with a technical dossier to enable the evaluation of the risks which the substance may create for people or the environment. Compliance with these Regulations would, in practice, be likely to protect a manufacturer or supplier from liability under s. 6 of the 1974 Act in respect of a category of substances; but liability could still arise in the case of a particular consignment not complying with the technical specification notified to HSE.

The general duties in the Act are only imposed in respect of things done in the course of a trade, business or other undertaking, but they apply whether or not the activity is carried on for profit.

40. Scope of duty imposed

A person's duty extends only to matters which are within that person's control. This suggests that the ambit of the manufacturer's duty might be different from that of, say, the supplier. In this respect s. 6 may be contrasted with the Consumer Protection Act 1987: under that Act the strict civil liability to compensate for injuries caused by unsafe goods is placed primarily upon the producer (i.e. the manufacturer), whereas the criminal liability rests primarily upon the supplier (i.e. generally the shopkeeper). However, under both consumer and occupational safety legislation the primary objective must be to identify unsafe goods before they have been supplied for use, and serve a prohibition or similar, notice to prevent their onward supply. Consumer protection legislation has focused on seizure of unsafe goods at the point of entry into the jurisdiction and has given customs officers power to seize and detain imported goods to facilitate the work of enforcement officers. The 1987 Act inserts s. 25A into the 1974 Act to give customs and excise officers similar powers in respect of articles and substances intended for use at work.

41. EC safety standards

It is not possible to invoke s. 6 against goods in relation to dangers directly consequential upon compliance with EC safety standards.

42. Written undertakings

Section 6(8) gives limited powers to persons who design, manufacturer, import or supply articles to reduce their obligations: it enables them to get a written undertaking from the person with whom they are dealing that that other person will take specific steps sufficient to ensure that the article will be used in compliance with the requirements of s. 6. This subsection cannot be interpreted as a general invitation to manufacturers and suppliers to enter into contracts transferring their statutory responsibilities to their customers. It is clear that the subsection is intended only to apply to limited circumstances where the nature and extent of the transfer of obligations is clearly spelled out; it seems likely that there would need to be established that there was some particular purpose for the arrangement other than lightening the obligations of the person taking the benefit of the undertaking. Possibly the special reason might be that the article was supplied for incorporation in some larger article the purchaser was constructing to a special specification, e.g. a guard might not be needed for a part of a machine where the whole, of which it was to be a part, would be covered by a protective device.

43. Risk not foreseeable

Section 6 originally contained a proviso exonerating manufacturers etc. from liability in cases where it could be shown that the article or substance in question had been rendered unsafe by being other than 'properly used'. The application of this proviso proved problematic and since the 1987 Act the expression is no longer used. Instead the exemption from liability is given in relation to what is reasonably foreseeable. Section 6(10) now provides:

> For the purposes of this section an absence of safety or a risk to health shall be disregarded in so far as the case in or in relation to which it would arise is shown to be one the occurrence of which could not reasonably be foreseen . . .

103

The addition of this proviso does not appear to add anything to the interpretation of *reasonably practicable* (which is the standard in s. 6) which was given in the *Mailer* v. *Austin Rover Group plc* [1989] case; it will be recalled that in that case it was suggested in the House of Lords that the defence of reasonable practicability might be established by showing that the risk was not foreseeable. Moreover, the wording of s. 6(10) suggests that the burden would be on the defendant to establish under that subsection that the risk was not foreseeable.

44. Articles and substances

Section 6 relates to articles and substances, whereas the Consumer Protection Act, in the tradition of consumer protection, relates to goods. It is probable that largely the same commodities are covered by both safety statutes. Certainly the EC's Directive on classification, packaging and labelling of dangerous substances resulted in similar regulatory provisions under both pieces of legislation (subject to provisions to accommodate the fact that substances are often supplied to industry in bulk). However, the 1974 Act envisages also equipment which would have no place in the supermarket and it (like the 1987 Act) contains its own definitions:

'article for use at work' means –
(a) any plant designed for use or operation (whether exclusively or not) by persons at work, and
(b) any article designed for use as a component in any such plant;

'substance' means any natural or artificial substance (including micro-organisms), whether in solid or liquid form or in the form of a gas or vapour (s. 53).

45. Relationship between s. 6 and employers' duties

It has always been apparent that s. 6 and s. 2 were related: s. 6 imposes upon suppliers etc. obligations to ensure that safe goods are supplied to the workplace accompanied by proper instructions as to their use, while s. 2 imposes upon the employer the duty to ensure that the articles and substances brought into the workplace are safe and used in accordance with any manufacturer's instructions. In particular employers need to ensure that information supplied with invoices, or on bulk packages, actually reaches the worker using them. They also need to ensure that the worker is trained, monitored and, if necessary, disciplined to ensure safety instructions are observed. The employers' general duties have now been strengthened by the duty to assess the safety of products which is imposed upon them by the Control of Substances Hazardous to Health Regulations 1994 and by the general duty to assess the safety of the workplace provided in the Management of Health and Safety at Work Regulations 1992.

OTHER DUTIES WHICH INVOLVE THE PUBLIC

46. Duty of employees

The duty imposed on the employee under s. 7 is wide enough to require employees to have regard for public safety when they are at work, since they are required to take reasonable care for the health and safety of other persons (without any qualification) who may be affected by their acts or omissions at work.

47. Duty of the general public

Similarly s. 8 imposes duties on the general public, since without qualification it places a prohibition on interference with anything provided in compliance with any of the relevant statutory provisions. However, there is only liability under this section for behaviour which is an intentional or reckless interference.

48. Limitation of the provisions

Section 8 (as indeed s. 7 or the other general duties) cannot be invoked by enterprises against any persons who, by their behaviour, create hazards. Such organisations will have to rely on any powers they may have by reason of contract or licence to control persons whose conduct is creating hazards. Organisations may need to exercise these powers if they are to avoid being in breach of ss. 2, 3 and even 4 of the 1974 Act. If members of the public who are creating hazards will not respond to requests to desist it may be necessary to call the police in order to restrain them. Any hazardous situation which has been created will have to be remedied by the organisation as speedily as possible, whatever the long-term possibilities of obtaining an indemnity from the wrongdoer.

Progress test 7

1. Within what parameters does the 1974 Act provide protection for the public?

2. In what circumstances does s. 4 provide protection for the public?

3. What statute made provision for the repeal of s. 5 of the 1974 Act?

4. To what extent is foresight relevant to liability under ss. 4 and 6?

5. What aspects of environmental protection are clearly beyond the ambit of the 1974 Act?

6. In what circumstances does s. 6 require articles and substances to be safe?

7. What responsibilities does s. 6 impose in respect of testing and research?

8. In what circumstances may a person on whom the s. 6 duties are imposed reduce their obligations?

8

OTHER RELEVANT STATUTORY PROVISIONS

1. Introduction

It was noted in Chapter 4 that s. 53, the general interpretation section of Part I of the 1974 Act, provides that the expression 'the relevant statutory provisions' used in the context of Part I means –

(*a*) the provisions of Part I of the Act
(*b*) the existing statutory provisions, and
(*c*) health and safety regulations.

The previous two chapters have considered the general duties contained in Part I of the Act and following chapters will consider some of the more important of the general regulations made since 1974. This chapter will:

- Briefly discuss the legislation which in 1974 was described as 'existing statutory provisions'. It is convenient to consider here regulations made further to, or to replace, these principal statutes, though this will to some extent overlap with the following chapters on regulations made under the Act.
- Note legislation which has been brought within the jurisdiction of the Health and Safety Commission since 1974.
- Consider very briefly some of the other regulatory codes which might overlap with the 1974 Act.

ACTS REPEALED BY THE 1974 ACT

2. The original 'existing' statutory provisions

Schedule 1 of the 1974 Act lists over 30 statutes, the whole or part of each, which were in 1974 both existing statutory provisions and, for the purposes of the Act, 'relevant statutory provisions'. However s. 1(2) of the Act states the intention that the Acts in this Schedule, and regulations made under them, should be:

Progressively replaced by a system of regulations and approved codes of practice . . . designed to maintain or improve the standards of health, safety and welfare established by or under those enactments.

It should be noted that s. 1(2) does not authorise de-regulation; it requires that any legislation which is repealed, or any regulations which are revoked, must be replaced.

3. The significant principal legislation

Of the statutes listed in Schedule 1 the following four were sufficiently important to warrant mention here, though all but one have now been wholly, or almost entirely, repealed:

The Mines and Quarries Act 1954
The Factories Act 1961
The Offices, Shops and Railway Premises Act 1963
The Mines and Quarries (Tips) Act 1969

However it is only necessary to make detailed comment about the mines and quarries legislation.

4. General philosophy of these Acts

The first three of the Acts listed above had in common that they dealt with the health and safety of employees in particular work situations. The Mines and Quarries Act and the Factories Act were but the most recent statutes in a tradition of legislative provision dating back more than a century. Interestingly the Offices, Shops and Railway Premises Act 1963, though the first legislation to cover these areas of employment, followed very closely the coverage and standards of the Factories Acts. All four acts had a piecemeal approach which reflected the empirical response to identified problems which typified nineteenth century safety legislation.

Many of the provisions were of strict liability; making for ease of enforcement in the magistrates' courts, something which was specially helpful as the employers on whom these duties were imposed would normally be corporate bodies lacking the 'mind' to commit offences where liability depended on proof of fault or intent.

5. On-going significance of repealed Acts

(a) *Special industries*: the general approach of the 1974 Act and of many of the regulations made under it has been to favour broad provisions for application across the whole workforce. In the case of mines and quarries the peculiar nature of this activity has necessitated that the pre-1974 principal legislation could not be completely replaced by regulations of general application. Specific regulations have been required to replace much of the Mines and Quarries Act and the so-called 'extractive industries' have been the subject of a special EC Directive.

(b) *Interim provisions*: most of those sections of the Factories Act 1961 which had not previously been repealed were repealed (as were many regulations made under the 1974 Act) with the implementation of the so-called 'Six Pack' of

Regulations (considered in a later chapter) on 1 January 1993. However the regulations did not, in every case, apply immediately to existing work situations; these continued to be governed by Factory Act standards even though the legislation had to all intents and purposes been repealed. However, from 1 January 1997 all the new regulations will apply to all workplaces, and all relevant work situations and work equipment, so there is no justification for setting out the old rules here (particularly as many of the old Factory Act standards are referred to in the new code of practice which accompanies the workplace regulations). It should be noted, though, that only the pre-1993 standards will be relied on in prosecutions taken after 1997 in respect of events which occurred in exempted work situations between 1 January 1993 and 1 January 1997.

(c) *Civil liability*: plaintiffs bringing civil claims for compensation for workplace accidents and work-related ill-health can only base their claims on the law which was in force at the time when their injury was suffered. For some years therefore the statutory provisions which have ceased to be relevant for the protection of the present workforce may be used in civil litigation in claims alleging injury caused by breach of statutory duty.

Interestingly a recent Scottish case hinged on the interpretation of s. 14(1) and s. 29(1) of the Factories Act 1961. In *Mains* v. *Uniroyal Englebert Tyres Ltd* [1995] the plaintiff had been injured when part of the machine with which he was working moved unexpectedly. The trial judge held that the movement of the machine was quite unforeseeable and rejected the plaintiff's claim against his employers for damages for breach of s. 29(1) of the Factories Act 1961, which required:

> There shall, so far as is reasonably practicable, be provided and maintained safe means of access to every place at which any person has at any time to work, and every such place shall, so far as is reasonably practicable, be made and kept safe for any person working there.

On appeal the issue between the parties was whether reasonable foreseeability of danger was a pre-requisite in the determination of whether or not a work place had been made and kept safe within s. 29(1). The appeal court were of the view that s. 29(1) was a rule of strict liability subject to the defence of reasonable practicability and therefore questions of foreseeability need not be addressed by the prosecution; if the defendants maintained the danger was not foreseeable they should plead this in their defence.

It is remarkable that the plaintiff relied on s. 29(1) in a claim concerned with a dangerous machine. Normally on the fact the plaintiff would have relied on s. 14(1) (a much litigated section) of the 1961 Act, which required

> Every dangerous part of any machinery . . . shall be securely fenced.

However there is good authority (stemming from *Hindle* v. *Birtwistle* [1897]) that in civil liability based on this section the burden is on the plaintiff to establish that the danger was foreseeable.

This case provides further support for the rigorous interpretation of statutory duties where the standard is that of reasonable practicability (*see* e.g. *R* v. *British Steel plc* [1995] referred to in discussion of s. 3 of the Act). It also demonstrates that even at this stage the Factories Acts are still the subject of interpretation in the civil courts.

(d) *Interpretation of concepts*: civil litigation for breach of the statutory legislation has, over the past century, contributed substantially to the judicial understanding of the statutory language. This has been particularly so because criminal prosecutions have largely been concluded in the magistrates courts. Now that offences can be tried upon indictment, and thus reported, the role of the civil courts in this respect is likely to be less significant than formerly, but the precedential value of the old reports, in so far as they relate to the interpretation of statutory concepts remaining in common usage (notably 'reasonably practicable'), will be unaffected by the repeal of the statutes under consideration when this important judicial guidance was delivered.

For example in *Galashiels Gas Co* v. *O'Donnell* [1949] the House of Lords held, in a civil claim, that the duty then in s. 22 of the Factories Act 1937, that every hoist or lift should be properly maintained, imported an absolute obligation, and it was a defence to establish that a reasonable system of routine inspection and repair was in force. The same strict interpretation might now be expected to be adopted in relation to Regulation 6(1) of the Provision and Use of Work Equipment Regulation 1992 which requires:

> Every employer shall ensure that work equipment is maintained in an efficient state, in efficient working order and in good repair.

6. Factories and offices

Many of the Factories Acts provisions, and regulations made under these Acts, had become obsolete with the passage of time (for example 'transmission machinery' is extremely rare now that steam-powered in-plant generating equipment is uncommon). The general provisions on health, safety and welfare in this and the Offices, Shops and Railway Premises Act 1963 remained of significance until the 1990s. The subject matter of these provisions is now covered by the Workplace (Health, Safety and Welfare) Regulations 1992 and the Provision and Use of Work Equipment Regulations 1992 and the older provisions were repealed on the commencement of the new regulations.

THE MINES AND QUARRIES ACT 1954

7. General

The Mines and Quarries Act 1954 has been largely replaced by the provisions of the 1974 Act, particularly in relation to administration, regulation-making, inspection and enforcement. However, the 1954 Act and its surviving codes of regulations remain for the time being a vital, if diminishing, source of technical safety standards and practices peculiar to mining conditions.

The 1954 Act was not greatly affected by the introduction of the 'Six Pack', but the Directive on the Extraction of Minerals in Mines and Quarries has been met by the introduction of the Management and Administration of Safety and Health at Mines Regulations 1993, the amending regulations of 1995, and the Mines Miscellaneous Health and Safety Provisions Regulations 1995.

8. The 1993 Regulations

The Management and Administration of Safety and Health at Mines Regulations 1993 as amended introduced far-reaching changes to the provisions of the 1954 Act dealing with the management and administration of mines. Thus, since 1 October 1993 provisions relating to management and control of mines are located in the new regulations, while basic safety standards are still to be found in the remaining provisions of the 1954 Act and regulations made under them.

9. Management and control

The owner of every mine has duties to ensure that the mine is both managed and worked in compliance with regulatory standards. These duties are spelt out in the Coal Mines (Owners Operating Rules) Regulations 1993. The duties must be discharged through the agency of a competent manager, possessing the prescribed qualifications, appropriate to the size and complexity of the mine (Regulations 8, 17–22).

The owner of every mine must ensure that a document is prepared and maintained that demonstrates that a risk assessment has been carried out and that adequate measures have been taken to safeguard the employees in response to the hazards revealed in the assessment (Mines Miscellaneous Provisions Regulations 1995, Regulation 4).

10. The manager-employer relationship

An important feature of mines legislation has long been the power to disqualify the holder of a statutory qualification.

Further, the relationships between mine owners and managers of mines are hedged with detailed provisions that are peculiar to the mining industry. The manager's primary duty is to have 'management, command, and control' of the mine, and to secure the discharge by all others of their statutory duties with regard to the mine (Regulation 9): thus the manager bears heavy personal responsibility in the event of accident or disaster. Nevertheless, he still remains subject to the command of his employer – but such commands, when they are not in writing, must be so reduced by the employer at the manager's request (Regulation 16). Additionally, the owner of a mine may not, except in an emergency or with the consent of the manager, give instructions to the manager's subordinates; where the owner exercises his right to give such instructions, he must be prepared to confirm them in writing to the manager (Regulation 16).

11. Management structure

A management structure must be established by the owner and manager in all mines, which will define the extent of the authority and responsibility of all persons in it – and all persons forming this structure must give precedence to health, safety and welfare over any other duties they may have (Regulation 10). The appointees must hold the specified qualifications, and, where appropriate, be liable to the same professional discipline, as the manager. Surveyors, officials, and technicians must be appointed for the mine from those possessing the required qualifications (Regulations 12, 27).

12. Duty to co-operate

Where there is more than one employer operating in a mine, a duty is imposed upon them to co-operate with each other so far as is necessary to enable each employer to comply with the requirements of the relevant statutory provisions applicable to him and his employees (Regulation 4).

13. Mine safety standards

Owners and managers of coal mines must comply with the detailed require-ments set out in the remaining provisions of the 1954 Act and regulations, in addition to the relevant provisions of the 1974 Act, and certain regulations of general application, such as the Electricity at Work Regulations 1989.

The special mining requirements include safe means of egress and ingress requirements – including a 'two means of egress' requirement (the Mines (Safety of Exit) Regulations 1988) and safety precautions in connection with shafts and entrances (ss. 30–32, 36–37, 39–47).

14. Other statutory duties

(a) A vital management duty is to ensure the support of the strata of every road and working place (ss. 48–54).

(b) The duty to secure the ventilation of the mine, both to protect the health of mineworkers, and to dilute the flammable gases present in the air of the mine, is imposed in the first instance upon the manager (ss. 55). A duty also exists to remove all potential sources of ignition against fire or explosion arising from lighting sources, electrical apparatus, blasting materials, or otherwise.

(c) Stringent precautions in the use of explosives in mines are contained in the Coal and Other Safety Lamp Mines (Explosives) Regulations 1993.

(d) Special arrangements must be made and maintained for fire precautions in mines, and for the organisation of central rescue stations where specially trained rescue personnel and equipment are available to assist following mine disasters (Escape and Rescue from Mines Regulations 1995).

(e) A most important provision requires the securing of the safety of employees against the dangers from underground water, mud or similar hazards, or from incursions from the sea or other surface water (ss. 81–87).

(f) Provisions relating to the safety of machinery and work equipment in mines are now contained in the Work Equipment Regulations discussed in Chapter 10.

(g) Mines safety regulations have in recent years also been made under the 1974 Act and certain general safety regulations applied specifically to mines (e.g. Equipment Intended for Use in Potentially Explosive Atmospheres Regulations 1996).

15. Standard of duties

Duties are generally to 'secure' or to 'take such steps as may be necessary to secure' (e.g. ventilation standards, roof support, lighting, protection against water) or to 'ensure' (e.g. dust precautions). This may be contrasted with the 'reasonably practicable' qualification governing the general duties under the 1974 Act.

16. Quarries

The 1954 Act, as amended by the Quarries Miscellaneous Health and Safety Provisions Regulations 1995, regulates all quarries in Britain. No quarry may be worked unless it is under the control of an appointed manager (s. 98), but this manager needs no formal qualifications. His duty is to manage and control the quarry, and to secure the discharge by all others of their statutory responsibilities, subject only to the instructions of the owner. As in the case of mines, the manager may insist upon written confirmation of orders, and is similarly protected against being 'bypassed' by the owner. The Act calls for the manager (or in his absence his substitute) to exercise 'close and effective supervision' over all operations in the quarry (s. 103).

There are stringent obligations for the safe operation of the quarry. The manager's duty is to secure that all quarry operations are carried out so as to avoid danger from falls (s. 108); to provide safe means of access to every working place (s. 109); to provide suitable and sufficient artificial lighting (s. 111); and, together with the owner, to secure the safe condition of machinery and apparatus (s. 115). Quarries near to a highway, or otherwise representing a danger to the public, must be fenced.

17. Supplementary legislation

The Act is supplemented by the Quarries (General) Regulations 1956, and the Quarries Miscellaneous Health and Safety Provisions Regulations 1995, which take much the same form as the Mines Miscellaneous Provisions Regulations already referred to. Danger from mechanical transport is addressed by the Quarry (Vehicles) Regulations 1970.

113

18. Shotfiring

The Quarries (Explosives) Regulations 1988 cover shotfiring, including the storage, handling, issue and return of explosives. Shotfiring must be carried out by 'authorised persons', using equipment provided by the quarry owner, following the procedures set out in the regulations, and generally in accordance with good practice. The shotfirer must delimit a 'safety zone' before firing, ensure that all persons are withdrawn to management-provided shelters, and observe the procedures for dealing with misfires. Shotfiring must only be carried out during daylight hours.

THE MINES AND QUARRIES (TIPS) ACT 1969

19. Safety of tips

The 1969 Act imposes upon mine management a duty to ensure that every tip to which the Act applies is 'made and kept secure'. This duty applies to active or disused tips connected with a still active mine or quarry. Management must also have specified information concerning such tips, must formulate and enforce 'tipping rules', and, on the abandonment of the mine, must send plans and sections of all the associated tips to the inspectorate. After abandonment, primary responsibility for tip safety passes to the relevant local authority, but subject to the ultimate liability of the tip owner. The duty to report accidents in connection with mine and quarry tips is now governed by the general Reporting of Injuries etc., Regulations 1995.

JURISDICTION ACQUIRED AFTER 1974

20. General

Since 1980 the HSC has acquired responsibilities for nine new areas of work, including carriage by road of dangerous substances, mains gas safety, asbestos licensing, control of pesticides and nuclear safety research. Most of this new work is accounted for in regulations, but there are three areas in which transfer of departmental responsibilities has brought additional statutes into a position analogous to the original relevant statutory provisions. These areas are railway safety, the offshore oil industry and fire precautions.

A. OFFSHORE INSTALLATIONS

21. The Mineral Workings (Offshore Installations) Act 1971

The Mineral Workings (Offshore Installations) Act 1971, the first UK statute to provide expressly for the health and safety of those engaged in this industry, recognised the similarities with merchant shipping. Regulations made under this Act built on shipping law while introducing construction and production systems comparable to those devised to regulate similar situations onshore. The Act required that every manned installation have a competent installation manager on board at all times and placed on this manager responsibilities similar to those held by the captain of a ship, including authority over all persons on board the installation (s. 4), and activities within the 500 metre safety zone surrounding the installation. The legislation imposes duties, the breach of which may result in criminal sanctions. In addition to the installation manager, responsibilities are placed upon the operator (i.e. the licensee conducting the activity – s. 5) and the owner of the installation who is primarily responsible for the structure and equipment of the installation.

22. Regulations under the 1971 and 1974 Acts

Regulations made under the Act covered such matters as the structure of the installation (the Offshore Installations (Construction and Survey) Regulations 1974); the systems of work on the installation (the Offshore Installations (Operational Safety, Health and Welfare) Regulations 1976); offshore emergencies, whether caused by weather or oil-related activities (the Offshore Installations (Emergency Procedures) Regulations 1976); and the provision of equipment for emergency situations (the Offshore Installations (Life-saving Appliances) Regulations 1977 and the Offshore Installations (Fire-fighting Equipment) Regulations 1978). These regulations have been repealed, or substantially modified, by the Oil and Pipeline Works (Management and Administration) Regulations 1995, Offshore Installations (Prevention of Fire, Explosion and Emergency Response) Regulations 1995 and the Offshore Installations and Wells (Design and Construction) Regulations 1996, made under the 1974 Act.

23. Enforcement of offshore safety legislation

Enforcement of the 1971 Act lay originally with the Department of Energy. Since 1977, a series of Orders in Council (currently the Health and Safety at Work etc. Act 1974 (Application outside Great Britain) Order 1995) have extended the 1974 Act offshore. Subsequently, increasing numbers of regulations made under the 1974 Act have been extended offshore (e.g. Diving at Work Regulations 1981 and the Offshore Installation and Pipeline Works (Management and Administration) Regulations 1995). (These latter regulations made extensive repeals to the 1971 Act and many of the regulations made under it.)

24. Jurisdiction of HSE

Since 1 April 1991 all enforcement offshore, of both the 1971 Act and its supporting regulations, and the 1974 Act and those of its regulations that have been specifically assigned offshore, has been carried out by the HSE inspectorate, exercising the powers of inspection and enforcement – including improvement and prohibition notices – granted by the 1974 Act.

Revocations have been effected through the Offshore Installations (Repeals and Modifications) Regulations 1993; one of the most significant of the new regulations has been the Offshore Installations (Safety Case) Regulations 1992 (as amended by the Offshore Installations and Wells (Design and Construction) Regulations 1996), introduced in the aftermath of the Piper Alpha disaster. These regulations impose a duty upon the employer, in addition to the normal risk assessment procedures, to document the risk/cost analysis of the operation and convince the inspectorate that it can be carried out safely.

All of the six pack except the Workplace (Health, Safety and Welfare) Regulations 1992 apply to offshore installations to which the 1977 Order in Council applies.

B. RAILWAYS

25. Railway safety legislation

Rail transport, like road transport, was already the subject of safety legislation when the 1974 Act was passed. Nevertheless, the statutes relating to safety of passengers and railway employees were not made relevant statutory provisions under the 1974 Act. However, the general duties in s. 2 clearly protect railway workers, while s. 3 duties protect passengers, and criminal charges brought against British Rail following the Clapham railway disaster were formulated in terms of ss. 2 and 3 of the 1974 Act. Moreover, many activities related to the operation of the railway system had been within the ambit of the Factories Act. Following a number of accidents and incidents on railways the railway inspectorate was transferred from the Department of Transport to the HSE in the autumn of 1990. HSE inspectors now enforce the 1974 Act in respect of rail transport, and enforce the earlier transport legislation as agents for the Department of Transport.

26. Duty to report incidents

The Railway Employment (Prevention of Accidents) Act 1900 applies to all railways used for public traffic including either goods or passengers. This Act imposes a duty upon railway management to report incidents in which persons have been killed or injured on the railway to the Department of Transport. All railway managements must also comply with the requirements of the Reporting of Injuries, Diseases and Dangerous Occurrences Regulations 1995.

27. Regulations under the 1900 Act

Regulations (which are the responsibility of the Department of Transport) have been made under the 1900 Act in a number of specific situations involving danger to persons from railway operations, e.g. Railway (Prevention of Accidents) Rules 1902.

116

28. Railways in factories and mines

Railways forming part of a factory or a mine are subject to regulations made under the Factories Acts or the mines legislation (currently Locomotives and Waggons on Lines and Sidings Regulations 1906 and Coal and Other Mines (Sidings) Order 1956). Quarry sidings are regulated under the Quarries (General) Regulations 1956. These regulations are framed for the protection of persons against the risks inherent in the movement of wagons and locomotives on mine and factory premises; their impact is much reduced at the present time due to the decline in the use of railway haulage in so many industries.

C. FIRE PRECAUTIONS

29. Fire Precautions Act 1971

By s. 1(2)(f) of this Act a fire certificate is required from the fire authority for premises put into use as a place of work. Paragraph (f) was added to the 1971 Act by s. 78 of the Health and Safety at Work Act.

30. Application for a fire certificate

Section 5 requires that an application for a fire certificate must be made to the fire authority in the prescribed form. The application:

(a) must specify the particular use or uses of the premises which it is desired to have covered by the certificate; and

(b) must give such information as may be prescribed about the premises and any prescribed rules connected with them; and

(c) if the premises consist of part of a building, must, in so far as it is available to the applicant, give such information as may be prescribed about the rest of the building and any prescribed matters connected with it.

31. Inspection of premises

The fire authority may require plans of the premises and must inspect the premises and satisfy itself as to:

(a) the means of escape . . .
(b) the means for securing the means of escape . . .
(c) the means for fighting fire . . .
(d) the means for giving warning . . . (s. 5(3)).

32. Issue of a certificate

If the authority is satisfied it must issue a fire certificate. Details of the matters outlined in (a) to (d) will be specified in the certificate. The fire authority may require that alterations be made to a building before a fire certificate is granted. Operating without a fire certificate (except between application to and approval by the fire authority) is an either way offence which carries, on conviction on indictment, a maximum penalty of two years imprisonment.

33. Regulations under the 1971 Act

Regulations may be made under the Act for the following purposes (s. 12(3)):

(a) the provision, maintenance and keeping free from obstruction of means of escape in case of fire

(b) the provision and maintenance of means for securing that any means of escape can be safely and effectively used at all material times

(c) as to the provision and maintenance of means of fighting fire and means of giving warning in case of fire

(d) as to the internal construction of the premises and the materials used in that construction

(e) for prohibiting altogether the presence or use in the premises of furniture or equipment of any specified description or prohibiting its presence or use unless specified standards or conditions are complied with

(f) for securing that persons employed to work in the premises receive appropriate instruction or training in what to do in case of fire

(g) as to the keeping of records of instruction or training given, or other things done, in pursuance of the regulations.

34. Enforcement

In the case of workplaces, the functions of the fire authority in enforcing the provisions of the fire certificate are normally performed by the inspectors with responsibility for enforcing the 1974 Act in those premises (s. 18). Moreover, if the fire authority proposes to require alterations to be made to work premises before granting a fire certificate, it will consult with the relevant health and safety inspectorate.

35. Duties to comply with the Act

R v. *Boal* [1992] provided an interesting interpretation of s. 23(1) of the Fire Precautions Act 1971. Section 23(1) (written in a form commonly found in regulatory legislation) states:

> Where an offence under this Act committed by a body corporate is proved . . . to be attributable to any neglect on the part of any director, manager, secretary or other similar officer of the body corporate . . . he as well as the body corporate shall be guilty of that offence . . .

Inspectors visited shop premises and found they did not comply with the statutory requirements. At the time of the visit the shop was in the charge of a relatively junior employee: he was charged with offences related to the breaches of the Act and was convicted under s. 23(1). When the defendant appealed against sentence the appeal court of its own motion expressed doubt as to whether such a junior person could be convicted under s. 23(1). This matter not having been argued in the lower court, the appeal court considered the conviction was unsound and set it aside.

36. Compliance with EC legislation

While the EC Framework Directive makes provision for fire precautions it has not been considered necessary, given the existing UK system, to make special provision for this in the Management of Health and Safety at Work Regulations 1992.

LEGISLATION DEALING WITH SIMILAR SITUATIONS

37. Other legislation which is substantively relevant

This chapter has so far considered only legislation which either falls within the 1974 rubric of 'relevant statutory provisions' or has been brought within the jurisdiction of the HSE for enforcement purposes. In Chapter 4 it was briefly noted that there are circumstances where persons may not be covered by, or for practical purposes within the jurisdiction of, the enforcement system set up under the 1974 Act.

The extension of HSE jurisdiction in relation to transport and offshore installations has, since 1974, reduced the situations in which the 1974 Act does not apply. But merchant shipping notably remains outside the system; though major catastrophes like the capsizing of *The Herald of Free Enterprise* and the sinking of *The Marchioness* emphasise that transport by water is an activity in which the public is likely to be at risk.

Where there are overlaps between the 1974 Act and other legislation it may be helpful to consider whether the alternative legislation contains that power, which the 1974 Act does, to deal with risks before there has been catastrophe. Interestingly road traffic legislation does: the principal offences of dangerous driving and driving without due care and attention can be committed without personal injury or damage to property having occurred.

The relevance of the general duties in relation to potential as opposed to actual injury may ensure the continued use of the 1974 Act, s. 3 in particular, even in relation to certain forms of air pollution, although as has been noted the enforcement of s. 5 of the 1974 Act has been transferred to the new Environment Agency: thus while *R* v. *Board of Trustees of the Science Museum* [1993] (discussed in Chapter 7) arose out of a situation which occurred before the formal transference of powers to the Agency (or its predecessor) it might well be that the HSE would still invoke s. 3 on similar facts.

It is therefore worth pondering whether there are situations which would normally be deemed to fall more readily into the province of other enforcement agencies, in which the 1974 Act might apply more effectively than the principal legislation intended to relate to that situation.

Progress test 8

1. What meaning did the 1974 Act give to the expression 'relevant statutory provisions'?

2. What statutes were 'existing statutory provisions'?

3. What was the obligation imposed by s. 14(1) of the Act?

4. What is the principal legislation for mines and quarries?

5. In what ways does mining legislation make the position of mine manager quite different from other managerial positions in Great Britain?

6. What areas of responsibility have HSC and HSE acquired since 1974?

7. What (apart from the 1974 Act) is the principal legislation for offshore installations?

8. Which body grants a fire certificate?

9. On what matters must the authority be satisfied before a certificate is granted?

9

FRAMEWORK REGULATIONS

1. Introduction

When the British Health and Safety at Work Act was enacted in 1974 it was intended to stay the course of time. It was deliberately couched in such wide and general terms that any subsequent needs could be met by regulations made under it. The EC Framework Directive had similar broad objectives. This chapter will demonstrate the way in which in Britain many of the provisions of the Framework Directive and some provisions of other related Directives have been implemented through the Management of Health and Safety at Work Regulations 1992.

2. Deadline for implementation

The Framework Directive had to be implemented in Member States by 31 December 1992.

NATURE OF THE DIRECTIVE

3. Object of Directive

Article 1 of the Directive declared that

(1) The object of the Directive is to introduce measures to encourage improvements in the safety and health of workers at work.

(2) To that end it contains general principles concerning the prevention of occupational risks, the protection of safety and health, the elimination of risk and accident factors, the informing, consultation, balanced participation in accordance with national laws and/or practices and training of workers and their representatives, as well as general guidelines for the implementation of the said principles.

4. Similarity between Act and Directive

It was initially argued in Britain that the Directive required nothing that was not already either expressly or impliedly covered by the 1974 Act. Be this as it may the decision was made to use the regulation-making powers in the 1974 Act to implement the Framework and other EC health and safety Directives in Great Britain. Whether this was a good strategy may be questioned because the Management of Health and Safety Regulations 1992 made in response to the Framework Directive sit somewhat uneasily under the umbrella of the 1974 Act and may not completely fulfil the intention of the Directive even in respect of those aspects of the Directive which they address. Particular concern has been expressed that duties under the Directive are strict, not being qualified by the British concepts of practicability or reasonable practicability but the Regulations do not expressly address this matter. In this chapter the provisions of both the Framework Directive and the Management of Health and Safety Regulations will be outlined and their relationship to the 1974 Act discussed.

5. Scope of the EC Directive

The Directive is concerned only with the safety and health of workers at their workplace. Thus it is narrower than the 1974 Act: there is nothing comparable to s. 5 of the 1974 Act for the Directive makes no provision for environmental protection. Nor does it make any provision for public safety.

The Directive focuses on the relationship between employer and worker but, in Article 3, defines that relationship more widely than the British relationship between employer and employee:

> Worker: any person employed by an employer, including trainees and apprentices but excluding domestic servants.

Article 5 provides that

> The employer shall have a duty to ensure the safety and health of workers in every aspect related to the work.

Thus the Directive has a wider scope than s. 2 of the 1974 Act. The principal obligations which the Directive seeks to impose on employers bridge ss. 2 and 3 of the 1974 Act.

The Directive is not concerned with the other roles which the employing organisation may fulfil, such as controller of premises or manufacturer of articles and substances.

PROVISIONS OF THE DIRECTIVE

6. Employer's primary obligations

The primary obligation of the employer, set out in Article 5, is:

> to ensure the safety and health of workers in every aspect related to the work.

The employer cannot escape this obligation by appointing competent external services or persons; nor will the employer's obligations be affected by the workers' obligations. In these respects Article 5 is similar to ss. 2 and 3 of the

1974 Act; similarly under that Act employers cannot avoid their legal duties by delegation of tasks.

7. General obligations on the employer

Within the context of his responsibilities the employer must take the measures necessary for the safety and health protection of workers, including prevention of occupational risks and provision of information and training. The Articles of the Directive spell out that the employer must:

(1) evaluate and combat risks (Article 6). The employer should do this on the basis of the following general principles of prevention:
   (a) avoiding risks;
   (b) evaluating the risks which cannot be avoided;
   (c) combating the risk at source;
   (d) adapting the work to the individual, especially as regards the design of work places, the choice of work equipment and the choice of working and production methods, with a view, in particular, to alleviating monotonous work and work at a predetermined work-rate and to reducing their effect on health;
   (e) adapting to technical progress;
   (f) replacing the dangerous by the non-dangerous or the less dangerous;
   (g) developing a coherent overall prevention policy which covers technology, organisation of work, working conditions, social relationships and the influence of factors related to the working environment;
   (h) giving collective protective measures priority over individual protective measures;
   (i) giving appropriate instructions to workers.

(2) provide protective and preventive services through the appointment of competent persons (Article 7). If there are no competent persons within the organisation the employer is required to 'enlist' competent external services. The Directive explains that the persons designated 'must have the necessary capabilities and the necessary means.'

(3) make provision for first aid, fire-fighting and evacuation of workers, where there is serious and imminent danger (Article 8)

(4) assess, respond to, and monitor the response to risks; including reporting of accidents (Article 9)

(5) provide workers with information about safety and health risks and protective and preventive measures (Article 10)

(6) provide for consultation with and participation by workers (Article 11)

(7) provide adequate safety training to workers (Article 12).

8. Workers' obligations

It is the responsibility of each worker to take care as far as possible of his own safety and health and that of other persons affected by his acts at work, in accordance with his training and the instructions given by the employer (Article 13). Workers are particularly required to:

(a) make correct use of machinery, apparatus, tools, dangerous substances, transport equipment and other means of production

(b) make correct use of the personal protective equipment supplied to them and, after use, return it to its proper place

(c) refrain from disconnecting, changing or removing arbitrarily safety devices fitted to machinery, etc.

(d) immediately inform the employer and/or the workers with specific safety responsibilities of any work situation they have reasonable grounds for considering represents a serious and immediate danger to safety and health and of any shortcomings in the protection arrangements

(e) co-operate, in accordance with national practice, with the employer and/or workers with specific responsibility for the safety and health of workers. . . .

9. Miscellaneous provisions

(a) *Health surveillance*

Measures must be introduced to ensure that workers receive health surveillance appropriate to the health and safety risks they incur at work. These measures must be such that each worker, if he so wishes, may receive health surveillance at regular intervals. Health surveillance may be provided as part of a national health system (Article 14).

(b) *Risk groups*

Particularly sensitive risk groups must be protected against the dangers which specifically affect them (Article 15).

THE BRITISH RESPONSE

10. Consultative Document

In the autumn of 1991 the Health and Safety Commission issued a Consultative Document together with a set of draft regulations and a draft approved code of practice. This Document summarised the Directive's requirements in the context of existing British law:

(a) The key requirement to assess risks for the purpose of identifying protective and preventive measures was already implicit in s. 2 of the 1974 Act and explicit in certain regulations.

(b) The new requirements on information and training did not go much beyond s. 2(2)(c) of the 1974 Act.

(c) Most workers affected by the new requirement for health surveillance were already covered by health surveillance requirements in existing regulations.

(d) The proposals regarding safety representatives were no more than modest extensions of existing provisions.

(e) The new provisions imposing duties on employees did not go much beyond s. 7 of the 1974 Act.

The regulations, published in draft form as the Health and Safety (General Provisions) Regulations, were enacted as the Management of Health and Safety at Work Regulations 1992; these and an accompanying Approved Code of Practice were brought into effect on 1 January 1993. (Codes of practice have less force than Regulations – see Chapter 12.)

MANAGEMENT OF HEALTH AND SAFETY AT WORK REGULATIONS

11. Scope of the Regulations

The Management of Health and Safety at Work Regulations 1992 reflect the particular obligations the Directive seeks to impose on employers, but for the most part impose obligations on employers only in respect of their own employees (e.g. Regulation 5, health surveillance; Regulation 8, provision of information; Regulation 10, training). However Regulation 3, introduced in order to comply with the EC requirement for risk assessment, is so worded as to cover the relationships envisaged by both ss. 2 and 3 of the 1974 Act; indeed its coverage includes all the general duties.

The Regulations do not deal with the first aid and fire-fighting requirements stipulated in Article 8, because it was considered that these were adequately dealt with elsewhere. Similarly that part of Article 9 which concerns reporting of accidents had already been covered by national regulations.

The Regulations did not address, except in a minimalist manner, the requirement of Article 10 and 11 concerning provision of information to workers and consultation with and participation of workers. It was considered that existing British regulations, providing only for worker involvement through trade union appointed representatives, were broadly sufficient to meet the Directive's requirement for 'balanced participation in accordance with national laws and/or practices' (Article 11). However, that view is no longer officially held and additional regulations have now been formulated to cover non-unionised work situations.

The Regulations did cover the special provision for temporary workers which was required by the Temporary Workers Directive.

12. Risk assessment

The principal duty imposed by the British regulations is Regulation 3: risk assessment. Many of the other regulations build on this Regulation. The Regulation is intended to fulfil the Framework Directive's requirement that employers identify the risks to which their workers are exposed while at work. The British regulation thus makes of very general application a concept already introduced into British law, in the narrower context of the control of dangerous substances, by the Control of Substances Hazardous to Health Regulations 1988 and also found in other Regulations. The HSC has identified eight sets of Regulations requiring risk assessment and in 1994 published a discussion document concerning rationalisation of these requirements. Arguably these assessment regulations only make explicit requirements which were already implied by ss. 2 and 3 of the 1974 Act.

In order to implement the EC Framework Directive's requirement, Regulation 3(1) requires:

(1) Every employer shall make a suitable and sufficient assessment of

(a) the risks to the health and safety of his employees to which they are exposed whilst they are at work; and

(b) the risks to the health and safety of persons not in his employment arising out of or in connection with the conduct by him of his undertaking.

Regulation 3(2) imposes on the self-employed virtually the same duty to assess risks as Regulation 3(1) places on employers.

By including public safety and also by imposing an obligation on the self-employed, the British regulation is in the spirit of the 1974 Act, but goes beyond the Directive's requirements. It should be noted that the risk assessment provision is itself a duty of strict liability; it simply states that the employer *shall* carry out the assessment, without any qualification as to reasonable practicability. However, the Regulations may fall short of the EC's wider intention to ensure the safety and health of workers as expressed in Article 5 in that they provide in 3(1) that the employer is required to carry out the assessment:

> for the purpose of identifying the measures he needs to take to comply with the requirements and prohibitions imposed upon him by or under the relevant statutory provisions.

Thus the assessment is to identify the necessary preventive and protective measures that the employer should take in order to comply with the existing British regulatory system.

In other words, the purpose of the employer's assessment is to ensure that they comply with the 1974 Act, the existing statutory provisions and Regulations made subsequent to, and under, the 1974 Act. Therefore while the obligation is a strict duty to identify any risks whatsoever in many instances the obligation is only to respond to them so far as is reasonably practicable. It is especially significant that, as has been noted in the previous chapter, the general duties under the 1974 Act may only impose on the employer a duty to deal with foreseeable risks. On the one hand it may be argued that this British interpretation of the EC's assessment requirement is a pragmatic solution to an otherwise unfathomable obligation; on the other it may be queried whether the British solution fully represents the EC intention. The Directive's strict requirement does not appear to be mitigated either by foreseeability or by other aspects of reasonable practicability.

Recent case law, particularly *R* v. *British Steel plc* asserting the onerous nature of those duties which incorporate the defence of reasonable practicability, may assuage the concerns of those who doubt whether the British standards are as rigorous as the EC appears to require.

13. Provision for pregnant women

After the EC had adopted the Framework Directive it adopted a further Directive (the tenth specific Directive under the Framework Directive), namely the Directive on the Protection of Pregnant Workers which had health and safety aspects and which had to be implemented by Member States by 19 October 1994. In a Consultative Document published in 1994 the Health and Safety Commission proposed to implement this Directive's health and safety requirements by amending regulations (Management of Health and Safety at Work (Amendment) Regulations 1994) adding new provisions to the Management of Health and Safety at Work Regulations by expressly making a requirement that employer's risk assessment includes assessment of risks to which pregnant women and mothers of young children might be exposed while at work.

The Management of Health and Safety at Work (Amendment) Regulations specify the measures that should be taken to ensure that employers' risk assessments identify any special risks to which new or expectant mothers may be exposed while at work: the group to which this special assessment applies is those who are pregnant, have given birth or miscarried in the last six months or are breastfeeding. The risk assessment regulation in the Management of Health and Safety at Work Regulations 1992 is extended by the inclusion of three extra paragraphs to Regulation 13.

Regulation 13(A) requires that if there are women of child-bearing age at the workplace, the employers must, as part of the general risk assessment, assess any aspects of the work or working conditions which might put the employee's or baby's health at risk and identify what measures should be taken to prevent those risks or protect the employee from them. If preventive or protective measure are not sufficient to prevent the risk, then the working conditions or hours of work must be altered so as to avoid the risk. If a risk remains or if the work is by definition dangerous for new or expectant mothers then the employee will have to be offered suitable alternative employment or be suspended from work with remuneration under the provisions of ss. 66–68 of the Employment Rights Act 1996.

Regulation 13(B) says that if a new/expectant mother does night-work, and has a medical certificate saying that this could damage her or the baby's health, then again she will have to be offered suitable alternative work or be suspended.

Regulation 13(C) specifies that any paid suspension will not extend to the maternity leave period and any action taken to protect a new/expectant mother will only be required so long as the circumstances require and provided the employer has been notified or is aware that the employee is pregnant, has recently given birth or is breastfeeding.

HSC guidance sets out a non-exhaustive list of working conditions, processes and agents which are identified in the Directive as being potentially or definitely hazardous to new or expectant mothers.

However, the ECJ ruled on 5 May 1994 in *Habermann-Beltermann* that a German law which totally prohibited pregnant women doing night-work was contrary to Articles 2(1) and 3(1) of the Equal Treatment Directive. The provision set out in Regulation 3(B) above would not seem to violate this Directive. Employers will need to ensure that they carefully steer a path which enables compliance with both Directives.

14. Duty to review findings

Regulation 3(3) imposes on the employer/self-employed person who made an assessment the duty to review the assessment if there is reason to suspect that it is no longer valid or there has been a significant change in the matters to which it relates; if necessary the assessment must then be modified.

15. Duty to record findings

Where an employer employs five or more employees Regulation 3(4) requires that he must record the significant findings of the assessment and any group of his employees identified by it as being especially at risk. The record does not have to be committed to paper; for example, it might be kept on a computer.

16. Explanation of the Regulation

The Approved Code of Practice states that the assessment should usually involve identifying the hazards present in any undertaking (whether arising from work activities or from other factors, e.g. the layout of the premises) and then evaluating the extent of the risks involved, taking into account whatever precautions are already being taken. In the Code,

(a) Hazards are defined as 'something with the potential to cause harm'.

(b) Risk 'expresses the likelihood that the harm from a particular hazard is realised'. The extent of the risk 'covers the population which might be affected by a risk; i.e. the number of people who might be exposed and the consequences for them.'

The Code thus concludes that

'Risk therefore reflects both the likelihood that harm will occur and its severity.'

The HSE's book *Essentials of Health and Safety at Work* gives the following useful explanation of the distinction between hazard and risk:

As an example, think about a can of solvent on a shelf. There is a hazard if the solvent is toxic or flammable, but very little risk. The risk increases when it is taken down and poured into a bucket. Harmful vapour is given off and there is a danger of spillage. Things are made much worse if a mop is then used to spread it over the floor for cleaning. The chance of harm, i.e. the risk, is then high.

The Code further states that a suitable and sufficient risk assessment should identify the significant risks arising out of work and this means focusing on those risks that are liable to arise because of the work activity. Trivial risks can usually be ignored as can risks arising from routine activities associated with life in general, unless the work activity compounds those risks, or there is evidence of significant relevance to the particular work activity.

Where employers have already made assessments under other regulations, such as the Control of Substances Hazardous to Health Regulations 1988, they need not repeat those assessments; on the other hand, in the case of highly hazardous plant which is required to present a 'safety case', the risk assessment made under Regulation 3 may well be incorporated in the safety case documentation.

The code states that the significant findings recorded as a result of an assessment should include:

(a) the significant hazards identified in the assessment
(b) the existing control measures
(c) the population which may be affected by the significant risks

The code incorporates, with some explanation and examples, the principles of preventive and protective measures set out in Article 6 of the Directive, namely:

(a) if possible avoid a risk altogether
(b) combat risks at source
(c) wherever possible adapt work to the individual
(d) take advantage of technological and technical progress
(e) make risk prevention measures part of a coherent policy and approach
(f) give priority to those measure which protect the whole workplace
(g) workers need to understand what they need to do
(h) ensure the existence of an active health and safety culture affecting the organisation as a whole.

Because these principles are incorporated in the code rather than in the regulations themselves they are merely statements of good practice – they are not mandatory rules of law. However some of these principles may be reflected in other relevant statutory provisions; for example the principle of adapting the work to the individual is addressed in part in s. 2(2)(e) of the 1974 Act, which requires the provision and maintenance of a healthy and safe working environment.

17. Health and safety arrangements

Regulation 4(1) requires:

Every employer shall make and give effect to such arrangements as are appropriate, having regard to the nature of his activities and the size of the undertaking, for the effective planning, organisation, control, monitoring and review of the preventive and protective measures

Where the employer employs five or more employees, he must record the arrangements he is making.

18. Safety is part of management

The Code of Practice proposes that the employer's safety arrangements should be integrated with the management system and that the system will include:

'(a) *Planning*: Adopting a systematic approach which identifies priorities and sets objectives. Whenever possible, risks are eliminated by the careful selection and design of facilities, equipment and processes or minimised by the use of physical control measures.
(b) *Organisation*: Putting in place the necessary structure with the aim of ensuring that there is a progressive improvement in health and safety performance.
(c) *Control*: Ensuring that the decisions for ensuring and promoting health and safety are being implemented as planned.
(d) *Monitoring and review*: Like quality, progressive improvements in health and safety can only be achieved through the constant development of policies, approaches to implementation and techniques of risk control.'

19. Health surveillance

Regulation 5 requires that:

Every employer shall ensure that his employees are provided with such health surveillance as is appropriate having regard to the risks to their health and safety which are identified by the assessment.

20. When is surveillance needed?

The code points out that the risk assessment will identify circumstances in which health surveillance is required by specific health and safety regulations like the Control of Substances Hazardous to Health Regulations. The code suggests that in addition health surveillance should be introduced where the assessment shows:

'(a) there is an identifiable disease or adverse health condition related to the work concerned;
(b) valid techniques are available to detect indications of the disease or condition;
(c) there is a reasonable likelihood that the disease or condition may occur under the particular conditions of work; and
(d) surveillance is likely to further the protection of the health of the employees to be covered.'

21. Benefits of surveillance

The code suggests that the benefits of surveillance include early identification of adverse health affects, so enabling further harm to be prevented. In addition it can provide a means:

'(a) of checking the effectiveness of control measures;
(b) providing feedback on the accuracy of the risk assessment;
(c) identifying and protecting individuals at increased risk.'

22. Competent persons

The concept of competence, which has had some place in the history of British safety legislation, has now been given particular significance because, as has been noted, Article 7 of the Framework Directive requires employers to appoint competent persons to carry out activities related to the protection of workers and prevention of occupational risks related to the undertaking. Regulation 6 of the Management of Health and Safety Regulations is intended to implement this. Regulation 6 requires:

> every employer shall . . . appoint one or more competent persons to assist him in undertaking the measures he needs to take to comply with the requirements and prohibitions imposed upon him by or under the relevant statutory provisions.

Further the employer is required to make arrangements for ensuring co-operation between individuals so appointed. The employer must also ensure that the number of persons appointed, the time available for them to fulfil their functions and the means at their disposal are adequate having regard to the size of the undertaking, the risks to which the employees are exposed and the distribution of those risks throughout the undertaking.

Regulation 6(4) envisages the possibility that persons appointed may be persons who are not employees of the organisation using their services. It requires the employer to ensure that any person appointed who is not in the employer's employment:

> is informed of the factors known by him [the employer] to affect, or suspected by him of affecting, the health and safety of any other person who may be affected by the conduct of his undertaking.

It may be noted that the obligation placed on the employer in Regulation 6(4) is not confined to employees, or even to persons other than employees working at the workplace. The concept 'affected by his undertaking' is that used in s. 3 of the 1974 Act and, in that context, is intended to extend protection to the general public as well as to persons at work. Presumably therefore Regulation 6(4) is intended to have a similarly wide effect and, indeed, this would relate to Regulation 6(1) where the employers' obligation is expressed in relation to the relevant statutory provisions which also extend in some instances to protection of the general public as well as protection of persons at work.

Regulation 6(5) will for the future provide a definition of competence. It states:

A person shall be regarded as competent for the purposes [of the Regulation] where he has sufficient training, experience, knowledge or other qualifications to enable him properly to assist in undertaking the protective and preventive measures or, as the case may be, to undertake the protective and preventive measures without any assistance.

23. Who is competent?

For the time being, employers are bound, in spite of Regulation 6(5), to feel some uncertainty both as to the situations for which they need to allocate responsibilities to competent persons and to the qualifications which such persons will need in order to comply with the regulation. The identification of standards for national vocational qualifications for personnel with safety responsibilities may clarify the meaning of 'competence' and indeed identify what is required in specific situations.

The code of practice points out that competence does not necessarily depend on the possession of particular skills or qualifications. Situations may require only:

'(a) an understanding of relevant current best practice;
(b) awareness of the limitations of one's own experience and knowledge; and
(c) the willingness and ability to supplement existing experience and knowledge.'

It would appear that, as in the past, the responsibility will lie with the employer to determine what expertise is needed for the task and, if events put the employer's judgment in issue, it will be for a court to determine on the facts whether the employer has in fact discharged his duty by making the particular appointments he has made.

The temptation must be for employers to regard their safety manager as the 'competent person' within their organisation and to delegate all safety matters to this manager. It may be appropriate to nominate such a manager as the competent person, but employers should not assume that such an appointment can relieve the organisation of its responsibilities in safety matters. The general duties, and many regulations, place their obligations on the employer and the recent case of *R* v. *British Steel plc* is a salutary reminder that delegation of a task to any manager, however competent, is not likely to amount to discharge of a duty to do what is reasonably practicable to achieve health and safety.

24. Procedures for serious and imminent danger

Regulation 7(1) requires employers to establish and where necessary give effect to appropriate procedures to be followed in the event of serious and imminent danger to persons at work in their undertaking. They have to nominate a sufficient number of competent persons to implement these procedures in so far as they relate to the evacuation of premises. The employer also has to ensure that none of their employees has access to any area occupied by the employer to which it is necessary to restrict access on grounds of health and safety: unless the employee concerned has received adequate health and safety instruction.

Regulation 7(2) provides that without prejudice to the generality of the regulation's requirements, the procedures shall:

(a) so far as is practicable, require any persons at work who are exposed to serious and imminent danger to be informed of the nature of the hazard and of the steps taken or to be taken to protect them from it;

(b) enable the persons concerned (if necessary by taking appropriate steps in the absence of guidance or instruction and in the light of their knowledge and the technical means at their disposal) to stop work and immediately proceed to a place of safety in the event of their being exposed to serious, imminent and unavoidable danger;

(c) save in exceptional cases for reasons duly substantiated (which cases and reasons shall be specified in those procedures), require the persons concerned to be prevented from resuming work in any situation where there is still a serious and imminent danger.

In most workplaces the most likely danger is the outbreak of fire; but in some cases there may be a risk of bombing. The employers' risk assessment should identify the risks and in complying with Regulation 7 the employer will need to make particular response to any special risks so identified.

While employment protection legislation protects from dismissal employees who leave their work in such circumstances, the employee must still establish that there was in fact a danger that warranted the action he had taken.

25. Information for employees

Regulation 8 requires that

Every employer shall provide his employees with comprehensible and relevant information on

(a) the risks to their health and safety identified by the assessment;

(b) the preventive and protective measures;

(c) the procedures referred to in Regulation 7(1)(a) [for responding to emergency situations];

(d) the identity of those persons nominated by him in accordance with Regulation 7(1)(b) [as competent to implement emergency procedures];

(e) the risks notified to him in accordance with Regulation 9(1)(c) [i.e. risks where employers share a workplace].

In addition to these general requirements, specific regulations may identify circumstances in which information has to be supplied to workers. The intention of these general requirements is that employees be given information necessary for the protection of their own health and safety: therefore no more information need be given than is necessary for that purpose. However information must be provided in a form in which it can be understood by the employee to whom it is given; not only does this mean that it must be given in sufficiently clear and simple language – in some instances it may be necessary to given the information in a language other than English.

This regulation makes more explicit certain aspects of the duty to provide information, instruction, training and supervision, which is, in s. 2(2)(c), at the heart of the 1974 Act. However, this Regulation is narrower than s. 2(2)(c) in that s. 2(2)(c) may require employers to provide information to persons other than their own employees: R v. *Swan Hunter Shipbuilders Ltd.*

26. Relationship with safety policy

Regulations 4, 5 and 8 of these Regulations make no express reference to s. 2(3) of the 1974 Act, which requires an employer who has more than 5 employees at an undertaking to produce, and bring to the notice of his employees, a safety policy; yet the relationship is clear.

27. Co-operation and co-ordination between employers

Regulation 9 requires co-operation and co-ordination when two or more employers share a workplace. The Regulation also applies when employers share a workplace with self-employed persons. This, while in response to the Directive, builds on s. 3 of the 1974 Act. It requires the employer to:

(a) co-operate with the other employers concerned so far as is necessary to enable them to comply with the requirements and prohibitions imposed upon them by or under the relevant statutory provisions;

(b) (taking into account the nature of his activities) take all reasonable steps to co-ordinate the measures he takes to comply with the requirements and prohibitions imposed upon him by or under the relevant statutory provisions with the measures the other employers concerned are taking to comply with the requirements and prohibitions imposed upon them by or under the relevant statutory provisions;

(c) take all reasonable steps to inform the other employers concerned of the risks to their employees' health and safety arising out of or in connection with the conduct by him of his undertaking.

This Regulation is another regulation which imposes its obligations for the purpose of achieving compliance with the relevant British statutory provisions: therefore it again (like s. 3 of the 1974 Act) requires co-operation and co-ordination for the protection of the public as well as for protection of persons at work. Recent cases (particularly *R* v. *Associated Octel Ltd* [1994]) demonstrate that section 3 of the Act imposes a stringent requirement for co-operation between contractor and subcontractor, through contractual arrangements and/or the enforcement of a permit to work system.

The code of practice recommends that where there is no controlling employer, the employers and self-employed persons should agree to appoint someone as health and safety co-ordinator. Again, it points out that the controller of premises has responsibilities under s. 4 of the 1974 Act and in order to discharge the s. 4 duties the controller may well need to secure the co-operation of other organisations present on the premises. Provisions made for co-operation and co-ordination will also need to take into account the requirements of Regulation 8 in respect of provision for emergency situations. The Construction (Design and Management) Regulations 1994, introduced to give effect to EC Directive 92/57/EEC, make special provision for the responsibilities of those engaged in large building construction works.

28. Persons working in host employers' undertakings

Regulation 10 is closely related to Regulation 9; but it will apply even where control of premises is not shared between two or more employers, as might be the case if a contractor sends workers to another employer's workplace, without itself assuming any control of the site. The Regulation imposes obligations on every employer and self-employed person to ensure that the employer of any employees from an outside undertaking who are working in their undertakings is provided with comprehensive information on:

(a) the risks to those employees' health and safety arising out of or in connection with the conduct by that first-mentioned employer or by that self-employed person of his undertaking; and

(b) the measures taken by that first-mentioned employer or by that self-employed person in compliance with the requirements and provisions imposed upon him by or under the relevant statutory provisions insofar as the said requirements and prohibitions relate to those employees.

The Regulation further requires that the resident employer/self-employed person shall provide appropriate instructions and comprehensive information regarding risks to persons visiting the workplace to work there, by communication to both the employer and the employee direct. Moreover the resident employer must take all reasonable steps to ensure that any employee from an outside undertaking receives sufficient information to enable the identification of any person who has been named as a competent person to implement evacuation procedures.

This Regulation will have particular significance in workplaces, such as offshore installations, where it is common for the employer to contract out some or many aspects of the operation of the enterprise, to organisations which will supply their own workforce, for the completion of the task. This Regulation would not appear to conflict with the interpretation placed upon s. 3(1) in *RMC Roadstone Products Ltd* v. *Jester* (see Chapter 6) since the risk in that case was not one connected with the conduct of the host employer's undertaking; though the ruling in that case on the concept of *conduct of undertaking* has been very much restricted by subsequent cases such as *R* v. *Associated Octel Ltd* [1994].

29. Capabilities and training

Regulation 11 imposes upon every employer the obligation, when entrusting tasks to his employees, to take into account their capabilities as regards health and safety and also to ensure that they are provided with adequate health and safety training. The employer is directed to ensure that adequate training is provided to employees:

(a) on their being recruited into the employer's undertaking; and
(b) on their being exposed to new or increased risks because of
   (*i*) their being transferred or given a change of responsibilities within the employer's undertaking,
   (*ii*) the introduction of new work equipment into or a change respecting work equipment already in use within the employer's undertaking,
   (*iii*) the introduction of new technology into the employer's undertaking, or
   (*iv*) the introduction of a new system of work into or a change respecting a system of work already in use within the employer's undertaking.

The Regulation requires that the training be repeated periodically where appropriate; be adapted to take account of any new or changed risks; and take place during working hours.

30. Employees' duties

Regulation 12 supplements s. 7 of the 1974 Act by spelling out that employees must not use things such as machinery or dangerous substances other than in accordance with any instruction and training respecting their use which has been provided by the employer. This latter provision has in fact some similarity to both ss. 7 and 8 of the 1974 Act. Section 7(b) requires the employee to co-operate with the employer so far as is necessary to enable the employer to comply with their statutory duties. Section 8 makes it an offence for any person to intentionally or recklessly interfere with or misuse anything provided in pursuance of any of the relevant statutory provisions.

Regulation 12(2) requires employees to inform their employer, or the employee to whom the employer has given specific health and safety responsibilities, where there is a dangerous situation, or a shortcoming in the employer's safety arrangements, which affects them personally. The employee's duty is however restricted to what might be expected in terms of risk identification from an employee who had received the instruction and training which the employee has received. Employment protection legislation provides some protection against dismissal or discrimination short of dismissal for employees who draw their employer's attention to dangerous or unhealthy situations.

31. Temporary workers

Regulation 12 relates to temporary workers and is, strictly speaking, intended to implement the Directive on temporary workers rather than the Framework

Directive. It imposes obligations on employers to provide information to temporary workers and to ensure they are trained for the tasks required of them. It is intended to ensure that workers who are not tenured employees receive the protection which is provided by the regulations. The combined effects of Regulations 9 and 12 should ensure (given a purposive interpretation) that the narrow concept of employment with which UK law is familiar does not prevent the Directive applying, as it is intended, to the entire workforce.

32. Exclusion of civil liability

Regulation 15 clarifies that breach of a duty imposed by these regulations shall not confer a right of action in any civil proceedings: thus Regulation 15 rebuts the presumption created by s. 47(2) of the 1974 Act that breach of regulations made under that Act will carry the right to bring a civil action for breach of statutory duty.

33. Extension of provision for consultation with safety representatives

Regulation 17 modifies the Safety Representatives and Safety Committees Regulations 1977 to extend the employer's obligation to consult with safety representatives appointed under those regulations. This issue, and other worker protection provisions referred to in this chapter, will be dealt with more fully subsequently in the chapter on worker involvement.

34. Draft young persons regulations

New regulations, the Health and Safety (Young Persons) Regulations, are intended for introduction before the end of 1996 to implement the health and safety provisions of the European Directive on the Protection of Young People at Work. The proposals are for insertion into the 1992 Management of Health and Safety at Work Regulations. In particular a new Regulation 3A will provide that no employer shall employ any young person without having made a risk assessment taking into account the inexperience, lack of awareness of risks and immaturity of young persons, paying special attention to –

(i) the fitting-out and layout of the workplace and the workstation
(ii) the nature, degree and duration of exposure to physical, biological and chemical agents
(iii) the form, range and use of work equipment and the way in which it is handled
(iv) the organisation of processes and activities
(v) the extent of the health and safety training provided or to be provided to the young persons concerned; and
(vi) risks from agents, processes and work listed in the Annex to the Council Directive.

STRICT OR FAULT LIABILITY?

35. Standard imposed by the Regulations

It is controversial whether or not the duties imposed in these regulations are strict. As noted, the Framework Directive undoubtedly intends that they should be. The duties in the regulations themselves are strict: there is no 'due diligence' or similar defence. There is no qualification, for example, of the employers' duty to make a suitable and sufficient assessment of risks: he must make an assessment suitable and sufficient for the circumstances.

It is not clear whether courts will mitigate these regulations by introducing concepts like reasonable foresight as a prerequisite of liability. Possibly in the particular example of Regulation 3(1) foreseeability and adequacy might be related concepts, i.e. to be adequate an assessment would need only to identify foreseeable risks.

On the other hand the purpose of making the assessment is to enable compliance with relevant statutory provisions which are often less than strict. If, as *Mailer* v. *Austin Rover Group plc* [1989] indicates, foresight is a criterion for what is reasonably practicable it might well be argued that the same criterion should apply to determining the nature and extent of the assessment which has to be undertaken in order to control the hazards which the statutory duties themselves require to be addressed.

Progress test 9

1. Distinguish hazard from risk.

2. In what circumstances should an employer carry out health surveillance?

3. In what circumstances should an employer record the findings of a risk assessment?

4. What is meant by 'competence'? For what purposes must an employer appoint competent persons?

5. In what respects are the Framework Directive's provisions wider/less wide than the Management of Health and Safety at Work Regulations?

6. What are the principles of preventive and protective measures as set out in the Framework Directive? To what extent are those principles repeated in the British code of practice? Does the code of practice have the full force of law?

7. What information is an employer required by the Management of Health and Safety at Work Regulations to give to his employees?

8. Do the words 'worker' and 'employee' have the same meaning?

9. What provision does the employer have to make for the health and safety of employees who are not in his employment in order to comply with the Management of Health and Safety at Work Regulations?

10. To what extent, and in what circumstances, do the Management of Health and Safety Regulations require two employers to co-ordinate their activities?

10

REGULATIONS

1. Introduction

This chapter will outline the five sets of Regulations which, together with the Management of Health and Safety at Work Regulations 1992, make up what in Britain has become known as the 'Six Pack'. It will also outline some of the other major sets of regulations made since 1974 (using the regulation-making power in s. 15 and Schedule 3 of the 1974 Act) which have not been dealt with in other chapters of this book. Thus it will include other regulations made to comply with European Directives, including certain Regulations made in relation to Directives subsidiary to the Framework Directive, but adopted and implemented after the Six Pack.

The five sets of Regulations

(a) Workplace (Health, Safety and Welfare) Regulations 1992
(b) Provision and Use of Work Equipment Regulations 1992
(c) Personal Protective Equipment at Work Regulations 1992
(d) Health and Safety (Display Screen Equipment) Regulations 1992
(e) Manual Handling Operations Regulations 1992.

Other major regulatory codes

(f) Control of Lead at Work Regulations 1980
(g) Control of Industrial Major Accident Hazards Regulations 1984
(h) Control of Asbestos at Work Regulations 1987
(i) Electricity at Work Regulations 1989
(j) Noise at Work Regulations 1989
(k) Dangerous Substances (Notification and Marking of Sites) Regulations 1990
(l) Notification of New Substances Regulations 1993
(m) Construction (Design and Management) Regulations 1994
(n) Control of Substances Hazardous to Health Regulations 1994
(o) Chemicals (Hazard Information and Packaging) Regulations 1994
(p) Health and Safety (Safety Signs and Signals) Regulations 1996

Further EC proposals

(q) Protection of Young People at Work
(r) Working Time

2. Pre-1974 regulations

This chapter will not include regulations made before 1974. The Robens Committee identified over 500 sets of regulations in existence in 1970 and the sheer weight of this subordinate legislation was one of their criticisms of the system then in existence. Many of the pre-1974 regulations have now been revoked but the number of Regulations needed recently to implement European Directives does raise the question as to whether the UK will not shortly have returned to the heavily state-regulated situation which Robens deplored. As against this it might be argued that the new Regulations do not have within them the rigid, narrow standards of the old regulations, but the generality of the Regulations themselves is in some cases (notably Chemicals (Hazard Information and Packaging) Regulations 1994 and Control of Substances Hazardous to Health Regulations 1994) negated by very detailed and complex schedules – which will not be reproduced in this text.

3. Systematic approach

The post-1974 Regulations, including those based on European Directives, tend to be general in their application and broad in their approach. It is the style of these Regulations which distinguishes them from the pre-Robens regulations, which contained detailed and precise standards and were of narrow application; indeed many of them did not even apply across industries, but applied only to specific mines, special categories of factories, or types of manufacturing activity. The new-style Regulations are often intended for application to workplaces generally and frequently require organisations to identify and respond to hazardous situations to make them as safe as is 'reasonably practicable.' They are frequently accompanied by approved codes of practice, which may suggest appropriate standards, though on occasion the emergence of standards may be left entirely to be determined by industry practice. Sometimes guidance has also been published by either HSC or HSE; such publications have no formal status when interpreting the requirements of the Regulations to which they relate.

The new broad-brush approach has in a number of instances enabled several industry-specific sets of regulations to be replaced by one set applying to virtually all workplaces; this is notably the case in relation to Control of Lead at Work Regulations, Reporting of Injuries, Diseases, and Dangerous Occurrences Regulations, and the Health and Safety (First Aid) Regulations.

4. Civil liability

Breaches of post-1974 Regulations are presumed to give rise to civil liability (s. 47(2) of the 1974 Act). Many of the Regulations discussed below relate to issues which may give rise to civil claims.

THE FIVE SETS OF REGULATIONS

5. Workplace (Health, Safety and Welfare) Regulations 1992

These Regulations were brought into effect on 1 January 1993 to implement the European Workplace Directive. In making them HSC took the opportunity to repeal ss. 1 to 7, 18, 29, 57–60 and 69 of the Factories Act 1961 and ss. 4–16 of the Offices, Shops and Railway Premises Act 1963 and to revoke part or all of 36 pieces of subordinate legislation, largely related to these two Acts.

The Regulations apply to every workplace except: ships, construction sites, mines. They have limited application to aircraft, locomotives, and vehicles and to any workplace in fields, woods or land forming part of an agricultural or forestry undertaking.

The Regulations set general requirements in four broad areas:

(a) *Working environment*:
temperature in indoor workplaces
ventilation
lighting, including emergency lighting
room dimensions and space
suitability of workstations and seating.

(b) *Safety*:
safe passage of pedestrians and vehicles
windows and skylights
transparent and translucent doors and partitions
doors, gates and escalators
floors
falling a distance and into dangerous substances
falling objects.

(c) *Facilities*:
toilets
washing, eating and changing facilities
clothing storage
drinking water
rest areas (including arrangements to protect people from the
    discomforts of tobacco smoke)
rest facilities for pregnant women and nursing mothers.

(d) *Housekeeping*:
maintenance of workplace, equipment and facilities
cleanliness
removal of waste materials.

Most of the above matters were provided for within the Factories Act and Offices, Shops and Railway Premises Act, but, of course, that legislation was not of general application. Arguably it was also (and still is!) an implied requirement in the general duties under the 1974 Act that every employer do what is reasonably practicable to secure appropriate working conditions in respect of the matters identified in these Regulations. While the Regulations are almost as broad and general as the provisions in the 1974 Act, Schedule 1 of the Regulations provides formulae for calculating workspace and determining the number of sanitary conveniences in existing factories and the Approved Code of Practice accompanying the Regulations gives, in most cases, a fairly general indication of how to comply with the Regulation. Compliance with the Code of Practice is not, of course, mandatory (see Chapter 11). In order to demonstrate the style of the Regulations and the Code, Regulation 8 on Lighting and the first of the five paragraphs of the related provisions of the Code are set out in full:

Regulation 8 Lighting

(1) Every workplace shall have suitable and sufficient lighting.
(2) The lighting mentioned in paragraph (1) shall, so far as is reasonably practicable, be by natural light.
(3) Without prejudice to the generality of paragraph (1) suitable and sufficient lighting shall be provided in any room in circumstances in which persons at work are specially exposed to danger in the event of failure of artificial lighting.

Approved Code of Practice

58. Lighting should be sufficient to enable people to work, use facilities and move from place to place safely and without experiencing eye-strain. Stairs should be well lit in such a way that shadows are not cast over the main part of the treads. Where necessary, local lighting should be provided at individual workstations, and at places of particular risk such as pedestrian crossing points on vehicular traffic routes. Outdoor traffic routes used by pedestrians should be adequately lit after dark.

Paragraph 62 of the Code notes that requirements on lighting are also contained in:

Docks Regulations 1988
Provision and Use of Work Equipment Regulations 1992
Health and Safety (Display Screen Equipment) Regulations 1992
Electricity at Work Regulations 1989.

Existing workplaces were not required to comply with the regulatory standards until January 1997.

6. Provision and Use of Work Equipment Regulations 1992

These Regulations which came into force on 1 January 1993 are to implement the European Provision and Use of Work Equipment Directive. HSC has taken the opportunity of these Regulations to repeal ss. 81 and 82 of the Mines and Quarries Act 1954, ss. 12–16 and 17–19 of the Factories Act 1961 and s. 17 of the Offices, Shops and Railway Premises Act 1963; the whole or part of 17 sets of regulations are also revoked, including parts of the Abrasive Wheels and Woodworking Machines Regulations.

Regulation 2 of the Regulations provides these interpretations:

'use' in relation to work equipment means any activity involving work equipment and includes starting, stopping, programming, setting, transporting, repairing, modifying, maintaining, servicing and cleaning, . . .

'work equipment' means any machinery, appliance, apparatus or tool and any assembly of components which, in order to achieve a common end, are arranged and controlled so that they function as a whole.

The Regulations place general duties on employers and list minimum requirements for work equipment to deal with selected hazards whatever the industry. Initially the Regulations will apply to equipment introduced to the workplace after 1 January 1993, but older equipment will have to comply with the new standards by 1997.

The general duties in these Regulations require employers to:

(*i*) make sure that equipment is suitable for the use that will be made of it;

(*ii*) take into account the working conditions and hazards in the workplace when selecting machinery;

(*iii*) ensure equipment is used only for operations for which, and under conditions for which, it is suitable;

(*iv*) ensure equipment is maintained in an efficient state, in efficient working order and in good repair;

(*v*) give adequate information, instructions and training; and

(*vi*) provide equipment that conforms with European product safety Directives.

There are specific requirements to cover:

(*vii*) guarding of dangerous parts of machinery;

(*viii*) protection against specific hazards (e.g. equipment catching fire);

(*ix*) work equipment parts and substances at high or very low temperatures;

(*x*) control systems and control devices;

(*xi*) isolation of equipment from sources of energy;

(*xii*) stability of equipment;

(*xiii*) lighting;

(*xiv*) maintenance operations; and

(*xv*) warnings and markings.

It is worth noting especially that Regulation 11 of these Regulations concerns dangerous parts of machinery and applies to, among other situations, the situations previously within the ambit of s. 14(1) of the Factories Act. Regulation 11 provides:

(1) Every employer shall ensure that measures are taken in accordance with paragraph (2) which are effective:

(a) to prevent access to any dangerous part of machinery or to any rotating stock-bar; or

(b) to stop the movement of any dangerous part of machinery or rotating stock-bar before any part of a person enters a danger zone.

(2) The measures required by paragraph (1) shall consist of:

(a) the provision of fixed guards enclosing every dangerous part or rotating stock-bar where and to the extent that it is practicable to do so, but where or to the extent that it is not, then

(b) the provision of other guards or protection devices where and to the extent that it is practicable to do so . . .

Possibly the most important sub-section is (3) which provides that all guards and protection devices must:

(a) be suitable for the purpose for which they are provided;

(b) be of good construction, sound material and adequate strength;

(c) be maintained in an efficient state, in efficient working order and in good repair;

(d) not give rise to any increased risk to health or safety;

(e) not be easily bypassed or disabled;

. . .

There has been a European proposal for a Directive to amend the Work Equipment Directive (Proposal for Directive 95/63/EC). The proposal reached a common position which text was adopted by the Social Affairs Council on 5 December 1995 and Members States are required to transpose it into national legislation no later than 5 December 1998. The new Directive is limited principally to requirements for mobile and lifting equipment. But other provisions aim to ensure that work equipment is inspected regularly, and at installation and after each new assembly; and that full account is taken of ergonomics in applying health and safety requirements.

Other Directives set out the standards which new equipment will have to meet; these Directives will be implemented in the UK by Regulations made by the Department of Trade and Industry.

7. Personal Protective Equipment at Work Regulations 1992

These Regulations came into effect on 1 January 1993 to implement the Use of Personal Protective Equipment Directive. They set out principles of selecting, providing, maintaining and using Personal Protective Equipment (i.e. PPE). They do not replace recently introduced law dealing with PPE (e.g. Control of Substances Hazardous to Health Regulations). They do not apply where there are specific regulations relating to PPE.

Regulation 2(1) interprets 'personal protective equipment' to mean:

all equipment (including clothing affording protection against the weather) which is intended to be worn or held by a person at work and which protects him against one or more risks to his health or safety, and any addition or accessory designed to meet that objective.

Regulation 3 lists certain PPE which is not within Regulation 2, principally ordinary working clothes and uniforms which do not specifically protect the health and safety of the wearer, and sports equipment. Certain of the Regulations do not apply to situations which are already within other Regulations, such as the Control of Lead at Work Regulations 1980.

PPE should be relied upon only as a last resort, where risks cannot be adequately controlled by other means. Where PPE is required it must be provided free of charge (a requirement of s. 9 of the 1974 Act). In order to be 'suitable' the PPE provided must effectively protect the particular wearer and it must be appropriate for the risks and the working conditions.

The employer's duties are in respect of employees to:

(a) assess the risks and assess the PPE selected to ensure that it is suitable for the situation;

(b) maintain, clean and replace PPE;

(c) provide storage for PPE when it is not being used;

(d) ensure PPE is properly used; and

(e) give training, information and instruction to employees on its use and how to look after it.

New PPE is subject to a European Directive on design, certification and testing and since 1 July 1995 all newly manufactured or imported PPE items must bear the CE mark.

8. Health and Safety (Display Screen Equipment) Regulations 1992

These Regulations brought into effect on 1 January 1993 are to implement the Display Screen Equipment Directive. The regulations are intended to encourage the ergonomic design of equipment, furniture, the working environment and the tasks performed.

The Regulations apply to display screens where there is a 'user', that is an employee who habitually uses display screen equipment as a significant part of normal work. Employers' duties are in relation to both employees and any self-employed who use display screen equipment in their undertakings. The Regulations cover equipment used for the display of text, numbers and graphics regardless of the display process used. Employers have duties to:

(a) assess display screen equipment workstations and reduce risks which are discovered by that assessment;

(b) make sure that workstations satisfy minimum requirements which are set for the display screen itself, keyboard, desk and chair, working environment and task design and software;

(c) plan display screen equipment work so that there are breaks or changes of activity; and

(d) provide information and training for users.

Display screen equipment users are entitled to ask for sight tests, and to have special spectacles if they are needed and normal ones cannot be used. It is the employer's responsibility to provide tests, and special spectacles if needed.

9. Manual Handling Operations Regulations 1992

These Regulations were brought into effect on 1 January 1993 in order to implement the Manual Handling of Loads Directive.

Regulation 4(1) requires the employer:

(a) so far as is reasonably practicable, to avoid the need for his employees to undertake any manual handling operations at work which involve a risk of their being injured;

(b) where it is not reasonably practicable to avoid the need for his employees to undertake any manual handling operations at work which involves a risk of their being injured:

(i) make a suitable and sufficient assessment of all such manual handling operations to be undertaken by them;

(ii) take appropriate steps to reduce the risk of injury to those employees arising out of their undertaking any such manual handling operations to the lowest level reasonably practicable.

In effect the employer is required to:

(a) consider whether the load has to be moved at all; then if it has to be moved

(b) consider whether it can be moved mechanically; if this is not possible

(c) assess the operation to minimise the risk.

Individual employees are required to notify their employer of any physical condition which may render them less able than other persons to handle loads. The Regulations make the self-employed responsible for their own safety during manual handling. The Regulations are accompanied by extensive guidance on manual handling. While such guidance has no legal, it clearly has considerable practical, significance.

OTHER MAJOR REGULATORY CODES

10. The Control of Lead at Work Regulations 1980

For the purposes of these regulations 'lead' means lead, lead alloys and compounds of lead which is liable to be inhaled, ingested or otherwise absorbed by persons. The objective of the regulations is to control the exposure of employees and other persons at work to such lead. Employers (and where relevant self-employed persons) are required to assess work where there is a risk of exposure to lead and to introduce and maintain control measures. Records must be kept of assessments. These control measures should as far as reasonably practicable be measures other than the use of respiratory equipment or protective clothing. In other words the primary duty is to protect the workers from exposure rather than to protect them from the consequences of exposure. Steps must be taken to avoid, so far as reasonably practicable, the spread of contamination from the place where the work is being carried out. The employer must provide adequate washing and changing facilities. The employer must take steps to secure (so far as reasonably practicable) that employees do not eat, drink or smoke in any place which is or is liable to be contaminated by lead. Employers must ensure that adequate information, instruction and training is given to employees who are liable to be exposed to lead. An employer is required to keep under medical surveillance any employees who are employed on work which significantly exposes them to lead.

In May 1996 HSC published a discussion document suggesting that the control of lead might be incorporated in the Control of Substances Hazardous to Health Regulations by an appropriate amendment of the latter.

11. Control of Industrial Major Accident Hazards Regulations 1984

These regulations were formulated, in part in response to the disaster at Flixborough in 1974, and in part in response to the EC 'Seveso' Directive. They apply where hazardous or ultra-hazardous activities might present a danger to employees or to the public. The regulations introduced into UK law the concept of the documented 'safety case'; they require manufacturers controlling certain industrial processes to:

(a) assess and document the hazards of their operations

(b) organise and document an adequate accident prevention system

(c) report major accidents to the HSE according to a special dossier

(d) prepare and update a detailed safety analysis of the more high-risk of their activities

(e) make provision (including disclosure of information to the public) for limiting the effects of major accidents.

These requirements are in a 'two-tier' classification of hazards. In the 'lower tier' – in specified, less-dangerous situations – manufacturers must have available the evidence, including documentation, to demonstrate that they have identified the major hazards, taken the necessary steps to control them, and to limit their consequences should they take place. They must also notify the HSE of any major accidents, and the results of their internal investigation, together with the steps proposed to alleviate their effects and to prevent their recurrence.

The 'upper-tier' duties, which apply only where substantial quantities of listed hazardous substances are involved, require manufacturers to notify the HSE three months prior to beginning the activity which falls under the regulations, submitting the specified 'safety case' relating to the activity, including details of the dangerous substances involved, the proposed management system for hazard control, the potential major accidents, and the laid-down emergency procedures. This 'safety case' must be updated every three years to take account of developments in safety and hazard assessment. The manufacturers' duty, as part of the upper-tier safety precautions, to formulate on-site and off-site emergency plans to deal with the consequences of a major accident, has already been referred to.

In R v. Associated Octel Ltd [1994], though the prosecution was brought under s. 3(1) of the 1974 Act, a major factor in determining the guilt of the company was that the accident involving visiting contractors occurred at premises subject to these regulations and it would not have occurred if the defendants had required the visitors to observe the 'permit to work' system which had been spelt out in the 'safety case' for the installation.

12. Control of Asbestos at Work Regulations 1987

These regulations, together with the Asbestos (Licensing) Regulations 1983 and the Asbestos (Prohibitions) Regulations 1985, form the regulatory code for the protection of persons against the risks associated with use of asbestos at work. They implement EC Directives.

They impose duties on employers for the protection of employees who may be exposed to asbestos at work, and for the protection of other persons who are liable to be affected by work involving asbestos. The first duty of employers is to identify the type of asbestos utilised in their work, and to assess the nature and degree of exposure to this asbestos, and the steps to be taken to reduce that exposure. They must then respond positively to the problem as identified by that assessment, by preventing the exposure at work of employees or other persons, or by reducing that exposure to the lowest level reasonably practicable. If exposure is not reduced to below the specified control limits, employees must be provided with respiratory protective equipment that will reduce their exposure below those limits.

The effectiveness of the employees' protection against exposure must be monitored, and, in the case of employees who are liable to be 'significantly exposed', the monitoring must be reinforced by regular medical surveillance.

Certain activities involving the use of asbestos, such as spraying, are prohibited by the regulatory code. All work involving the use of asbestos must be notified to the enforcing authority.

These regulations are noteworthy because they provide the only example so far of a person being convicted to serve an actual (as opposed to suspended) prison sentence for breach of occupational health and safety laws. The conviction (reported in *Health and Safety Information Bulletin* for March 1996) occurred at Bristol Crown Court in January 1996: Roy Hill was sentenced to three months imprisonment for releasing asbestos during demolition work. He had put his employees and the public at risk. He was found guilty of breaches of the Asbestos (Licensing) Regulations and the Control of Asbestos at Work Regulations. He had failed to identify the type of asbestos present; make a risk assessment; prevent or reduce to the lowest level reasonably practicable the risk of exposure to employees and the spread of asbestos from the place of work.

An HSC discussion document published in May 1996 suggests that the control of asbestos might be incorporated in the Control of Substances Hazardous to Health Regulations by an appropriate amendment of the latter.

13. Electricity at Work Regulations 1989

These replace 75 outmoded codes of regulations dealing with particular applications of electricity in the work situation. They apply to all aspects of work, including mining, involving the use of electricity. They require 'safe systems' of working. They place responsibilities upon, *inter alia*, employers and self-employed persons, managers of mines and quarries, and employees while at work, for the protection of employees, as well as third persons, against electrical dangers. The essence of these regulations is in their simplicity and flexibility. Typical of this approach is Regulation 16, which stipulates:

> No person shall be engaged in any work activity where technical knowledge or experience is necessary to prevent danger, or where appropriate, injury, unless he possesses such knowledge or experience or is under such degree of supervision as may be appropriate having regard to the nature of the work.

The regulations are supported by three sets of guidance.

14. Noise at Work Regulations 1989

These regulations implement the EC Directive on noise. They apply to all workplaces within the UK, other than ships and aircraft, and impose duties upon employers, the self-employed, employees, and machine designers and suppliers. The primary duty they impose is to reduce the risk of hearing damage at work to the lowest level reasonably practicable.

Additionally, further duties, of increasing orders of stringency, are imposed upon employers at the 'first and second action levels', which are defined as 85 DBA and 90 DBA respectively. At these higher levels the employers' obligations are based upon the concept of 'assessment and response' made familiar by the Control of Substances Hazardous to Health Regulations (*see* 12).

At these levels, it is the duty of employers to ensure that a noise assessment is carried out by a competent person, and that workers who are found by that assessment to be at risk above the lower action level are provided with suitable and efficient personal hearing protection. At the higher action level, it is, additionally, the employers' duty to reduce, so far as is reasonably practicable, this exposure to noise by means other than personal hearing protection.

It is also the duty of the employers, at first or second level of exposure, to provide all employees exposed with all relevant information relating to the noise hazard.

The obligations to protect hearing are, generally, modified by a 'reasonably practicable' defence, but it is noteworthy that in certain respects – such as the duty to provide personal hearing protection, the duty to ensure that all relevant equipment, other than personal hearing protection, is fully and properly used, and the duty to ensure that adequate noise assessments are carried out – the duties are not so modified.

15. Dangerous Substances (Notification and Marking of Sites) Regulations 1990

These regulations apply to any site upon which more than 25 tonnes of danger-ous substances (as listed in the Chemicals (Hazard Information and Packaging)

Regulations) are kept at any one time. They oblige the person in control of such sites to notify the local health and safety enforcing authority, and also the fire authority, giving the information specified in the regulations. Warning signs must also be displayed at the sites.

The object of the regulations is to ensure that the safety and fire authorities are in possession of information that will assist them in organising their inspection programmes, and also in alerting the emergency services personnel as to the hazards they are likely to encounter at a particular site where dangerous substances are stored.

16. Notification of New Substances Regulations 1993

These regulations came into force 31 January 1994: they replaced the 1992 regulations of the same name.

These regulations impose a duty on any manufacturer, importer or supplier of a new substance (within the meaning of the regulations) to notify the HSE of the particulars of the substance, as laid down in Schedule 1 of the regulations, before that person supplies that substance in a quantity of one tonne or more in any period of 12 months.

As part of that notification, the results of standard toxicity tests on that substance, carried out in accordance with the principles of good laboratory practice, must be given to HSE.

The regulations flesh out s. 6 of the 1974 Act. They also implement the EC Directive on the notification of substances.

17. Construction (Design and Management) Regulations 1994

These regulations were introduced, somewhat belatedly, on 31 March 1995, to implement an EC Directive on minimum safety and health requirements at temporary or mobile construction sites.

These regulations are to ensure that effective direction and co-ordination of health and safety matters takes place throughout the duration of a construction project. Companies have to appoint a health and safety co-ordinator and also to incorporate health and safety protection at project design stages. Clients and designers as well as contractors have key obligations. The regulations are to be supported by an Approved Code of Practice.

18. Control of Substances Hazardous to Health Regulations 1988

These regulations were first published in 1988 and like the Packaging regulations (in the paragraph below) to which they are cross-referenced, they seek to implement a series of complex EC Directives and have had to be updated to keep abreast of amendments to the EC laws.

The regulations require all employers to carry out a thorough assessment of the risks to their employees arising from the use in their work of a wide range of hazardous substances as identified by the regulations, as well as other substances creating hazards comparable to those identified within the regula-tions. Employers are under a similar duty towards persons not in their employ-ment who may be affected in like manner by those substances.

Employers must respond positively to the risks identified by the assessment, by controlling the exposure through their system of working. Wherever possible employers should adopt a system of control which does not involve the use of personal protective equipment by the persons at risk (i.e. 'engineering controls'). Only in the situation where no other system of protection is effective must personal protective equipment be provided by employers and used by employ-ees. Employers are under a duty to 'take all reasonable steps' to ensure that this equipment is properly used.

Where the nature of the hazard requires it, employers must, in addition, monitor the performance of the system both generally, and, in appropriate cases, through health surveillance of employees.

The regulations are supported by codes of practice and guidance. Since the original regulations came fully into force on 31 December 1989, one of their most striking effects has been the demand they have created for trained and competent persons to carry out their complex requirements.

The principal requirements are of strict liability.

It is now proposed to extend the regulations below ground at mines but the Coal Mines (Respirable Dust) Regulations 1975 together with the general duties on dust control in the Mines and Quarries Act 1954 s. 74 would be retained.

A recent HSC consultative document proposes further amendments to these regulations: these amendments would be introduced by amending regulations to come into force in 1997.

19. Chemicals (Hazard Information and Packaging) Regulations 1994

These regulations came into effect on 31 January 1995, replacing regulations of the same name, dated 1993. The subject matter of the regulations is related to a series of EC Directives dating back to 1967 and with the various EC amending Directives it has been constantly necessary to update the British regulations. Originally the regulations were known as the Classification, Packaging and Labelling of Dangerous Substances Regulations. Yet a further (the 21st) adapta-tion to the original Directive (67/548/EEC) required further amendments to the regulations before the end of 1996. (See Chemical (Hazard Information and Packaging) (Amendment) Regulations 1996.)

The objective is to improve the information provided when chemicals are supplied; remove barriers to trade; and reduce animal testing. They aim to protect both people and the environment from dangerous chemicals. They require chemicals to be classified according to the categories of danger listed in the Schedule: the categories cover explosions, flammability, toxicity, carcinogenicity, danger to the environment.

The regulations mainly affect suppliers and consignors of chemicals, requir-ing them to label and package dangerous chemicals safely. They require that the inherently dangerous properties of the chemicals are classified, before supply or carriage: it is an offence to supply or consign for carriage a chemical which has not been classified. Unless the chemical is not dangerous (or within the class of preparations to which particular labelling requirements apply) a safety data sheet may have to be provided when it is supplied, and it will have to be appropriately labelled. Chemicals also have to be classified to identify those which are dangerous for carriage. In some circumstances a supplier may rely on a classification made by a manufacturer, but only if the supplier has exercised 'all due diligence'.

20. Health and Safety (Safety Sign and Signals) Regulations 1996

These regulations came into effect on 1 April 1996. They implement the EC Safety Signs Directive (92/58/EEC) and apply to all places and activities where workers are employed, but exclude signs and labels used in connection with the supply of substances, products and equipment or the transport of dangerous goods. HSE has published a guidance leaflet. Employers are required to use a safety sign whenever there is a risk to health and safety that cannot be avoided or properly controlled by other means. Signs need to contain a pictogram to convey the message instead of relying solely on text. The EC objective is to harmonise signs in all the Member States.

FURTHER EC PROPOSALS

21. Protection of Young People at Work

Regulations are proposed to implement the health and safety provisions of the EC Directive (94/33/EC) on the Protection of Young People at Work. As was noted in the previous chapter the proposed regulations build on the risk assessment and information requirements of the Management of Health and Safety at Work Regulations 1992. They would also remove a number of existing provisions relating to the health and safety of young people which are considered to be outdated and unnecessary.

The regulations will require employers to take particular account of the implications of lack of experience and absence of awareness of risks. In the case of school-age children, employers will have to inform parents (or those with parental authority) of the outcome of risk assessments and control measures introduced. Employment in certain hazardous situations would be prohibited, e.g. where there might be exposure to radiation.

22. Working Time Directive

If the UK challenge to this Directive (93/104/EC) is overruled by the European Court of Justice – as seems likely, given the Advocate General has given an opinion that the Directive, being concerned with health and safety, was properly based on Article 118A of the Treaty of Rome – the UK will have to implement it within a very short space of time. The Directive was adopted by a majority vote on 23 November 1993; therefore implementation should be in November 1996, but leeway is likely to be granted to the UK.

Regulations to implement the Directive would have to address:

- a maximum 48 hour working week, including overtime, over a four-month period
- a maximum average 8 hour shift for night-workers
- rest breaks after every 6 hours worked
- rest periods of 11 hours daily
- a minimum 4 weeks' paid leave (3 weeks until 1999).

There are, however, many exceptions to these requirements; for example, managing executives, family workers and those employed in hospitals, residential institutions and prisons are largely exempt.

Progress test 10

1. Which of the post-1974 regulations implement EC Directives?

2. What are the principal requirements of the Control of Substances Hazardous to Health Regulations?

3. To what work situations do the Electricity at Work Regulations apply?

4. Which of the post-1974 regulations set out above provide for public safety?

5. Which of the regulations require a 'safety case' to be made out?

6. What matters are covered by the 'individual' EC Directives?

11

IMPLEMENTATION AND ENFORCEMENT OF THE 1974 ACT

1. Introduction

Responsibility for implementation and enforcement of the 1974 Act lies with the Health and Safety Commission (HSC) and the Health and Safety Executive (HSE); certain responsibilities and powers are also given to a Secretary of State (for example the Secretary of State for the Environment). This chapter will identify the constitution, responsibilities and powers of the HSC and the HSE with particular reference to powers to make regulations and codes of practice, powers and responsibilities of HSE-appointed inspectors, and the system of enforcement under the Act.

ESTABLISHMENT AND FUNCTIONS OF THE HSC AND THE HSE

2. General

Section 10 declares that there shall be two bodies corporate: the Health and Safety Commission and the Health and Safety Executive and sets out their constitutions.

3. The Health and Safety Commission

The HSC is a 'quango', established to specialise in occupational health and safety and thus to rectify the problems which the Robens Report had attributed to the previous situation where responsibilities for occupational health and safety had been spread over a number of Ministerial portfolios. The HSC is largely independent, acting on behalf of the Crown, but reporting to Parliament through relevant Secretaries of State.

4. Composition of the HSC

The HSC consists of a chairman and between six and nine other members, all appointed by the Secretary of State. Before appointing members the Secretary of State is required to hold consultations: in respect of three members with employers' organisations; in respect of three members with employees' organisations (i.e. trade unions); and before appointing the other members, with organisations representing local authorities and other organisations, including relevant professional bodies.

5. The Health and Safety Executive

The HSE must consist of three persons, appointed by the HSC with the approval of the Secretary of State. One is to be appointed to be the director of the HSE; the others are to be appointed after consultation with the director of the HSE.

Detailed provisions concerning the appointment, tenure of office, remuneration, etc., of members of the HSC and HSE are set out in Schedule 2 of the Act.

6. Role of the HSC

It is the general duty of the HSC 'to do such things and make such arrangements as it considers appropriate for the general purposes of' Part I of the Act (s. 11). Section 11(2) (somewhat paraphrased here) requires the HSC to:
(a) assist and encourage persons concerned with furthering the purposes of the Act;
(b) make arrangements for carrying out research, publishing the results thereof, and the provision of training and information in connection therewith;
(c) make arrangements for the provision of information and advice to government departments, and employers and employees and organisations representing them;
(d) submit proposals for the making of regulations.

The HSC is required to report to the Secretary of State on its proposals, ensure that its activities accord with proposals the Secretary of State has approved, and give effect to any directions given to it by the Secretary of State.

7. Role of the HSE

It is a duty of the HSE to provide staff for the performance of HSC functions. In practice this means that a proportion of the work of the HSE's inspectorate is concerned with conducting the research and identifying the information required to enable the HSC to remain properly informed. Notwithstanding this, the HSC is also empowered to appoint and pay persons to provide specialist advice, and to pay for research (s. 13).

The HSE is further required to provide information to any Minister of State in connection with any matter with which he is concerned, and to provide him with advice, where relevant expertise is available in the HSE, even if the matter is not relevant to any of the general purposes of the Act. It would appear, therefore, that the HSE could be requested to give an expert opinion on such matters as whether plant and equipment used on merchant ships engaged in fishing was comparable, in safety terms, with that used onshore, or whether mechanical toys could be deemed to be safe.

The HSE may be required by the HSC to investigate and report on any accident or occurrence which the HSC considers necessary or expedient to investigate for any of the purposes of the Act, including the making of regulations, whether or not the HSE is directly responsible for enforcement of the Act in the situation in question.

8. Responsibilities for enforcement

It is the duty of the HSE to make adequate arrangements for the enforcement of the relevant statutory provisions, except to the extent that some other authority has been made responsible, or by agreement with the HSC assumed responsibility for their enforcement (s. 18(1)). The Secretary of State may make regulations giving local authorities specified enforcement duties (s. 18(2)(a)). Local authorities have retained their duties of enforcing health and safety legislation in those premises which were formerly within the scope of the Offices, Shops and Railway Premises Act 1963, and were given responsibility for enforcing the 1974 Act in those premises by the Health and Safety (Enforcing Authority) Regulations 1977. By the Health and Safety (Enforcing Authority) (Amendment) Regulations 1985 they were given responsibility for a large number of other 'low risk' premises and work situations (e.g. leisure premises).

Section 19 empowers enforcing authorities to appoint (and terminate the appointment of) inspectors.

REGULATIONS AND CODES OF PRACTICE

9. Powers of the Secretary of State

Section 15 of the 1974 Act empowers the Secretary of State to make regulations for the purposes of Part I of the Act, i.e. to secure the health and safety of persons at work, to protect other persons from risks created by the activities of people at work (s. 1(1)), and to update the earlier safety legislation (s. 1(2)).

10. Purposes for which regulations may be made

Schedule 3 specifies purposes for which regulations may be made, but s. 15(2) makes it clear that Schedule 3 in no way restricts the general regulation-making power.

The schedule covers such matters as the regulation or prohibition of manufacture, use or supply of any plant or substance; the testing, labelling, or marking of articles; the transport of articles or substances; and the licensing of activities.

Regulations may also be made about the premises in which people work, the taking of fire precautions, and the provision of protective clothing.

Regulations must not conflict with EC requirements, e.g. prohibit the import into the UK of articles or substances contrary to the EC's objective of securing free movement of goods between Member States.

11. Scope of regulations

Section 15 identifies certain matters which may be dealt with by, and limitations which may be imposed on, the application of regulations. In particular regulations may vary statutory provisions. Thus the existing statutory provisions may be repealed or modified (and indeed have been especially with the introduction of the six pack to implement important EC Directives!), and situations may be removed from the ambit of the general duties of the 1974 Act itself, by regulations. Similarly exemptions from the requirements of any of the relevant statutory provisions may be granted (this latter power has, in the past, been used fairly extensively in respect of mining legislation in relation to specified mines). The Offshore Safety Act 1992, s. 1(2) makes specific provision for regulations concerning the offshore oil industry and much has since been done to bring the older regulations made under the Mineral Workings (Offshore Installations) Act 1971 into the more modern regulatory and enforcement system (e.g. The Offshore Installations and Pipeline Works (Management and Administration) Regulations 1995).

12. Breach of regulations

Regulations may also state the persons or classes of persons who are to be guilty of offences in the event that regulatory duties are breached, make provision for defences available in proceedings, exclude proceedings on indictment, and restrict the punishment which may be imposed.

13. Proposals for regulations

Section 50 empowers the Secretary of State to make regulations further to proposals submitted by the HSC, or independently of such proposals. However, the Secretary of State may not act on proposals other than those submitted by the HSC without having consulted the HSC. Regulations do not become operative unless they have been laid before Parliament.

14. Codes of practice

Section 16 empowers the HSC to approve and issue such codes of practice (whether prepared by it or not) as are, in its opinion, suitable for the purpose of providing practical guidance as to the requirements of any of the general duties of health and safety regulations, or of any of the existing statutory provisions. It can also, where it considers this appropriate, approve codes of practice which have been issued by other bodies.

15. Approval of a code of practice

While approved codes of practice take their authority from the actions of the HSC rather than the Secretary of State, the HSC is nevertheless required to obtain the consent of the Secretary of State before approving a code of practice. Moreover, before seeking the consent of the Secretary of State, the HSC must consult any government department that appears to the HSC to be appropriate.

When the HSC approves a code of practice it must issue a written notice identifying the code, stating the date on which its approval is to become effective, and specifying the statutory or regulatory provisions for which it provides practical guidance. The HSC may withdraw its approval from a code of practice.

16. Regulations and codes of practice

Many regulations brought into force under the 1974 Act have been accompanied by codes of practice. It has become the practice for the HSC to publish draft regulations and codes in the form of a consultative document, to seek the widest possible comment, as part of the process of drawing up and bringing into force these instruments.

Nevertheless in its *Review of Health and Safety Regulation* (published in 1994) HSC accepted that 'The respective roles of regulations, Approved Codes of Practice and guidance are unclear. One result is that businesses – especially small firms – and others have difficulty in finding out exactly what legal requirements they must follow . . .' However HSC concluded that it should continue to issue both Approved Codes of Practice and guidance.

17. Breach of a code of practice

Failure to observe a code is not in itself an offence (s. 17). However, where in any criminal proceedings someone is alleged to have committed an offence by reason of a contravention of any requirement or prohibition imposed by or under a statutory provision to which an approved code of practice has properly been related, then that code may be relevant to the proceedings. Where a code appears to the court to be relevant that code is admissible in evidence in the proceedings. If it is proved that there was a failure to observe any provision of the code which is relevant to any matter which it is necessary for the prosecution to prove in order to establish a contravention of the law, that matter shall be taken as proved unless it is proved that the law was complied with otherwise than by observance of the code. Thus if the prosecution shows that the accused has not observed the code, then a presumption is raised that the law to which the code relates has been broken, but this presumption may be rebutted by the accused showing that he has observed the law in some other, and equivalent, way.

POWERS OF INSPECTORS

18. Appointment and exercise of powers

Inspectors appointed under s. 19 of the 1974 Act, and also local authority inspectors responsible for enforcing occupational health and safety, may enforce the 1974 Act and other relevant statutory provisions and regulations. Inspectors appointed under s. 19 must be appointed in writing and the instrument of appointment must specify which of the powers conferred on inspectors by the relevant statutory provisions are to be exercisable by the person appointed. An inspector is entitled to exercise only such powers as are specified in the instrument of appointment and then only within the field of responsibility of the authority which appointed him. Thus local authority inspectors can only exercise their powers in premises and situations which are within the jurisdiction of local authorities. Where it is intended that HSE inspectors shall exercise powers which the HSE has acquired under agency agreements (e.g. with the Department of Transport in relation to railway legislation), this must be stipulated either in the instrument of appointment, by amendment of it (under s. 19(3)) or in a separate document. An inspector may be required to produce his instrument of appointment or an authenticated copy of it, when exercising his powers (s. 19(4)).

19. Powers of inspectors

Section 20 sets out the powers of an inspector. Under s. 20(2) these are broadly:

(a) at any reasonable time (or in a situation which in his opinion is, or may be dangerous, at any time) to enter any premises which he has reason to believe it is necessary for him to enter;

(b) to take with him a constable if he has reasonable cause to apprehend any serious obstruction;

(c) on entering any premises in the course of his duty to take with him –

(i) any other person duly authorised by his (the inspector's) enforcing authority; and

(ii) any equipment or materials required for any purpose for which the power of entry is being exercised;

(d) to make such examination and investigation as may in any circumstances be necessary;

(e) to direct that premises shall be left undisturbed for as long as is reasonably necessary for the purpose of any examination or investigation;

(f) to take measurements and photographs;

(g) to take samples of any articles or substances found in any premises, and of the atmosphere in, or in the vicinity of the premises;

(h) to cause an article or substance found in premises to be dismantled or subjected to testing (but not to damage or destroy it if this is avoidable) where he believes these commodities to have caused or to be likely to cause danger to health or safety;

(i) to take possession of any article or substance he believes to be dangerous and to detain it for so long as is necessary for any of the following purposes:
   (*i*) to examine it and do to it anything he is empowered to do;
   (*ii*) to ensure that it is not tampered with before his examination is completed;
   (*iii*) to ensure that it is available for use as evidence in any proceedings in relation to enforcement of the relevant statutory provisions;
(j) to require any person to answer any relevant questions and to sign a declaration as to the truth of the answers given;
(k) to require the production of, inspect, and take copies of or of any entry in –
   (*i*) any books or documents which the relevant statutory provisions require to be kept;
   (*ii*) any other relevant books or documents;
(l) to require any person to afford him such facilities and assistance with respect to any matter or things within that person's control or in relation to which that person has responsibilities:
(m) any other power which is necessary.

Arguably these powers are wider than those given to a police constable. In common law jurisdictions constables normally need a special warrant in order to enter premises, and in the USA it has been held that federal health and safety inspectors need a warrant before entering premises, should the occupier insist on the point. The statutory authority of inspectors under s. 20 is such that no such proposition could be raised in Great Britain. Similarly the powers of the police in Great Britain to take evidence are probably more constrained by the Police and Criminal Evidence Act 1984 than those of HSE and local authority inspectors operating under s. 20.

20. Constraints on the exercise of inspector's powers

Section 20 does, however, actually or potentially, place some constraints on the exercise by inspectors of their powers. Section 20(3) enables the making of regulations as to the procedure to be followed when taking samples, including the way in which samples are to be dealt with when taken. Section 20(4) provides that when inspectors propose to exercise their powers under s. 20(2)(h) to dismantle or test something then they must (subject to questions of national security), if so requested by that person, carry out these processes in the presence of the person who has responsibilities in relation to the premises. They must also consult such persons as appear to them to be appropriate to find out what dangers, if any, there may be in dismantling or testing the thing (s. 20(5)). Where inspectors take possession of something under s. 20(2)(i) they must leave at the premises, either with a responsible person, or if that is impracticable, fixed in a conspicuous position, a notice giving particulars of the article or substance of which they have taken possession. Wherever it is practicable for them to do so, they must take a sample of any substance they intend to take into possession, and give that sample to a responsible person at the premises in question.

No answer given by a person under s. 20(2)(j) is admissible in evidence against that person or the husband or wife of that person in any proceedings (s. 20(7)).

ENFORCEMENT OF THE LAW

21. General advisory role of the inspectorate

An important feature of the British safety inspectorates has been the emphasis placed on giving advice rather than merely invoking the law. The merits of the approach become apparent when the relationship between the British inspectorate and those at the workplace is compared with the adversary relationship which can exist in other jurisdictions, such as the USA.

The advisory role is authorised by s. 11(2)(c) which imposes upon the HSC the duty to provide an information and advisory service. This duty is carried out by the publication of explanatory leaflets, and more substantial reports and works of guidance.

The inspector must be circumspect in giving advice because, in the final analysis, legal requirements can only be determined in court, by a judge interpreting the law. Inspectors do, however, provide information as to available expert literature, and may, upon occasion, express an opinion about how situations might be improved.

22. HSC enforcement policy statement

HSC has recently published an important *enforcement policy statement*. It states that its **four principles of enforcement** are:

- Action should be **proportionate** to any risks and the seriousness of the breach of the law.
- **Consistency** of approach does not mean uniformity. It means taking a similar approach in similar circumstances to achieve similar ends.
- **Transparency** means helping duty-holders to understand what is expected of them.
- **Targeting** means making sure that inspection is targeted primarily on those whose activities give rise to the most serious risks or where the hazards are least well-controlled.

HSC states that prosecution will be considered when:

'it is appropriate in the circumstances as a way to draw general attention to the need for compliance with the law and the maintenance of standards required by law, especially where there would be a normal expectation that a prosecution would be taken or where, through the conviction of offenders, others may be deterred from similar failures to comply with the law'; *or*

'there, is judged to have been potential for considerable harm arising from the breach; *or*

'the gravity of the offence taken with the general record and approach of the offender warrants it.'

The decision to prosecute will also take into account criteria set out in the Code for Crown Prosecutors or, in Scotland the Procurator Fiscal.

Enforcing authorities will:

'identify and prosecute or recommend prosecution of individuals, including company directors and managers, if they consider a conviction is warranted and can be secured.'

'Where there has been a breach of the law leading to a work-related death enforcing authorities need to consider whether the circumstances of the case might justify a charge of manslaughter'.

A leaflet has also been published, as part of the Citizen's Charter initiative, entitled *Your rights when health and safety inspectors take action*. This leaflet spells out:

'If an inspector tells you to do something – you have a right, if you ask, to be given a letter explaining what needs to be done, when and why. You have two weeks to make representations to the inspector's manager.'

23. Level of enforcement

Prior to the implementation of the 1974 Act if an inspector did not get coopera-tion from an employer in maintaining workplace standards, the only way forward for the inspector was the expensive and time-consuming process of prosecution. Moreover, in most instances a dangerous state of affairs could not be stopped pending the outcome of the prosecution. The 1974 Act enables inspectors to deal speedily and effectively with both hazardous situations and persistent non-compliance with the statutory standards, by serving improve-ment and prohibition notices. The level of effective enforcement has risen greatly since the 1974 Act, although there has been no great increase in the number of prosecutions. Prosecutions have tended to be reserved either for situations where there has been personal injury, or where, even though there has been no accident, there has been very unacceptable behaviour. This is in the spirit of the Robens Report, which recommended that the criminal process should only be used where there had been a wilful or reckless disregard for safety.

24. Improvement notices

Inspectors may serve an improvement notice when they are of the opinion that a person is contravening one or more of the relevant statutory provisions or has contravened one or more of those provisions in circumstances that make it likely that the contravention will continue or be repeated (s. 21). The notice states the inspector's opinion, identifies the statutory provision(s) which has been broken, gives reasons for the view that it is broken and requires that the situation be remedied within the period stated in the notice. The notice must be served on the person under the duty to ensure that the statutory standard in question has been met. For example, if the inspector's concern is that the organisation has either no, or an unsatisfactory, safety policy it will specify s. 2(3) as being contravened; as the s. 2(3) duty is placed on the employer, the notice will be served on the employer.

Under the new procedures set out in the Citizen's Charter leaflet referred to above it is now spelt out that if the inspector intends to issue an improvement notice:

'You have a right to have your point of view heard by the inspector's manager if you consider that the notice should be changed or should not be issued. You have two weeks in which to make representations, which will be considered on a fair and fresh basis.

'When a notice is issued – you will be told in writing about your right of appeal to an Industrial Tribunal, and given a form to use to appeal. You will be told:

- how to appeal
- where and within what period an appeal may be brought
- that an appeal may be brought on any grounds; and
- that action required by an improvement notice is suspended while an appeal is pending.'

25. Prohibition notices

Section 22 enables an inspector to serve a prohibition notice when of the opinion that activities which are, or are likely to be, carried on involve a risk of serious personal injury. The activities must be ones to which relevant statutory provisions apply. But it is not necessary for the inspector to identify that a statutory duty is being flouted or broken – the criterion is the apparent danger, not the violation of the law. As no particular legal rule need be invoked by the inspector it is not relevant to require the service of the notice on a person with identified statutory duties. Therefore the notice is served on the person 'in control' of the activities to which the notice relates: who this should be will be a factual matter to be determined by the inspector.

The new Citizen's Charter initiative will, apparently, have no impact on the serving of prohibition notices. The leaflet states that when an inspector intends to take immediate action:

' – for example by issuing a prohibition notice, you have a right to a written explanation as soon as practicable of why this is necessary. Prohibition notices include such explanation.'

26. Content of prohibition notices

The notice must state that the inspector is of the opinion that there is a danger of serious personal injury; specify the matters which in the inspector's opinion give, or as the case may be, will give rise to the risk; where statutory duties appear to be contravened, specify the provisions in question; give the inspector's reasons for having formed the opinion that these provisions are being broken; and direct that the activities shall not be carried on by, or under the control of, the person on whom the notice is served unless the situation has been remedied.

27. Time scale

A prohibition notice either takes effect at the end of the period specified in the notice (a deferred notice) or immediately. In practice the majority of notices are immediate prohibition notices.

28. Additional matters

Sections 23 and 24 provide additional information about notices.

(a) Section 23 clarifies that a notice may include directions about the measures which are to be taken to remedy any contravention or danger and such directions may be framed by reference to an approved code of practice. The notice may specify alternative ways of dealing with the situation, leaving a choice to the person on whom the notice is served.

(b) Notices relating to the structure of a building must not impose requirements more onerous than the building regulations currently in force; notices which might lead to measures affecting the means of escape in case of fire must not be served unless the inspector has consulted the fire authority.

(c) An immediate prohibition notice, once served, may not be withdrawn. So the controller on whom it is served remains at risk should work be resumed before the required standard has been achieved, or, if work has been resumed, the standard is allowed to fall again below that required by the notice.

(d) The time granted for complying with an improvement notice or a deferred prohibition notice may be extended by an inspector.

29. Appeals

A person upon whom a notice is served may appeal to an industrial tribunal against it (s. 24); regulations stipulate that the appeal must be lodged within three weeks of the service of the notice (the Industrial Tribunals (Improvement and Prohibition Notices Appeals) Regulations 1974). The tribunal may either affirm the notice, modify it or cancel it. Where an appeal is brought against an improvement notice the bringing of the appeal suspends the notice until the appeal is finally disposed of, or the appeal is withdrawn. In the case of a prohibition notice the appeal only suspends the notice if the tribunal so directs. Assessors may be appointed to assist the tribunal in evaluating the notice.

Appeal against a notice may be taken from the industrial tribunal to the High Court and ultimately to the House of Lords. The number of appeals against notices is not high in relation to the number of notices which are served and the proportion of successful appeals is small.

In *Belhaven Brewery Company Ltd* v. *A McLean (HM Inspector of Factories)* [1975] the appellants appealed against an improvement notice which required screens to be provided to prevent access to transmission machinery and other parts of the company's automatic kegging plant. The appellants claimed that the work would be more expensive than they could afford. The tribunal held that the requirement was only to do what was reasonably practicable and it had no regard to the suggestion that the work would be too costly for the particular employer.

On the other hand in *West Bromwich Building Society Ltd* v. *Townsend* [1983] a notice had required fitting bandit screens. The tribunal found that the risk to employees from robberies was more than minimal and the measures required by the notice were both physically and financially within the society's capacity; so the tribunal upheld the notice. The High Court found that in reaching its decision the tribunal had erred because it had not weighed the risk at the particular premises against the cost of providing the screens. Had it made this evaluation it would have concluded that, though possible for the employer to install the screens, it was not reasonably practicable for them to do so.

30. Burden of proof

In *Readmans Ltd* v. *Leeds City Council* (1992) it was held that the burden is on the inspector who serves a prohibition notice to show that the law has been broken: it is not for the person receiving the notice to establish that the situation was lawful.

A prohibition notice had been served in relation to shopping trolleys provided by the company which operated a large cash-and-carry clothing store; the environmental health officer considered that the trolleys, fitted with child seats, involved a risk of serious personal injury. The company appealed first to an industrial tribunal and then to the High Court. The High Court held that as the notice alleged a breach of a criminal duty it was for the council who had issued the notice to establish the existence of the risk, not for the appellant to have the burden of proving that there was no such risk.

31. Criminal procedures

Service of a notice does not activate the criminal law; however, failure to comply with a notice, whether an improvement or a prohibition notice, is a criminal offence and can result in imprisonment even though tried summarily.

32. Inspectors' responsibilities

The commitment of inspectors to the use of their powers to serve notices, especially immediate prohibition notices, has been commendable, bearing in mind that such notices may involve organisations on whom they are served in very great expense – often more expense than might be incurred by a prosecution in a magistrates' court. HSE inspectors cannot but be aware that if they do not observe highly professional standards when serving a notice an action for damages might be brought against them personally. Should such an action be brought against an inspector the relevant enforcing authority may, but need not necessarily, indemnify the inspector (s. 26). In a climate in which the public is increasingly likely to seek redress against public bodies whenever there is the least suggestion of failure properly to carry out public duties, the possibility of civil litigation cannot be ignored. There is no recorded case of either an inspector, or the HSE, being successfully sued under the 1974 Act.

WORK OF CUSTOMS OFFICERS

33. Assistance for HSE inspectors

The work of HSE inspectors in enforcement of s. 6 of the 1974 Act is assisted by customs officers who are empowered by s. 25A to seize and detain any imported article or substance. Though customs officers may only detain such goods for two working days this is sufficient time to enable HSE inspectors to decide whether to serve a notice or take other enforcement measures in relation to the articles and substances in question.

OBTAINING AND DISCLOSING INFORMATION

34. Powers of the HSC

Section 27 empowers the HSC (with the consent of the Secretary of State) to serve on any person a notice requiring that person to provide specified information, either to the HSC or the relevant enforcement authority. Information thus obtained must only be used for the purposes of the HSC or HSE.

35. Confidentiality of information

Section 28 applies both to information obtained under s. 27 and to any other information provided by persons in compliance with a requirement imposed by any of the relevant statutory provisions. It provides that such information must not normally be disclosed without the consent of the person who provided it. Section 28(3) provides exceptions to this safeguard enabling information to be disclosed for the purposes of functions conferred under the relevant statutory provisions, and to officers of certain other public bodies, such as the police. There is a particular restriction on the disclosure of trade secrets.

36. Disclosure of information

Notwithstanding the rigorous emphasis of the provisions of s. 28 on the confidentiality of information obtained by the HSC and the HSE, s. 28(8) requires disclosure of information to employees or their representatives for the purpose of assisting in keeping them adequately informed about matters affecting their health, safety and welfare. For this purpose the following descriptions of information must be supplied:

(a) factual information which the inspector has obtained which relates to the premises where they are employed, or to anything which is in the premises or was or is being done there; and
(b) information with respect to any action which the inspector has taken or proposes to take in or in connection with those premises in the performance of his/her functions.

Where an inspector supplies such information the same information must be given to the employers of the persons in question.

PROVISIONS AS TO OFFENCES

37. Institution of proceedings

Section 38 of the 1974 Act provides that in England and Wales proceedings for an offence under any of the relevant statutory provisions may not be instituted except by an inspector, or by or with the consent of the Director of Public Prosecutions. This provision remains in force although the Crown Prosecution Service has been created since 1974. Section 39 empowers inspectors to prosecute before a magistrates' court even though they are not qualified lawyers. Proceedings, even to final appeal to the House of Lords, may well be in the name of the inspector who initiated the prosecution (e.g. *Mailer* v. *Austin Rover plc* [1989]). In Scotland offences are prosecuted through the Procurator Fiscal.

38. Types of offence

Section 33 of the Act sets out the circumstances in which offences may be committed. The section is not well framed, but broadly it is an offence to fail to discharge a general duty or to contravene any health and safety regulation, or to contravene an improvement or prohibition order. There are also other offences such as obstructing an inspector, disclosing information, making a false statement, intentionally making a false entry in any register etc. required by law, or forging a document.

39. Penalties available

The majority of these offences are either way offences; that is to say that they may be prosecuted either summarily or upon indictment. The normal maximum penalty on summary conviction is now £5,000; but under the Offshore Safety Act 1992, s. 4, magistrates are empowered to impose penalties of up to £20,000 for breaches of ss. 2–6 of the 1974 Act, breaches of improvement or prohibition notices, or of a court's remedial order, and any court may impose up to six months' imprisonment for breaches of any notice or court order. The penalty where trial is on indictment is usually an 'unlimited' fine (i.e. in this respect the court's jurisdiction is unlimited).

In a few instances the Crown Court may impose a prison sentence of up to two years. Such a prison sentence may be imposed:

(a) where the accused has done without a licence something which requires a licence (e.g. stripping asbestos – *see* the Asbestos (Licensing) Regulations 1983)

(b) contravened a term of, or a condition or restriction attached to, a licence

(c) acquired or attempted to acquire, possessed or used an explosive article or substance in contravention of any of the relevant statutory provisions

(d) contravened a requirement or prohibition imposed by a notice

(e) used or disclosed any information obtained further to ss. 27 or 28 of the Act (i.e. obtained by the HSC or the HSC by notice issued with the consent of the Secretary of State, or other information obtained in relation to enforcement activities).

While most prosecutions are tried summarily, the majority of the offences are either way offences. It has been held that when an either way offence under the Act is tried summarily the usual limits on the time within which summary prosecutions must be brought do not apply.

40. Use of penalties by the courts

It might be thought that the powers of the Crown Court to impose very heavy fines, coupled with the majority of the offences being triable either way, would result in very substantial penalties being imposed for health and safety offences. However, there has in recent years been some dissatisfaction, which the HSE has shared, that the level of fine is not sufficiently high to bring home the seriousness of health and safety offences. There appear to have been few imprisonments under the legislation, though there have been suspended sentences, particularly in the context of asbestos licensing requirements.

41. Alternatives to penalties

On convicting a person, in addition to, or as an alternative to, imposing a penalty for an offence, the court may order that person, within such time as may be fixed, to take such steps as may be specified in the order, to remedy matters (s. 42).

42. Common law not available

Inspectors may not prosecute under the common law. Therefore, while homicide charges might be brought where workplace accidents have resulted in death, such proceedings could not be instituted or conducted by the HSE or local authority inspectors. Such prosecutions would be instituted in England and Wales by the police and conducted through the Crown Prosecution Service. The police are likely to learn that someone has been killed either through the involvement of emergency services (e.g. calling an ambulance through the telephone service) or the coroner's inquest.

43. European Agency for health and safety at work

Council Regulation (EC) No. 1643/95 of 29 June 1995 amending the Council Regulation (EC) No. 2062/94 provided for the establishment of a European Agency for health and safety. The purpose of the Agency will be to promote improvements in health and safety at work by raising awareness and improving the availability of health and safety information. It will supply the Community institutions, Member States and those involved in the field of health and safety at work with technical, scientific and economic information. The agency will also have a role in assessing the impact of health and safety legislation on small and medium sized companies. It will encourage the exchange of experts between Member States and will hold seminars. The work of the Agency will also include the establishment of a network to provide and disseminate relevant information within the EU, and to co-operate with other countries and international organisations. The network will comprise Member States, research institutes and other bodies concerned with health and safety. There will be a national focal point – HSE for UK.

The regulations provide for an Administrative Body comprising 15 government representatives, 15 representatives from each side of industry and 3 representatives from the EC. The government representatives will have two votes to the social partners' one. So far meetings of the Administrative Board have been concerned with setting up the system.

Progress test 11

1. What are the principal responsibilities of:
   (a) the HSC;
   (b) the HSE?

2. Which has the greater powers, to carry out their respective roles, HSE inspectors or the police?

3. What are the principal differences between improvement and prohibition notices?

4. What information must an inspector provide to workers?

5. To what extent, and by what means may an employer contest the inspector's action in issuing either an improvement or a prohibition notice?

6. What rights has an HSE inspector to prosecute a case?

7. In what ways is the inspector's advisory role inhibited?

8. What effect has the Citizens Charter Initiative had upon the policy of the HSE in enforcing current health and safety legislation?

12

WORKER INVOLVEMENT

1. Introduction

In the 1960s it was believed that workplaces would be safer if they had safety committees. There were attempts to enact legislation requiring such committees in every factory employing more than 50 persons. Many progressive organisations voluntarily introduced them.

Following the enactment of the 1974 Act regulations were made to enable the appointment of safety representatives in unionised workplaces. In the 1990s European Directives require the UK to have a more comprehensive system of worker participation in health and safety, and other matters, at the workplace.

FROM ROBENS TO REGULATIONS

2. The Robens Committee

The debate about worker involvement was a reason why the Robens Committee was set up; the Committee's terms of reference included consideration of what changes were necessary in 'the nature and extent of voluntary action' for health and safety. The Report advocated involvement by management of workers to counter the apathy which the Committee believed to be a principal cause of accidents at the workplace.

3. Worker involvement

Parliament accepted the value of worker involvement. Nevertheless one of the matters most vigorously debated was whether provision should be made for every workplace or only for workplaces at which there was a trade union presence. The 1974 Act contained two separate enabling provisions: one for worker representation through trade unions (s. 2(4)); the other for representation through employee-elected persons (s. 2(5)). Section 2(6) imposed a broad obligation on employers to consult with worker safety representatives and s. 2(7) made provision for safety committees.

4. Implementation strategy

It would have been possible to have implemented both s. 2(4) and s. 2(5) and permitted organisations to decide which system to adopt. However, a Labour government of the late 1970s, committed to developing the role of trade unions, repealed s. 2(5) and then encouraged the implementation of s. 2(4). The draft regulations as proposed in the initial Consultative Document satisfied neither trade unions nor employers. The final regulations, the Safety Representatives and Safety Committees Regulations 1977, did not differ greatly from the original draft and would appear to be a compromise between the aspirations of the two sides of the collective bargaining process at that time.

5. Alternative systems

It remains lawful to operate an alternative system to that laid down in the regulations for unionised workplaces. Some unionised workplaces have negotiated an alternative system. However, the lack of statutory provision for non-unionised workers makes it difficult for them to have any system of representation other than one which their employer may choose to provide. The Offshore Installations (Safety Representatives and Safety Committees) Regulations 1989 have already made a comprehensive system of worker involvement offshore mandatory. Regulations have now been made to provide for non-unionised workplaces onshore.

EMPHASIS ON SAFETY REPRESENTATIVES

6. Appointment of safety representatives

Section 2(4) enables regulations for the appointment of safety representatives, and it states that safety representatives:

> shall represent the employees in consultations with the employers . . . and have such other functions as may be prescribed.

It makes no specific mention of any relationship between safety representatives and safety committees, though membership of a safety committee might be one of the functions of safety representatives.

7. Employers' obligation to consult

Section 2(6) reiterates the emphasis of s. 2(4), making it the employer's primary obligation to consult with safety representatives. The subsection then goes on to state the purposes for which, but not the means by which, such consultation must take place. The employer is required to consult:

> with a view to the making and maintenance of arrangements which will enable him and his employees to cooperate effectively in promoting and developing measures

to ensure the health and safety at work of the employees, and in checking the effectiveness of such measures.

In the original Regulations there was a notable failure to provide for involvement of the workforce in planning for safety as opposed to monitoring the system the employer had set in place. This situation has been changed, it will be seen, by a widening of the concept of consultation in Regulation 4A(1).

8. Provision of facilities

Regulation 17 and the Schedule to the Management of Health and Safety at Work Regulations insert Regulation 4A into the Safety Representatives and Safety Committees Regulations 1977. Paragraph 2 of the new regulation requires that every employer shall provide such facilities and assistance as safety representatives may reasonably require for the purpose of carrying out their functions under section 2(4) of the 1974 Act and under these Regulations.

9. Safety committees

Section 2(7) makes minimal provision for safety committees:

> In such cases as may be prescribed it shall be the duty of every employer, if requested to do so by the safety representatives . . . to establish, in accordance with regulations made by the Secretary of State, a safety committee having the function of keeping under review the measures taken to ensure the health and safety at work of his employees and such other functions as may be prescribed.

Thus the employer is only required to set up a safety committee if safety representatives ask him to do so, and regulations have prescribed that safety representatives may require a committee. The committee need only exercise the functions prescribed by the regulations.

RIGHTS OF TRADE UNIONS

10. 'Recognised trade union'

Section 2(4) enables regulations to give rights to 'recognised trade unions'. The value of the rights under s. 2(4) to trade union members depends on the legal significance of the expression 'recognised trade union'.

It is necessary to turn to other employment protection legislation to give a meaning to the words 'recognised trade union', an expression related to status in negotiation with an employer. The Trade Union and Labour Relations (Consolidation) Act 1992, s. 1, states that a trade union is an organisation of workers (whether permanent or temporary):

> whose principal purposes include the regulation of relations between workers and employers or between workers and employers' associations, or include the regulation of relations between its constituent or affiliated organisations.

11. Certification of trade unions

If a trade union is on the list of unions maintained by the Certification Officer it may, under s. 6 or the Trade Union and Labour Relations (Consolidation) Act 1992, apply for certification by the Certification Officer as an independent trade union. The certificate will be granted if the union meets the criteria of independence given in s. 5 of the Act. For this purpose it must be a trade union which:

(a) is not under the domination or control of an employer or a group of employers or of one or more employers' associations; and

(b) is not liable to interference by an employer or any such group or association (arising out of the provision of financial or material support or by any other means whatsoever) tending towards such control.

12. Recognition of trade unions

Recognition is recognition by an employer for any of the purposes set out in s. 244(1) of the Trade Union and Labour Relations (Consolidation) Act 1992:

(a) terms and conditions of employment, or the physical conditions in which any workers are required to work;
(b) engagement or non-engagement, or termination or suspension of employment or the duties of employment, of one or more workers;
(c) allocation of work or the duties of employment as between workers or groups of workers;
(d) matters of discipline;
(e) the membership or non-membership of a trade union on the part of a worker;
(f) facilities for officials of trade unions; and
(g) machinery for negotiation or consultation, and other procedures, relating to any of the foregoing matters, including the recognition by employers or employers' associations in any such negotiation or consultation or in the carrying out of such procedures.

A certified independent trade union could at one time seek formal recognition by an employer for purposes of negotiation; it could invoke procedures set out in the Employment Protection Act 1975 to obtain a ruling that it had a sufficient presence at a workplace for it to be entitled to be recognised at that workplace (though this would not necessarily ensure that the employer would actually recognise it!). The statutory procedures for recognition have been repealed. Whether a trade union can claim to be recognised is now therefore no more than a matter of fact: it will be recognised only if it can persuade an employer to recognise it for one or more of the matters set out above.

13. The present position

The formal abolition of all statutory protection for closed shop arrangements, and the introduction of statutory provisions which are intended to prevent an employer making any contractual stipulations concerning an employee's membership or non-membership of any trade union, have made it difficult for any union to acquire recognition. It seems unlikely therefore that workers who have not already achieved a system of trade union appointed safety representatives will be able to persuade an employer to grant them the floor of rights set out in the regulations made under s. 2(4). Indeed employers who have sympathy with the concept of safety representatives may be reluctant to endorse the statutory system because such *de facto* trade union recognition might in due course involve them in recognition of trade unions for other purposes such as consultation in relation to redundancies (Trade Union and Labour Relations (Consolidation) Act 1992, ss. 188–198). Thus any new system of safety representatives set up now is likely to be established within a framework laid down by the employer, with perhaps some consultation with the workforce.

STATUS OF SAFETY REPRESENTATIVES

14. Role of the safety representative

The safety representative, being a worker's representative, is not a part of the employer's management team. Safety representatives must not be confused with the competent persons whom the employer is required to designate by Article 7 of the Framework Directive to carry out safety activities. This provision of the Directive, now reflected in Regulation 6 of the Management of Health and Safety at Work Regulations 1992, has not hitherto been expressly paralleled in the UK system, but clearly the article has in view management nominees. The safety representative's function is also quite distinct from the function of the safety manager, who is engaged to advise the employer on, or deal with, safety issues, and may be regarded by the employer as the competent person required by Regulation 6. The worker safety representative's role is primarily a policing role, monitoring the performance of management. Carried to ultimate conclusions it may be, in the UK system, a conflict role, i.e. the safety representative may oppose, rather than cooperate with, management.

15. Experience required for the post

In many instances trade unions have chosen to give the responsibility of acting as safety representative to shop stewards. It is argued that, as such persons are 'officials' of the union, they can bring to the role experience and power. An alternative argument is that the special functions of safety representative are best performed by someone with more narrow technical expertise who is not burdened with the responsibilities which a shop steward carries.

RELATIONSHIP OF SCHEME WITH 1974 ACT

16. General

The Safety Representatives and Safety Committees Regulations take their authority from legislation which bears criminal sanctions. This is anomalous because the system is essentially concerned with industrial relations as much as safety. Theoretically an inspector might serve an enforcement notice on, or even prosecute, an employer who failed to recognise and consult with safety representatives; the prospect of this happening is very remote.

17. Floor of rights

The regulations are not mandatory as are other regulations made under the 1974 Act. They represent a floor of rights which recognised trade unions might require of an employer; the employer is under no obligation to set up a system for safety representatives – he is required only to recognise those who have been properly appointed. Also, it is open to employer and union to negotiate a system somewhat different from the system set out in the regulations. Even if they agree to adopt the statutory system there are areas in which they will need to negotiate the way in which the system is to operate in the particular workplace.

18. Result of failure to apply regulations

The most likely result of a failure on the part of an employer to set up and maintain a safety representatives system to the requirements of the relevant trade union, or unions, is a breakdown in industrial relations, possibly a strike. Alternatively a claim might be made by a particular safety representative, to an industrial tribunal (*see* below).

THE REGULATORY PROVISIONS

19. General

The Safety Representatives and Safety Committees Regulations 1977 were published in conjunction with an Approved Code of Practice on Safety Representatives and two sets of guidance notes, one on the operation of the safety representatives system and the other on the functioning of safety committees. A further approved code of practice published in 1978 dealt with time off for the training of safety representatives. The system has the following provisions.

20. Appointment of safety representatives

Regulation 3(1) empowers a trade union to appoint safety representatives from amongst the employees where one or more employees are employed by an employer by whom it is recognised; this regulation does not take precedence over the provisions in the Mines and Quarries Act 1954, s. 123, for safety representatives in mines. An appointment takes effect when the employer has been notified in writing and will continue until either the trade union concerned notifies the employer in writing that the appointment has been terminated, or the representative leaves the employer's employment at the workplace(s) for which he/she was appointed or he/she resigns. The method of appointment is for the trade union to decide but regulation 3(4) stipulates that so far as is reasonably practicable the person appointed shall either have been employed by the employer throughout the preceding two years, or have had at least two years' experience in similar employment.

21. Where there is more than one union

Where there is more than one union at a workplace it is not usual for one to cede its rights to appoint representatives to the other; but trade unions often deal with matters concerning a worker who is not a union member, since it is in the union's interest to have the hazard controlled. This is in contrast to compensation claims where a union is most unlikely to concern itself with assisting the claim of someone who is not a member.

22. Numbers of representatives

The code of practice suggests that appropriate criteria for determining numbers of representatives should include:

(a) the total numbers employed

(b) the variety of different occupations

(c) the size of the workplace and the variety of workplace locations

(d) the operation of shift systems

(e) the type of work activity and the degree and character of the inherent dangers.

Employers cannot resist the appointment of a disproportionate number of safety representatives but might reasonably respond by allowing only minimal time for any particular representative to perform safety functions.

23. Scope of functions

Safety representatives have no function in relation to workers who are not employees of their own employer (except that such workers might be putting their employer's employees at risk) and no right to recognition by, or consultation with, an employer other than their own. These limitations put some restrictions on the operation of safety representative systems when employees are sent to work at premises which are not occupied by their own employer, or otherwise where they are required to work together with employees of another employer. This problem has been addressed in the system set up for those working in the North Sea on offshore installations.

24. Situations where safety representatives need not be employees

Regulation 8 provides that safety representatives representing members of the British Actors' Equity Association or of the Musicians' Union need not be employees of the employer of members of the group they represent.

25. Functions of safety representatives

Regulation 4 states that a safety representative has certain functions in addition to the function given to them under s. 2(4) and (6) of the Act, which is to represent the employees in consultation with the employer. These additional functions are to:

(a) investigate potential hazards and dangerous occurrences at the workplace (whether or not they are drawn to his attention by the employees he represents) and to examine the causes of accidents at the workplace;

(b) investigate complaints by any employee he represents relating to that employee's health, safety or welfare at work;

(c) make representations to the employer on matters arising out of subparagraphs (a) and (b) above;

(d) make representations to the employer on general matters affecting the health, safety or welfare at work of the employees at the workplace;

(e) carry out inspections in accordance with regulations 5, 6 and 7 [see **37-39** below];

(f) represent the employees he was appointed to represent in consultations at the workplace with inspectors of the HSE and of any other enforcing authority;

(g) receive information from inspectors in accordance with s. 28(8) of the 1974 Act; and

(h) attend meetings of safety committees where he attends in his capacity as a safety representative in connection with any of the above functions.

The code of practice suggests that safety representatives should take all reasonably practicable steps to keep themselves informed of legal requirements, the particular hazards of the workplace and the measures deemed necessary to eliminate or minimise the risk deriving from these hazards, and the health and safety policy of their employer. The code further suggests that they should encourage cooperation between their employer and its employees in promoting and developing essential measures to ensure the health and safety of employees and in checking the effectiveness of such measures.

26. Reporting unsafe systems

The code of practice suggests that safety representatives should bring to the employer's notice (preferably in writing if the matter is a serious one) any unsafe or unhealthy conditions or working practices or unsatisfactory arrangements for welfare at work which come to their attention.

Regulation 12 of the Management of Health and Safety at Work Regulations 1992 requires every properly trained and suitably instructed employee to inform his employer 'or any other employee of that employer with specific responsibility for the health and safety of his fellow employees . . .' (presumably the safety officer rather than the safety representative):

(a) of any work situation which a person [with such training and instruction] would reasonably consider represented a serious and immediate danger to health and safety; and

(b) of any matter which a person [with such training and instruction] would reasonably consider represented a shortcoming in the employer's protection arrangements for health and safety

'in so far as that situation or matter either affects the health and safety of . . . [the] employee or arises out of or in connection with his own activities at work, and has not previously been reported to his employer or to any other employee of that employer . . .'

27. Safety representatives' legal responsibilities

Regulation 4 provides that no function given to a safety representative by regulations shall impose any duty on him. However, this provision is without prejudice to duties imposed by ss. 7 and 8 of the Act. The duties under s. 7, to take care for themselves and others, to cooperate with persons such as their employer, and (under s. 8) not to interfere with any thing provided for purposes of safety, need to be borne in mind in discussions as to whether safety representatives should be empowered to stop operations which in their view are dangerous. However, as pointed out in Chapter 9, the Management of Health and Safety at Work Regulations 1992 have now formulated specific rights and obligations for individual workers, and these need to be weighed against any agreement made by management in relation to the powers and functions of safety representatives: under Regulation 12 employees are required to inform their employer of any serious and immediate danger and under Regulation 7 they are empowered to stop work in such circumstances. However these new regulations would not seem to detract from earlier case law which held that even then such withdrawal should be after carrying out shut-down procedures which can safely be undertaken (*see Gannon* v. *Firth Ltd* [1976]).

The guidance notes give reassurance that a safety representative who accepts, agrees with, or fails to object to a course of action taken by an employer to deal with a health or safety hazard does not take on legal responsibility for that course of action.

The guidance notes also point out the need for representatives to be able to communicate with management without delay.

28. Powers of safety representatives

A safety representative is in some respects given more authority, in UK law, than a shop steward. There is no regulatory provision for shop stewards comparable to the detailed identification of functions of safety representatives: this disparity is the more apparent now that safety representatives have been given similar protection to that enjoyed by shop stewards against discrimination against them by their employer on account of their activities.

29. Former lack of protection against discrimination

Until recently employees enjoyed a general protection against discrimination against them by the employer on account of trade union membership or activities (see Trade Union and Labour Relations (Consolidation) Act 1992 s. 146–167) which a safety representative or anyone else seeking to enforce safe systems did not necessarily enjoy. Thus in *Chant* v. *Aquaboats Ltd* [1978] organising a petition about safety standards was held not to be a trade union activity, and therefore the worker was not protected from discrimination, even though the TU vetted the petition (*see also Gardner* v. *Peeks Retail Ltd* [1975] and *Drew* v. *St Edmundsbury BC* [1980]).

Employees refusing to carry out work which placed them in danger were usually only protected against dismissal if they had the continuous employment necessary to bring them within the jurisdiction of industrial tribunals for the purposes of unfair dismissal proceedings (*see*, for example, *Austin* [1978]).

The Framework Directive, Article 11, required UK law on discrimination against those engaged in safety activities to be clarified.

30. Protection under the current law

The Trade Union Reform and Employment Rights Act 1993, s. 28 and Schedule 5, amended the Employment Protection (Consolidation) Act 1978 (now re-issued as Employment Rights Act 1996) in order to provide protection for employees against dismissal, and being subjected to other detriment, in health and safety cases.

31. Right not to suffer detriment

The Employment Rights Act 1996 s. 44 provides that an employee has the right not to be subjected to any detriment by the employer on the grounds that:

(a) having been designated by the employer to carry out activities in connection with preventing or reducing risks to health and safety at work, he carried out, or proposed to carry out, any such activities;

(b) being a representative of workers on matters of health and safety at work, or a member of a safety committee ... he performed, or proposed to perform, any functions as such a representative or a member of such a committee;

(c) being an employee at a place where

(i) there was no such representative or safety committee, or

(ii) there was such a representative or safety committee but it was not reasonably practicable for the employee to raise the matter by those means,

he brought to his employer's attention, by reasonable means, circumstances connected with his work which he reasonably believed were harmful or potentially harmful to health or safety;

(d) in circumstances of danger which he reasonably believed to be serious and imminent and which he could not reasonably have been expected to avert, he left, or proposed to leave, or (while the danger persisted) refused to return to, his place of work or any dangerous part of his place of work; or

(e) in circumstances of danger which he reasonably believed to be serious and imminent, he took, or proposed to take, appropriate steps to protect himself or other persons from the danger.

However an employee will not be regarded as having been subjected to any detriment if the employer shows that the employee had acted in such a negligent manner that the employer had acted reasonably.

Employees who believe they have suffered a detriment on the grounds set out above may complain to an Industrial Tribunal and if the IT finds in their favour it must make a declaration to that effect and may make an award of compensation.

32. Dismissal in safety cases

Section 100 of the Employment Rights Act 1996 provides that the dismissal of an employee by an employer shall be regarded as having been unfair if the reason for it (or, if more than one, the principal reason) was the employee's safety activities. The activities set out in s. 100 are the same as those listed in s. 44.

It will be noted that while ss. 44 and 100 are aimed primarily at protecting safety representatives, para (c) provides that if there is no representative any employee will be protected against discrimination in relation to steps which they personally take. Cases on the interpretation of this section indicate, however, both that there must have been an actual dismissal and, if the dismissal is constructive, the employee's belief that the situation was unsafe was a reasonable one.

In *Baddley* v. *Mehta t/a Supscoop* [1995] (6 Jan. 1995, Case No.46041/94) the employee resigned and complained to an industrial tribunal that her employer had caused her physical and mental stress by requiring her to undertake duties beyond her physical capacity. The tribunal found that she could not claim under s. 57A (now s. 100 of 1996 Act); it was only intended to protect employees who had either been actually dismissed or suffered a fundamental breach of contract as a punishment for their health and safety activity.

In *Kerr* v. *Nathan's Wastesavers Ltd* [1995] an employee who had been dismissed was no more successful in his claim than was Ms Baddley. In this case the employee was a driver whose job involved collecting bags of used clothing from charity shops. The employer had 2 vehicles: this employee usually drove the larger. One day he was told to drive the smaller: he said it would not carry a full day's load so he would not use that but would use the larger one as he usually did. His reply was immediately followed by his dismissal. The IT accepted that he had reasonably estimated that the smaller van would be overloaded by the end of the run. It also accepted that he had brought his concern to the company's attention by reasonable means. But the tribunal concluded that he had not reasonably believed that the circumstances were potentially harmful to safety. Although he had honestly believed that they were, he had not had reasonable grounds for that belief in all the relevant circumstances: he knew that if he believed his van was going to be overloaded he could return to the depot.

33. Protection for whistleblowers

The provisions inserted into the Employment Protection (Consolidation) Act 1978 (now Employment Rights Act 1996) gave no express protection to employees who disclosed their concern about safety at their workplace to persons other than their employer. The need to protect individuals from being penalised for disclosing information about significant misconduct or malpractice was addressed in the Public Interest Disclosure Bill before Parliament in 1996. To gain the protection intended by the Bill the courts would have had to be satisfied that the disclosure was in the public interest and the alleged victim would normally have had to have failed to get satisfaction by raising the matter with the employer before making a public disclosure. The Bill fell. It is possible that s. 100 of the 1996 Act could already provide a similar protection, but the levels of compensation may be different. In *Harris* v. *Select Timber Frame Ltd* the complainant, who was employed by his father, drew the latter's attention to a safety matter; shortly after, an HSE inspector visited the workplace and it seemed likely that the son had alerted the inspector to the unsafe working conditions. Soon after the son was dismissed: he complained to an industrial tribunal. The tribunal found that the dismissal was within what is now s. 100: it did not believe the employer's contention that the employee had been dismissed for misconduct.

34. Rights to time off and training

Regulation 4(2) provides that an employer shall permit a safety representative to take such time off with pay during the employee's working hours as shall be necessary for the purposes of:

(a) performing his functions as a safety representative; and
(b) undergoing such training in aspects of those functions as may be reasonable in all the circumstances.

A schedule to Regulation 4(2) provides that an employer must pay a safety representative remuneration at his normal rate while he is carrying out his safety representative's duties, and if there is no normal rate, then an amount calculated by reference to the average hourly earnings for that work.

35. Failure by the employer to permit time off

Regulation 11 enables a safety representative to present a complaint to an industrial tribunal that:

(a) an employer has failed to permit him to take time off to carry out his functions under Regulation 4(2); or

(b) has failed to pay him for the time in which he was carrying out those functions.

A complaint must be presented to an industrial tribunal within three months of the date when the failure occurred or within such further period as the tribunal considers reasonable in a case where it is satisfied that it was not reasonably practicable for the complaint to be presented within the period of three months. Where an industrial tribunal finds a complaint that time off has not been allowed is well founded, it shall make a declaration to that effect and may make an award of compensation to be paid by the employer to the employee. The compensatory award is to be of such amount as the tribunal considers just and equitable in all the circumstances having regard to the employer's default in failing to permit time off to be taken by the employee and to any loss sustained by the employee which is attributable to the matters complained of. Where a complaint concerning failure to pay is established then the tribunal must make an order requiring the employer to make the due payment.

36. Other disputes

The procedure of complaint to a tribunal might prove a way of settling a dispute in which the allegation is that the employer refuses either to recognise the appointment of the complainant as a safety representative or to agree the amount of time needed for the performance of the representative's safety functions.

37. Code of practice on training

The Code of Practice on Time Off for the Training of Safety Representatives proposes that as soon as possible after their appointment safety representatives should be permitted time off with pay to attend basic training facilities approved by the TUC or by the independent union or unions who appointed the representative. Moreover, further training, similarly approved, should be undertaken where the safety representative has special responsibilities or where such training is necessary to meet changes in circumstances or relevant legislation.

The Code proposes that when a trade union wishes a safety representative to receive training it should inform management of the course it has approved and supply a copy of the syllabus, indicating its content, if the employer asks for it.

The number of safety representatives attending training courses at any one time should be that which is reasonable in the circumstances, bearing in mind such factors as the availability of courses and the operational requirements of the employer. Unions and management should endeavour to reach agreement on the appropriate numbers and arrangements and refer any problems which may arise to the relevant agreed procedures.

White v. *Pressed Steel Fisher* [1980] concerned a dispute about attendance at a training course. The appellant's union wanted him to attend a course at a local technical college, but the employer wanted him to attend the company's own in-company course which did not include a trade union input because, so the employers alleged, the union had refused to contribute to it. The employers refused permission to attend the technical college, because they considered their own course was appropriate. The industrial tribunal rejected the employee's claim that he had been unreasonably refused time off to attend the course and found that the company's course was adequate for the purposes of the regulations. The EAT noted that, while the code of practice refers to training through a union-approved course, the requirement of union approval was not in the regulations themselves. However, the EAT found that a union refusal to participate in an employer's course was not automatically an answer to a claim for time off to attend a TU course. On the other hand the union refusal to work with the employer did not automatically mean the employer's course was defective. The EAT considered there was not sufficient evidence to know whether the employer's course was adequate and the case was sent back to the tribunal for further consideration of the evidence.

In *Gallagher* v. *The Drum Engineering Co. Ltd* (1991) an industrial tribunal found employers had breached the regulations when they failed to allow safety representatives to take paid time off to attend a TUC course on the implementation of the Control of Substances Hazardous to Health Regulations. It was held unreasonable for the employer to allow only one of the three representatives to attend the particular course: the regulations were new and important, the course was only offered three times a year and there was no evidence that the employer would have been greatly inconvenienced if all the men had attended at the same time.

Training provided by the TUC and unions in the late 1970s and early 1980s ensured that the first generations of safety representatives were well informed – often better informed than first line management, whom employers did not generally train sufficiently to enable them to respond effectively to informed safety representatives. Any advantage at that time gained by the workforce has probably been lost by now.

38. Inspections at the workplace

Regulation 5 entitles safety representatives to inspect the workplace (or part of it) if they have given the employer reasonable notice in writing of their intention to do so and have not inspected it in the previous three months. More frequent inspections may be carried out by agreement. Inspections may also be carried out within the three-month period where there has been a substantial change in the conditions of work, or new information has been published by the HSC or HSE. The employer is required to provide such facilities and assistance as the safety representatives may reasonably require (including facilities for independent investigation by them and private discussion with the employees). The employer may be present at the workplace during the inspection.

Regulation 6 provides for inspections following notifiable accidents, occurrences and diseases. In these circumstances an inspection may be carried out only if it is safe for it to be carried out and the interests of employees in the group or groups which safety representatives are appointed to represent might be involved.

39. Guidance on inspections

The guidance suggests that normal inspections should be carried out on an agreed routine basis and also that there may be advantages in employer and representatives carrying out such inspections together, provided such arrangements do not prevent the representatives from carrying out independent investigations or having private discussions with employees. In the view of the HSC, where a post-accident investigation is carried out, the main purpose should be to determine the causes so that the possibility of action to prevent a recurrence can be considered. For this reason it is important that the approach to the problem should be a joint one by the employer and the safety representatives working together.

40. Inspection of documents etc.

Regulation 7 gives safety representatives the right (provided they have given the employer reasonable notice) to inspect and take copies of any document relevant to the workplace or to the employees the safety representatives represent, being documents which the employer is required to keep by virtue of any relevant statutory provision, except a document consisting of, or relating to, any health record of an identifiable individual.

The employer is required to make available to safety representatives information which is both within the employer's knowledge and necessary to enable them to fulfil their functions except:

(a) any information the disclosure of which would be against the interests of national security, or

(b) any information which the employer could not disclose without contravening a prohibition imposed by or under an enactment, or

(c) any information relating specifically to an individual, unless that individual has consented to its being disclosed, or

(d) any information the disclosure of which would, for reasons other than its effect on health, safety or welfare at work, cause substantial injury to the employer's undertaking or, where the information was supplied by some other person, to the undertaking of that other person, or

(e) any information obtained by the employer for the purpose of bringing, prosecuting or defending any legal proceedings.

The employer is not required by this regulation to produce or allow inspection of any document which is not related to health, safety or welfare.

41. Guidance on disclosure of information

The guidance suggests that safety representatives will need to be given information over and above that given to individual employees by employers in discharge of their duty under s. 2(2)(c).

42. Safety committees

Regulation 9 provides that the prescribed cases referred to in s. 2(7) of the Act, where safety committees must be established by an employer, are cases in which at least two safety representatives request the employer in writing to establish such a committee.

The regulation further provides that where an employer is requested to establish a safety committee he shall establish it in accordance with the following provisions:

(a) they shall consult with the safety representatives who made the request and with the representatives of recognised trade unions whose members work in any workplace in respect of which he proposes that the committee should function:

(b) the employer shall post a notice stating the composition of the committee and the workplace or workplaces to be covered by it in a place where it may be easily read by the employees;

(c) the committee shall be established not later than three months after the request for it.

43. Guidance on safety committees

In guidance published in association with this regulation, the HSC suggests the detailed arrangements necessary to fulfil the regulations should evolve from discussion and negotiation between employers and safety representatives, since they are best able to interpret the needs of the particular workplace. The HSC further opines that safety committees are most likely to prove effective where their work is related to a single establishment. They also consider that the work of the committee should have a separate identity from that of other works' committees.

EC REQUIREMENTS

44. General

The EC Framework Directive on health and safety at work attaches some significance to worker involvement and envisages a worker safety representative system. Article 3 of the Framework Directive defines a workers' representative as a person elected, chosen or designated in accordance with *national laws and or practices* to represent workers where problems arise relating to the safety and health protection of workers at work.

45. Requirements of the Directive

Article 11 of the EC Directive requires employers to consult with workers and/or their representatives and allow them to take part in discussions on questions relating to safety. It intends that all workers and/or their representatives will have the right to make proposals and engage in balanced participation with employers on safety matters. Employers are specifically required to consult with their workers about:

(a) any measure which may substantially affect safety and health

(b) the designation of workers with special safety responsibilities, such as first-aid or fire-fighting

(c) safety risks and the way they are being controlled

(d) the enlistment of competent persons from outside the enterprise

(e) the planning and organisation of training.

Moreover, workers and or their representatives must be allowed by the employer the opportunity to submit their observations during inspection visits by the enforcing authority.

46. UK response

The Management of Health and Safety at Work Regulations 1992, Regulation 17 and the schedule extend the employer's duty to consult with safety representatives as set out in s. 2(6) of the 1974 Act. It adds Regulation 4A to the Safety Representatives and Safety Committees Regulations 1977. Paragraph 1 of Regulation 4A requires every employer to consult safety representatives in good time with regard to:

(a) the introduction of any measures at the workplace which may substantially affect the health and safety of the employees the safety representatives concerned represent;

(b) his arrangements for appointing or, as the case may be, nominating [competent] persons in accordance with . . . the Management of Health and Safety at Work Regulations 1992;

(c) any health and safety information he is required to provide to the employees the safety representatives concerned represent by or under the relevant statutory provisions;

(d) the planning and organisation of any health and safety training he is required to provide to the employees the safety representatives concerned represent by or under the relevant statutory provisions; and

(e) the health and safety consequences for the employees the safety representatives concerned represent of the introduction (including the planning thereof) of new technologies into the workplace.

47. Offshore system

It had been a cause of dissatisfaction to the trade union movement that the onshore regulations were not extended to offshore installations, where in any case the workforce tends not to be unionised. A distinct set of regulations has now been made under the Mineral Workings Act – namely the Offshore Installations (Safety Representatives and Safety Committees) Regulations 1989. These require the implementation of a system to allow representatives to be elected without reference to whether the workforce is unionised. Safety representation offshore is further complicated because of the number of different employers with employees present on an installation and the offshore system differs from the onshore in that it attempts to provide for representation of the interests of that part of the workforce not in the direct employment of the employer controlling the site at which they are working.

The Offshore Safety (Protection Against Victimisation) Act 1992, which came into force on 16 March 1992, made provision to protect employees working on offshore installations from victimisation when acting as safety representatives or members of safety committees. This Act was repealed with the implementation, through s. 28 of the Trade Union Reform and Employment Rights Act 1993, of a general system for protection against victimisation.

OUTSTANDING ISSUES

48. Representation of non-unionised employees

It must be doubted whether the *national system* in the UK has hitherto met the expectations of the EC Directive, since the latter appears to presuppose that there will be a more comprehensive system of representation than the trade union orientation of the UK system provides.

The problem with the UK system was not that the regulations provided for a system of trade union representation; it was that the system imposed no alternative duty on an employer to consult with the non-unionised sector of the workforce. It is true that the general duty in s. 2(2)(c) could be deemed to impose on the employer an obligation to provide information to every individual employee, even if there is no trade union at the workplace in question. The s. 2(2)(c) duty does not, however, necessarily extend to consultation with individual employees, i.e. entering into dialogue with them.

Although currently the culture of the workplace in the UK is to prefer direct dialogue between employer and employee to dialogue through worker representatives, it was inescapable that UK law would have to be changed to give a safety representatives system to non-unionised workers, if the Directive were to be honoured. It was not necessary to reinstate s. 2(5) to do this; the general regulation-making power of the 1974 Act is wide enough to support such regulations.

49. New regulations

The Health and Safety (Consultation with Employees) Regulations 1996 provide for safety representatives in non-unionised workplaces. They come into force 1 October 1996. They are a direct response to the Framework Directive and require employers to consult generally as well as specifically on a number of matters required under the Directive. The mandatory matters for consultation are:

- the introduction of any workplace measure that may substantially affect the health and safety of employees
- arrangements to be made in compliance with the Management of Health and Safety at Work Regulations 1992 concerning the appointment of competent persons
- any information the employer must provide to employees under health and safety law
- the health and safety consequences for employees of the introduction of new technologies into the workplace
- planning of health and safety training.

The employer is required to consult either employees directly or person(s) elected to represent a group of employees. Employers are required to make information available to allow effective participation in consultation.

The functions of representatives are to make representations to the employer on general matters affecting the health and safety of the group and about potential hazards and dangerous occurrences at the workplace. They may represent the group in consultation with inspectors. Employers have to ensure their training, meet training costs, allow paid time off, and provide them with the facilities and assistance which they require for the discharge of their function. Such representatives are protected against victimisation for standing for election or otherwise taking part in consultation.

The regulations do not cover self-employed persons working on the employer's premises, but they may be consulted voluntarily.

There are no rights for representatives to carry out investigations or inspections or to have a safety committee.

Progress test 12

1. What is a 'recognised trade union'?

2. What are the primary functions of a safety representative?

3. Does a safety representative enjoy protection against discrimination?

4. What systems for safety representatives other than that created under s. 2(4) exist in the UK?

5. When is a safety committee required?

6. Why does the UK system not match the requirements of the EC Framework Directive?

7. What new provision is there for safety representatives (onshore) where there is no recognised trade union?

Part Three

COMPENSATION FOR INDUSTRIAL ACCIDENTS

13

INTRODUCTION: NATURE AND PURPOSE OF CIVIL LIABILITY

1. Introduction

Claims for common-law damages are based either on the tort of negligence or on breach of statutory duty. These forms of liability will be discussed in the two succeeding chapters: this chapter will deal with principles which are relevant to these forms of liability. It will cover:

(a) the role and purpose of civil liability

(b) strict and fault liability

(c) personal and vicarious liability

(d) distinction between employers' liability and public liability.

THE ROLE AND PURPOSE OF CIVIL LIABILITY

2. General

There has been a long-standing debate about the purpose of litigation for damages for personal injury.

3. Damages are to compensate

Litigation is intended to provide the accident victim with damages to compensate for the injury that has been suffered, though it may be disputed whether a monetary value can be placed on physical injury, as opposed to loss of income which results from physical injury. English law has hitherto rejected awarding sums greater than the loss suffered by the plaintiff in order to punish the defendant for callous, irresponsible or reckless behaviour (*see A B* v. *SW Water Services Ltd* [1993]), although exemplary damages, as such awards are called, are available in other kinds of civil litigation (*see Rookes* v. *Barnard* [1964]).

In the nineteenth century workers argued that payment of damages to injured workers should cause hardship to the wrongdoer to punish for the suffering which had been endured by the accident victim. Subsequently it was realised that there was a conflict between the need to compensate the victim and the desire to punish the wrongdoer; if wrongdoers did not have the funds to pay the damages then accident victims got neither financial compensation nor emotional satisfaction.

4. Third-party insurance

Until the purpose of civil liability had been clarified, the legality of third-party insurance was doubted: it was argued that a contract of insurance would be illegal if it relieved the insured of the obligation personally to compensate. Later, it was realised that there was merit in using insurance to ensure availability of funds for compensation. In the twentieth century legislation has made third-party insurance compulsory in respect of road traffic generally, and to some extent in relation to work-related injuries.

5. Relationship with social security

An employee who is incapacitated from work by reason of accident or disease is entitled to receive statutory sick pay in the terms set out in statutory sick pay legislation. Employers are responsible for making payments of the sums required by the legislation for the first 28 weeks of incapacity for work. Since the coming into force, in April 1995, of the Social Security (Incapacity for Work) Act 1994, all employers are entitled to recover the amount of statutory sick pay given in any tax month which exceeds a specified percentage (in 1995–96 13%) of their gross national insurance contributions in the same month.

The statutory sick pay scheme provides income maintenance to incapacitated employees irrespective of whether or not their injury or illness is work related. Formerly those who suffered an accident arising out of and in the course of employment, or were incapacitated by a prescribed industrial disease (i.e. a disease recognised under the scheme as capable of being work-related), received rather more than the standard rate sickness benefit. Since the Social Security and Housing Benefits Act 1982 industrial injuries benefit claims have been abolished and subsequent legislation has further narrowed the scope of the industrial injuries scheme. However it still provides a pension for those who suffer a long-term disablement of at least 20%; it is especially important in providing for the victims of industrial diseases and its role in this respect may be expanding.

The changing nature of employment makes the risk of employment-related disease more statistically significant than in the past and increased medical knowledge enables the causation of illness to be more easily identified. The range of prescribed diseases continues to be expanded, compensation has recently been made available for certain work-related upper limb disorders, and the basis for claiming for occupational deafness and various respiratory conditions has been extended.

Payments made under statutory schemes are unrelated to contractual arrangements made between employer and employee for the payment of salary during illness or for a pension in the event of long-term incapacity.

6. The Pearson Commission

The debate about the purposes of compensation is not entirely dead. One of the arguments against paying all compensation through the social security system is that litigation is therapeutic for victims; it enables them to enjoy a sense of 'getting even with' the wrongdoer. This, as well as the overwhelming cost of providing adequate compensation through social security, was the reason that the Pearson Commission advocated retaining the present common-law system in tandem with the social security system. So while the system of suing for common-law damages for personal injury has been described as 'the forensic lottery' (T.G. Ison (1967)), the right to sue remains.

The Pearson Commission demonstrated that, as far as can be estimated, given the uncertainty over how many cases are settled out of court, about 15% of industrial injury victims obtain common-law damages. But nevertheless, for personal injuries generally, about 50% of money payments (primarily in respect of income maintenance) come from the social security system and less than 20% come from common-law litigation.

7. EC initiative

The EC's Foundation for the Improvement of Living and Working Conditions has been exploring possible ways of compensating the victims of industrial injury and in a newsletter published in 1994 (No. 42) expressed enthusiasm for workmen's compensation schemes of the kind which were provided for in Britain between 1897 and 1948, under Workmen's Compensation Acts, before the introduction of the 'Welfare State'. Such schemes provide only for a degree of income maintenance. The Foundation was very impressed by the workmen's compensation scheme operated in Canada, in British Colombia. Under that scheme organisations are grouped into industries, and groups are rated according to performance. Individual organisations have to pay a percentage of their payroll to fund the scheme, but the organisation's payroll tax is dependant on its personal performance as well as its industrial grouping. The theory is that thus relating insurance premium to performance provides an economic incentive to employers to operate safely.

8. Victim support groups

The victim's desire to impose a financial penalty on the wrongdoer is illustrated by the victim support groups which are nowadays frequently formed in the aftermath of major catastrophes. These groups publicise the problems of the victims with quite surprising outcomes. One such outcome has been the revival of the suggestion that exemplary damages should be awarded, even if such damages were not paid to the victims, but used for other suitable purposes which the court might name (such as research). Such an idea could, presumably, only be implemented by legislation; particularly since in *AB* v. *SW Water Services Ltd* [1993] the Court of Appeal refused to add to the categories of case in which exemplary damages might be awarded.

A controversial outcome of the publicity which catastrophes receive is that victims of them often get favourable out-of-court settlements. Alleged wrong-doers presumably conclude that it is better, and perhaps cheaper, to settle rapidly, without admission of liability, rather than face ongoing publicity in the litigation process. By contrast, the solitary victim of an accident may face lengthy and expensive proceedings.

Such support groups have been noticeably more active in the wake of catastrophes which have killed members of the public rather than workers.

9. For what injuries is compensation paid?

Damages are awarded in respect of personal injury. Personal injury is interpreted widely to include fatal accidents; it includes other accidental injury and injury suffered by reason of deterioration in health, i.e. disease.

The former Workmen's Compensation Acts which provided compensation for any *accident* arising out of and in the course of employment, but only provided compensation for *certain prescribed diseases* contracted in like circumstances, gave rise to a great deal of case law about the meaning of the word accident. Suffice it to say that an accident was defined as some unlooked-for mishap or untoward event which was not expected or desired by the victim: an accident normally happens only once and has fairly immediate consequences. Diseases generally occur over a period of time from continual exposure to adverse conditions.

Historically much disease has been caused to the workforce by exposure to dust: this has typically caused respiratory diseases and skin complaints such as dermatitis. Changing work patterns, and advances in medical science, have shifted the focus to deafness caused by noise, muscular and skeletal strain caused by repetitive work and poisoning caused by toxic substances such as lead. The realisation that work can cause cancer and related diseases, such as asbestosis, also causes concern.

10. Difference between accident and disease

There is little purpose here in distinguishing accidents from diseases, since either may entitle the victim to claim common-law damages. In practice it remains more difficult for the victim of long-term exposure to bad working conditions to recover damages than it is for one who has suffered an accident whose occurrence was at a particular time and probably witnessed. However, back injuries are difficult to prove, even where allegedly caused by an accident rather than repetitive strain – because there is often a lack of evidence of the occurrence!

11. Nervous shock

The courts have for many years awarded damages to persons who have suffered nervous shock (now more accurately described as post traumatic stress disorder) as a result of an accident causing injury to other persons. Since *Chadwick* v. *British Railways Board* [1967] it has been accepted that a claim may be made by those who suffer PTSD as a result of coming to the aftermath of a disaster and undertaking rescue work.

In *Alcock* v. *Chief Constable of South Yorkshire Police* [1992] (a case arising out of the Hillsborough football stadium disaster) Lord Oliver stated:

> It is well established that the defendant owes a duty of care not only to those who are directly threatened or injured by his careless acts but also to those who, as a result, are induced to go to their rescue and suffer injury in so doing. The fact that the injury suffered is psychiatric and is caused by the impact on the mind of becoming involved in personal danger or in scenes of horror and destruction makes no difference.

This was apparently successfully tested in *Hale* v. *London Underground* where the plaintiff was a fireman who had been exposed to horrific scenes during the fire, in November 1987, at King's Cross Underground Station. He had suffered no physical injury but had entered the blaze several times, finally collapsing from exhaustion. Subsequently he needed counselling and his condition gradually deteriorated; he was at times a hospital in-patient and he eventually reached the position where he had no future prospect of employment in the fire service. The High Court found for him and awarded him substantial damages.

Recent case law has limited the range of claimants in the situations of being present at, or coming to the immediate aftermath of, disaster to: those in fear of personal injury (*McFarlane* v. *EE Caledonia* [1994]), those with close emotional links with the primary victims (*Alcock* v. *Chief Constable of South Yorkshire Police* [1992]), or those actively involved in rescue work (*Frost and others* v. *The Chief Constable of South Yorkshire and Others* [1995]).

But case law has not allowed that the relationship between two workers employed on the same task is sufficiently close to give rise to employer's liability as the following case illustrates. In the Scottish case, *Robertson and Rough* v. *Forth Bridge Joint Board* [1995] it was held that an employee was not entitled to damages for psychiatric injury suffered as a result of witnessing a fatal accident during the course of his employment in which a fellow employee was killed due to the employer's negligence. The court considered that the plaintiff employees were merely bystanders whom the employer was entitled to assume were sufficiently robust to withstand the shock of witnessing such an accident.

However, *Walker* v. *Northumberland County Council* [1995] has opened a new area of liability because the defendant employer was found liable for mental illness caused by long-term exposure to stress in employment. (In *Johnstone* v.

Bloomsbury Health Authority [1991] the High Court granted a junior house doctor permission to sue to establish that excessively long hours had caused mental breakdown and the Health Authority subsequently made an out-of-court settlement.)

12. Assessment and payment of damages

Compensatory damages are intended to put the defendant in the position in which he would have been had he not sustained the injury. There are generally two aspects to a claim: unliquidated damages and special damages.

13. Unliquidated damages

The claim for unliquidated damages is generally supported by medical evidence. On the basis of the evidence, and also by reference to the 'tariff' established by other judges in like cases, the judge puts a monetary figure on the pain, suffering and loss of amenity suffered by the plaintiff.

14. Special damages

These damages are for the financial burden which the injury has imposed on the plaintiff. Principal items of special damages are the cost of medical attention and care attendance, the cost of adapting to the injury (e.g. installing a lift in a house) and the loss of earned income. The plaintiff is allowed to look into the future and claim in respect of financial benefit which might have been expected to accrue to him if the accident had not occurred; this is an exception to the general reluctance of courts to award damages for economic loss negligently caused.

15. Recoupment of social security

The Law Reform (Personal Injuries) Act 1948, s. 2(1), required that deductions be made of half of the benefits received for a five-year period (if the disability lasts this long) as sickness benefit, invalidity benefit, non-contributory invalidity pension, injury benefit or disablement benefit. This is now relevant only to small claims. In other cases the Social Security Act 1989, s. 22 requires the compensator completely to reimburse the Secretary of State out of sums otherwise payable to the victim whether by way of damages or out-of-court settlement. In *Hassall* v. *Secretary of State for Social Security* [1995] where the plaintiff had been unemployed at the time of his accident and therefore did not claim loss of wages by way of special damages, it was held that the Department of Social Security were entitled to recoup out of the general damages awarded.

The significance for the state of the recoupment provisions will be considerably less in future now that under the Social Security Act 1994 the burden of the statutory sick pay has been imposed more heavily upon employers.

Under s. 5 of the Administration of Justice Act 1982 any saving to the injured person which is attributable to his maintenance wholly or partly at public expense in a hospital is set off against any income lost to him as a result of the injuries sustained.

16. Loss of expectation of life

Formerly substantial damages were awarded for 'the lost years' where the victim's life expectancy was shortened as a result of the injury. The Administration of Justice Act, s. 1(1), has considerably curtailed such claims by providing:

(a) no damages shall be recoverable in respect of any loss of expectation of life caused to the injured person by the injuries; but

(b) if the injured person's expectation of life has been reduced by the injuries, the court, in assessing damages in respect of pain and suffering caused by the injuries, shall take account of any suffering caused or likely to be caused to him by awareness that his expectation of life has been so reduced.

Section 1(2) provides that s. 1(1)(a) does not affect the right to claim for loss of income, confirming the House of Lords decision in *Pickett* v. *British Rail Engineering Ltd* [1980]. The plaintiff was the victim of asbestosis contracted at work. He died before his appeal on *quantum* of damages could be heard; the House held an award should have been made for loss of income appropriate to the length of his life expectancy prior to the accident. Their Lordships were no doubt mindful that any other finding would have been unfavourable to the widow who might otherwise have been left with less provision than if she had made a claim in her own right under the Fatal Accidents Act 1976.

17. Periodical payments

Identifying the appropriate amount for an award is a difficult task, necessitating a calculation of the plaintiff's needs, over an uncertain period of time, when the prognosis of the plaintiff's future physical condition may be unclear, and inflation may affect the value of the award. The Supreme Court Act 1981, s. 32A, assists the court to award provisional damages in cases where there is a chance that the injured person will develop some serious disease or suffer some serious deterioration in his physical or mental condition as a consequence of the injury under consideration. Where the award is provisional the plaintiff may return to court to make a further claim if the contingency occurs.

The courts welcome any arrangement between the parties, in the form of structured settlements, for investment of money to enable periodical payments to be made to meet the needs of the plaintiff; while courts are reluctant themselves to rely on actuarial evidence in calculating awards, they are happy that the parties should rely on this kind of evidence to agree a suitable arrangement for endorsement by the court.

18. Fatal accidents

The Fatal Accidents Act 1976 acknowledges the needs of widows and other dependents deprived by a fatal accident of income support from the deceased. It must be established that:

(a) if the victim had been injured rather than killed he would have had a claim in his own right (i.e. the claimant must establish liability of the defendant to the deceased in negligence or for breach of statutory duty)

(b) the claimant comes within the class of persons to whom the statute gives rights (i.e. be either a spouse or child, or other person within the recognised list of relationships)

(c) the claimant was actually dependent on the deceased for income maintenance (e.g. an adult married child would not normally be able to claim); and

(d) awards are calculated in relation to the income support which the deceased might have been expected to provide.

A claim under this legislation is normally brought by the personal representative of the deceased; this person need not, of course, be a person actually entitled under the Act.

Section 1A of the Fatal Accidents Act enables a claim of a small sum for bereavement; such sums are only payable to the benefit of the husband or wife of the deceased, or to the parents of a minor who had never married.

19. Limitation of actions

Normally a plaintiff may not start an action for personal injury more than three years after the cause of action arose, i.e. the date when the accident occurred. In cases arising from exposure to circumstances which cause ill-health, the cause of action ought logically to arise at the time of the exposure, but if this rule were applied the limitation period might have expired long before the victim was aware that he might sue (*see Cartledge* v. *Jopling & Sons Ltd* [1963]). Parliament has revised the limitation rules to assist persons in this situation. The task proved difficult and the problem had to be addressed on more than one occasion to produce legislation that was satisfactory. The position is now governed by the Limitation Act 1980, ss. 11(4)(b), 14 and 33.

20. Knowledge of right to sue

Section 11(4)(b) prevents time running until the plaintiff has knowledge that he has a right to sue.

Section 14 defines knowledge for this purpose as knowledge of the following facts:

(a) that the injury in question was significant

(b) that the injury was attributable in whole or in part to the act or omission which is alleged to constitute negligence, nuisance or breach of duty; and

(c) the identity of the defendant; and

(d) if it is alleged that the act or omission was that of a person other than the defendant, the identity of that person and the additional facts supporting the bringing of an action against the defendant.

When the plaintiff has the relevant knowledge he must start the action within three years unless he can persuade the court to exercise its power under s. 33 further to extend the period; the court will only exercise this discretion if it is equitable to do so and the defendant would not be prejudiced by the extension of time.

STRICT AND FAULT LIABILITY

21. General

The debate about the purposes of civil liability has led to questioning whether civil liability should be strict or fault liability. If the purpose is entirely compensatory then arguably damages should always be recoverable by an injured person regardless of whether the injury was the result of his own folly, the fault of another person, or occurred without fault.

22. Liability of the state

The Pearson Commission pointed out that the state's liability to pay social security benefits is 'no fault liability': the claimant who can establish that he suffers from the incapacity is entitled to the benefit. The primary source of income maintenance for incapacity arising from work-related injuries is the social security 'no fault' system, providing benefits, in the short term at least, from the general sickness benefit scheme.

23. Statutory sick pay

Since the implementation of the Social Security and Housing Benefits Act 1982, payments due to employees from the state scheme for incapacitating sickness in respect of the first 28 weeks of incapacity are paid to the employee by the employer. The Statutory Sick Pay Act 1991 restricted the employers' entitlement to recoup payments made to employees under this scheme, in most instances (there are exceptions for small employers) to 80% of the benefits paid. The Statutory Sick Pay Act 1994 deprived all but small employers of any right to recoup payments made to sick employees. Thus an element of strict liability for income maintenance of employees has been placed on employers, independently of any contractual scheme for income maintenance which the employer may operate and irrespective of whether or not the incapacity has been caused by work or is in any way related to it.

24. Contractual sick pay

The statutory sick pay scheme described above must not be confused with any contractual scheme which the employer may enter into with the employee, either to pay wages, or a proportion of them, during absence from work due to illness, or to insure to provide income maintenance or a pension in the event of long-term or permanent incapacity due to an accident or illness. The entitlement of the employee under such a scheme will be entirely dependent on interpretation of the terms of the contract, as the following cases demonstrate.

In *Franklin* v. *British Railways Board* [1993] the plaintiff had suffered an accident during the course of his employment, which resulted in his being off work for over a year. His contract of employment provided for sick pay equivalent to his normal basic wage, less national insurance benefit, with the proviso that where absence was due to an accident the payment would be by way of loan which would be repayable to the employer in the event of damages being recovered. Mr Franklin was paid damages including a sum for loss of earnings, calculated net of tax and national insurance contributions. Mr Franklin repaid his employers the loan he had received. The employers then claimed that he was also obliged to repay to them sums which they had paid to the Inland Revenue and the DSS in relation to his salary. The Court of Appeal found for the employee noting that the Inland Revenue had always made it plain that in circumstances such as these they were content to reimburse either the employer or the employee according to which was the more appropriate recipient in the light of the arrangements which had been made between them.

Similarly in *Bews* v. *Scottish Hydro-Electric plc* (1992) the Scottish Outer House of the Court of Session held that an *ex gratia* payment made by employers to the executor of a deceased employee could not be deducted from a compensation claim made by the widow and sons of the deceased against that employer. This was so although the employers had advised all their employees that they were insured and that payments of insurance proceeds were made to dependents of employees at the employer's discretion and might be taken into account in the event of a claim against the employers. The court considered that as the employers had not been legally bound to make the payment, but had done so *ex gratia* without any provision for recovery, they were not entitled to deduct the sum.

25. Breaches of statutory duties

In situations where claims are based on breach of statutory duty, strict liability may be imposed on defendants. The plaintiff is unlikely to have to establish that the defendant's conduct has been negligent: the only alleged 'fault' of the defendant is failure to ensure that the duty imposed by the statute has been observed. The plaintiff must bring the evidence necessary to show the statutory duty has been broken: what the plaintiff has to prove will vary according to the requirements of the provision relied upon, but negligent conduct is rarely a criterion of liability.

26. Vicarious liability

Vicarious liability (dealt with more fully below) is imposed upon employers in respect of the wrongdoing of their employees. This is an example of strict liability. It is generally related to, but not entirely consistent with, fault-based common law liability.

27. Common-law system of damages

The common-law system of compensatory damages is a fault-based system. The plaintiff must establish that the defendant's conduct was at fault in order to win his case. Where the claim is based in negligence the plaintiff must establish that the defendant's conduct was negligent. The possibility of imposing strict liability in common-law industrial injury claims was proposed to, and rejected by, the House of Lords in *Read* v. *J & C Lyons & Co Ltd* [1946] where the plaintiff had suffered personal injury in an explosion in the munitions factory where she worked. The matter was put by Lord Macmillan:

> The action is one of damages for personal injuries . . . I am of the opinion that, as the law now stands, an allegation of negligence is in general essential to the relevancy of an action of reparation for personal injuries.

In rejecting the proposition that there might be special rules of strict liability imposed on anyone who engaged in hazardous activities his Lordship continued:

> Strict liability, if you will, is imposed upon him in the sense that he must exercise a high degree of care, but that is all. The sound view, in my opinion, is that the law in all cases exacts a degree of care commensurate with the risk created.

28. Damages as a result of disease

It is often difficult for the victim of disease to recover damages because of the problems associated with establishing that the disease was caused by work. The ruling of the House of Lords in *Bonnington Castings Ltd* v. *Wardlaw* [1956] is of assistance to plaintiffs in establishing that unlawful working conditions have caused their illness. The respondent, who had worked for eight years in the appellants' foundry, contracted pneumoconiosis through inhaling air containing silica dust. Some of the dust came from swing grinders because the dust-extraction plant for these grinders had not been kept free from obstruction as required by statutory regulations. Their Lordships held the respondent should recover damages for breach of statutory duty as the dust from the swing grinders had contributed materially to his condition.

This approach was developed in *McGhee* v. *National Coal Board* [1972] where the House considered the case of a worker who had suffered a skin disease apparently attributable to cycling home from a workplace where (in breach of the employer's statutory duty) there were no washing facilities. It was established that the lack of washing facilities increased the risk of catching the disease, but not that the plaintiff would not have suffered from it if his employers had provided washing facilities. Their Lordships nevertheless allowed the plaintiff's claim.

It thus appears that if the circumstances of an employer's breach of duty could cause the plaintiff's ill-health the courts are prepared to find a causal link sufficient to sustain a claim in damages.

29. Appreciation of the danger

Another problem which frequently besets the plaintiff in ill-health cases is of showing that the employer ought to have appreciated the risk at the date when the worker was exposed to it. Illnesses which manifest themselves today may have been caused by exposure to dangers many years ago; in the past the dangers may not have been appreciated. The victim can only impose liability on a defendant for conduct which was unlawful at the time the injury occurred; in relation to some causes of ill-health which have been much litigated the courts have established the date at which employers ought first to have been aware of the risk to which they were exposing their workers. In the case of noise-induced deafness the courts have refused to attach liability for exposure to noise before the mid-1970s.

In some situations the employer's personal experience is relevant to whether the risk should have been appreciated: thus in *Stokes* v. *GKN* [1968] when Mr Stokes died of scrotal cancer, it was relevant to his employer's liability that there had been a previous case of scrotal cancer at his workplace. Similarly in *Walker* v. *Northumberland County Council* when Mr Walker suffered the second of two nervous breakdowns and was forced to retire, it was deemed to be foreseeable after the first breakdown that he would suffer another breakdown if the defendant employers did not reduce his workload.

30. Identification of disease

In order to succeed in a claim for work-related ill-health the plaintiff must satisfy the court that they are suffering from a recognised disease. In *Mughal* v. *Reuters Ltd* [1993] the plaintiff alleged that he had suffered pain in his fingers, hands, arms and shoulders because of the length of time he had to work with his visual display unit. Mr Justice Prosser, QC, suggested that repetitive strain injury was not a condition known to medical science, having neither an identifiable pathology nor an existence as a clinical condition, and accordingly could not form the basis of an action against an employer alleging negligent working methods or environment. Tenosynovitis and peritendonitis were clear clinical conditions; hands could also become cold, dry, pale, stiff and lose function as a result of reflex sympathetic dystrophy, otherwise known as sympathetically maintained pain. In each case it had to be determined what a plaintiff was suffering from and what had caused it.

On the other hand in *Mountenay (Hazzard) and Others* v. *Bernard Matthews plc* (1993) the company was found liable to several of the plaintiffs for upper limb disorders (i.e. repetitive strain injuries). Liability was attached because on the evidence the employers had not maintained a safe system of warning employees about and controlling their exposure to a known risk.

31. Risk outside the workplace

Finally the difficulty of establishing the cause of ill-health is compounded if the particular disability from which the plaintiff suffers is one, like asthma or deafness, which might have been caused by exposure to risk outside the workplace.

PERSONAL AND VICARIOUS LIABILITY

32. General

Most employers are corporations; while the law recognises such legal entities as 'persons' it is somewhat fanciful to imagine them as actually performing any actions, since they have no physical being. However, the law places duties on corporations personally.

33. Types of organisational liability

In civil law two kinds of organisational liability have been recognised: the personal liability of the organisation and its liability for the acts of others (vicarious liability). Strictly speaking vicarious liability has no place in criminal law, but if a strict duty is imposed by the criminal law, and the person on whom it is placed is not allowed either to delegate responsibility for performance of that duty or to bring evidence that another person is the actual wrongdoer, the effect will be much the same as under the civil law relating to vicarious liability. In this chapter personal and vicarious liability will be considered solely in the context of the civil law; but reference to the position at criminal law is pertinent because the duties on which civil liability for breach of statutory duty is placed are primarily a part of the criminal law.

34. Demise of the doctrine of common employment

The doctrine of common employment formerly prevented an injured employee from claiming damages from his employer if the actual wrongdoer were a fellow servant in the service of the victim's own employer at the time when the injury was suffered. In *Wilsons & Clyde Coal Company Ltd* v. *English* [1937] the House of Lords imposed liability on an employer in circumstances where the, by this time discredited, doctrine of common employment should logically have protected him from liability. Their Lordships achieved this by discovering a 'non-delegable' duty on the employer to provide a safe system of work. The matter was put by Lord Wright:

> . . . I do not mean that employers warrant the adequacy of plant, or the competence of fellow-employees, or the propriety of the system of work. The obligation is

fulfilled by the exercise of due care and skill. But it is not fulfilled by entrusting its fulfilment to employees, even though selected with due care and skill. The obligation is threefold, 'the provision of a competent staff of men, adequate material, and a proper system and effective supervision' . . .

I think the whole course of authority consistently recognises a duty which rests on the employer, and which is personal to the employer, to take reasonable care for the safety of his workmen, whether the employer be an individual, a firm, or a company, and whether or not the employer takes any share in the conduct of the operations.

35. Duty to provide a safe system of work

Subsequent case law added other facets to this personal duty, such as the requirements of training and supervision, but the essence of the duty is to provide a safe system of work. The abolition of the doctrine of common employment might have seen the demise of the concept of the personal duty: that it did not is because an employer can only be made vicariously liable for the actual wrongdoings of an employee when acting in the course of his employment. The employer's personal duty therefore remains important:

(a) where the wrongdoer is not an employee, though the courts are reluctant to find an employer liable for the wrongdoing of one who is not their employee (e.g. *Davie* v. *New Merton Board Mills Ltd* [1959])

(b) where the wrongdoer was not acting in the course of employment, e.g. a practical joker who tripped a fellow worker was not in the course of employment when thus skylarking, but the employer was liable for keeping in his employment someone with the known propensity for practical joking (*Hudson* v. *Ridge Manufacturing Company Ltd* [1957])

(c) a hazard may be created because no person is detailed to a task, or persons given the task cannot perform it because they lack adequate equipment, training or supervision (*see Jones* v. *Manchester Corporation* [1952]).

36. Various forms of liability

The employer does not incur *personal* liability unless his conduct has been negligent in failing to provide a safe system. On the other hand, an employer may be *vicariously* liable for the wrongdoing of his employee even though that employer has exercised every degree of care possible. For example, in *Lister* v. *Romford Ice & Cold Storage Co. Ltd* [1957] employers were found liable for the negligence of their lorry driver in running down his mate although the employers were themselves faultless.

37. Vicarious liability

The prerequisites of vicarious liability are:

(a) the wrongdoer must have been an employee (*see* **38**)

(b) the employee must have committed a tort (which will generally, but not necessarily, be the tort of negligence) (*see* **39**); and

(c) when committing the tort that employee must have been acting in the course of his employment (*see* **40**).

It is, since the abolition of the doctrine of common employment, no longer relevant whether the victim was also an employee, or another worker, or a member of the public.

38. Status of employee

It was noted when outlining the development of safety law that the task of identifying a test by which the status of employee might be determined has exercised the courts for more than a hundred years. The origin of the modern multiple test is *Ready Mixed Concrete (South East) Ltd* v. *Minister of Pensions* [1968] where a firm had dismissed all its lorry driver employees and purported to re-engage them as self-employed drivers.

McKenna J held that there were three conditions necessary to establish that a contract of employment existed:

(a) the worker agreed to provide his own work and skill in the performance of a service for the employer

(b) there was an element of control exercisable by the employer

(c) that the other terms of the contract must not be inconsistent with the existence of a contract of employment.

In the event, the facts that the drivers were buying their own lorries, thus giving them a considerable capital investment in the enterprise, and that they were allowed to delegate the work to other persons, led his Lordship to find the drivers were not employees.

Subsequent case law has focused on identifying contractual terms which may be inconsistent with there being a contract of employment. These have included the intention of the parties (*Massey* v. *Crown Life Insurance Company* [1978]), and an obligation on the employer to provide, and the worker to accept, work (*Nethermere (St Neots) Ltd* v. *Gardiner & Taverna* [1984]), but no single factor is conclusive and the decision of the trial court or industrial tribunal is a question of fact which cannot normally be challenged on appeal (*O'Kelly* v. *Trusthouse Forte plc* [1984]); but see *Duke* v. *Martins Retail Group plc* [1994] where two ITs had taken different views of the status of the defendants' managers.

The question of the status of the worker is only in dispute in a very small proportion of cases.

39. The wrongful act of the employee

Vicarious liability does not arise unless the employee has committed a tort, normally, but not necessarily, the tort of negligence. An employee's conduct will be considered in the context of the training he has had, and the resources available to him. There may be cases where the employer is deemed to be personally rather than vicariously liable because he has placed more responsibility on the employee than the circumstances warrant. For example, in *Jones* v. *Manchester Corporation* [1952] a hospital was found at fault for allowing a junior doctor to administer an anaesthetic without supervision from a more experienced practitioner (though in this case the liability was still vicarious – for the wrongdoing of the senior man!).

40. In the course of employment

In the older cases the courts were frequently concerned narrowly to define the task which the employee was engaged to do and to find that if the employee had deviated from that task he was no longer in the course of employment. Nowadays the courts tend to take a broader view and find that the employee is in the course of employment if what he is doing is for the employer's benefit. Thus formerly an employee would not be in the course of employment if he did something other than what he was employed to do, e.g. a conductor driving the bus (*Beard* v. *London General Omnibus Company* [1900]). Similarly employees sent on an errand ceased to be in the course of their employment when they deviated from the route on 'frolic of their own' (*Storey* v. *Ashton* (1869)).

In contrast to these older cases a warehouseman was in the course of his employment when he, though not employed as a driver, moved a lorry which was in the way (*Kay* v. *ITW Ltd* [1967]); maintenance men remained in the course of their employment when they took a meal break and also went off (on a motorbike) to fetch extra tools (*Harvey* v. *O'Dell Ltd* [1958]); and a tanker driver remained in the course of his employment when he smoked a cigarette (a forbidden action) while delivering petrol (*Century Insurance Co Ltd* v. *Northern Ireland Road Haulage Transport Board* [1942]).

41. Basis of doctrine of vicarious liability

The doctrine of vicarious liability really rests on the policy that the employer should pay for injuries caused when something is being done for his benefit; *Rose* v. *Plenty* [1976] recognised this. A boy was injured by the negligent driving of a milkman he was assisting to deliver milk: the milkman knew that it was forbidden for him to seek the assistance of young persons, but the employers were, in the view of the majority of the Court of Appeal (Lawton LJ dissenting), liable because the milkman, though doing something which was prohibited, was nevertheless working for the employers' benefit. Lord Denning MR said:

> In considering whether a prohibited act was within the course of the employment, it depends very much on the purpose for which it is done. If it is done for the employers' business, it is usually done in the course of his employment, even though it is a prohibited act . . .

A fairly extreme example of employees being deemed to be in the course of employment is *Smith* v. *Stages* (below).

42. Action against actual wrongdoer

The fact that the employer may be vicariously liable does not prevent an action being brought against the actual wrongdoing employee (though the victim cannot recover damages twice for the same injury). Sometimes the victim may join both employer and employee as co-defendants, though this will normally only be an attractive strategy if the employee is a professional person, like a doctor, or a driver, who has his own insurance cover. If both employer and employee are brought before the court, responsibility may be allocated between them according to the extent to which each is at fault. If an employer is found liable in these circumstances the liability placed upon him is personal.

DISTINCTION BETWEEN EMPLOYERS' AND PUBLIC LIABILITY

43. General

Traditionally, compensation law has distinguished between employers' and public liability. Early case law distinguished the employers' liability to one who had a contract of employment with them from their liability to those who rendered services under other arrangements, whether or not provided under a direct contract between the employers and the workers concerned. The contract of employment (or contract of service) had an implied term that the employers would take reasonable care for the safety of their employee.

44. Action in contract

It is still possible for an injured employee to frame a personal injury claim against the employer in contract (*Matthews* v. *Kuwait Bechtel Corporation* [1959]). This option has a superficial attraction where the accident victim was engaged in the UK but was, at the time of the accident, working overseas. But the courts may, in such cases, recognise that the employer has little power to ensure workers are safe (*see Cook* v. *Square D Ltd* (1992)).

45. Maintenance of injured workers

The Workmen's Compensation Acts imposed liability on employers to make payments towards income maintenance of injured workers. This liability only arose in relation to certain of their workers who were their employees.

46. Difference between contract and other relationships

Twentieth-century case law, particularly before about 1970, further demonstrated the differences between employment relationships based on a contract of employment and other relationships. Cases like *Wilsons & Clyde Coal Company*

Ltd v. *English* [1937] identified special obligations for the employer in respect of the safety of employees. Similarly civil actions for breach of statutory duty normally benefited only employees of the defendant since these duties were usually imposed on employers to protect their employees. The historic limitations on liability continue to be reflected in the statutes which require liability insurance.

The distinction between employer's and public liability has been largely whittled away with the development of the law of negligence and has recently been almost entirely lost. Of particular significance is *Margereson* v. *JW Roberts Ltd, Hancock* v. *Same* [1996]. In this case it was held that the owner of an asbestos factory should reasonably have foreseen a risk of some injury to children playing in the factory loading bay and was therefore liable when they developed mesothelioma, because the factory had deposited very large amounts of asbestos dust outside its perimeters. The Court of Appeal was of the opinion that no distinction could sensibly be drawn between the position of employees working within the factory and the plaintiffs playing outside the factory. The case is the more remarkable because the plaintiff children had been exposed to the risk in the 1930s and had they suffered an immediate injury at that time, say broken bones, it is fairly unlikely that the factory would have then been liable to compensate them!

47. Compulsory liability insurance

The Employers' Liability (Compulsory Insurance) Act 1969, s. 1(1), requires that:

> Every employer carrying on any business in Great Britain shall insure and maintain insurance, under one or more approved policies with an authorised insurer or insurers against liability for bodily injury or disease sustained by his employees, and arising out of and in the course of their employment in Great Britain in that business . . .

The circumstances in which liability to pay damages may arise remains governed by case law. The statute only determines when insurance monies should be available to meet liability which the courts impose. The provision:

(a) requires insurance only in respect of injuries to employees of the employer – it makes no provision in respect of other persons

(b) the policy only has to cover 'accidents arising out of and in the course of their employment'. It may not cover, for example, accidents on the way to work, on the employer's premises during lunch breaks, or after clocking out.

48. Effectiveness of the legislation

The effectiveness of this legislation in providing funds must depend on the extent to which the legislative provisions are observed. The HSE and other occupational health and safety inspectors are authorised to ask for evidence that an effective policy is in force, but there is no fund comparable to that operated by the Motor Insurers' Bureau in respect of road traffic insurance, to meet claims against a person who does not have the cover which the law requires.

49. Additional legislation

This Act must be considered in conjunction with the Employer's Liability (Defective Equipment) Act 1969. This enables employees to claim against their own employer in respect of injury caused by equipment which is defective due to the negligence of someone other than the employers (typically the manufacturer). Section 1(1) provides that where:

(a) an employee suffers personal injury in the course of his employment in consequence of a defect in equipment provided by his employer for the purposes of the employer's business; and
(b) the defect is attributable wholly or partly to the fault of a third party (whether identified or not), the injury shall be deemed to be also attributable to negligence on the part of the employer . . .

This statute makes the employer strictly liable for the fault of another (i.e. it is a statutory extension of vicarious liability). The employer may seek an indemnity from the actual wrongdoer. The statute has been interpreted broadly. In *Knowles* v. *Liverpool City Council* [1993] it was held that the statutory definition of 'equipment' included the materials (in this case a flagstone) which an employee was given by his employer to use to do his job.

50. Extent of insurance cover

Wise employers will take out more third-party liability insurance than these statutes require. They are likely to insure at least against liability to persons other than employees injured on their premises or by the activities of their employees. If they are manufacturers they will also need to consider product liability insurance.

Road traffic legislation also requires that drivers of vehicles have insurance to cover the vehicle for the purposes for which it is being driven. Employers need to ensure that they are not held liable for injuries caused by their employees when driving their own vehicles in the course of their employment without insurance cover appropriate for the circumstances.

In *Smith* v. *Stages* [1989] the House of Lords held an employer liable to compensate an employee for personal injury suffered when being driven by a fellow employee from a workplace in Wales to their work base in the Midlands, in an uninsured vehicle. The employees were held to be in the course of their employment although they were supposed to travel by train, and at the time of the accident they were in a paid rest break at the end of a very long period of work without sleep. As the employer was paying them during the hours in question they were deemed to be in the course of employment. The decision undoubtedly ensured compensation was available to the accident victim. It may, however, be considered that this was only achieved by transfering what was really liability under road traffic insurance to employers' liability. This may not have been unjust: possibly the employer should have insisted that the vehicle was properly insured, or, better still, taken effective steps to prevent his employees from starting on a long cross-country drive directly after the completion of a 90 hour work shift.

Progress test 13

1. What is the primary purpose of civil litigation following personal injury?

2. What matters are generally covered in awards of 'special damages'?

3. To what extent is compensation made for 'loss of expectation of life'?

4. How does the Limitation Act apply in disease cases?

5. How do the courts assist plaintiffs to overcome the problem of establishing causation in disease cases?

6. In what circumstances is an employer 'vicariously liable'?

14

LIABILITY IN NEGLIGENCE

1. Introduction

Most personal injury claims are founded in negligence. This is partly because there are few situations to which the tort of negligence is not applicable, and partly because judges are unsympathetic to attempts to establish other forms of liability for personal injury. (*See Bolton* v. *Stone* [1951] and *Read* v. *Lyons* [1946].)

The exceptions to the general rule occur when the plaintiff either alleges that the defendant intended to injure him or else builds his case on the defendant's breach of statutory duty. Breach of statutory duty will be considered in the following chapter; other exceptions to the general rule can be dealt with very quickly here.

2. No strict liability at common law

In the Court of Appeal in *Letang* v. *Cooper* [1965] (where the plaintiff had been run over while sunbathing in a car park!) Lord Denning MR stated:

> If one man intentionally applies force directly to another, the plaintiff has a cause of action in assault and battery ... If he does not inflict injury intentionally, but only unintentionally ... only cause of action is in negligence, and then only on proof of want of reasonable care.

There is little likelihood of an employer being found personally liable for assault and battery. Similarly an employer is not likely to be vicariously liable for assault and battery committed by one of his employees. In *Warren* v. *Henleys Ltd* [1948] where a garage forecourt attendant struck a customer whom he believed to be leaving without paying for the petrol he had received, it was held that the employee was not in the course of his employment when he struck the customer.

3. From employers' liability to negligence

In *Donoghue* v. *Stevenson* [1932] the House of Lords established that there was a general concept of tortious liability for negligence. This case did not overrule earlier case law on liability for negligent conduct. For the immediate future the new tort was perceived as relevant to various categories of relationships of which master/servant and occupier/visitor relationships were examples and to which *Donoghue* v. *Stevenson* itself added the manufacturer/consumer relationship. In the 60 years which have elapsed since *Donoghue* v. *Stevenson* the category approach has ceased to be valuable in personal injury litigation. Old cases on employers' liability have not necessarily been overruled, but it must be asked whether the distinctions these often suggest between employers' liability and other forms of negligence liability still exist.

4. The ingredients of negligence

In order to succeed in an action for negligence the plaintiff must prove:

(a) the defendant owed the plaintiff a duty of care

(b) the defendant broke that duty by negligent conduct

(c) the defendant's negligent conduct caused damage to the plaintiff.

THE DUTY OF CARE

5. Basis of the duty of care

Whether the defendant is under a duty to take reasonable care not to injure the plaintiff is a matter of law for the judge.

The essence of Lord Atkin's dictum in *Donoghue* v. *Stevenson* was that a person had to take reasonable care not to injure his neighbour. This raises two questions. First, who is the 'neighbour' to whom this duty of care is owed? Secondly, what has to be done to discharge the duty? Strictly the first question relates to the duty issue while the second question relates to the conduct issue, but it has not proved easy to keep the two distinct.

The difficulty was not assisted because his Lordship's speech bound the two issues together with a foresight test thus:

> You must take reasonable care to avoid acts or omissions which you can reasonably foresee would be likely to injure your neighbour. Who then in law is my neighbour? The answer seems to be – persons who are so closely and directly affected by my act that I ought reasonably to have them in contemplation as being so affected when I am directing my mind to the acts or omissions which are called in question.

6. Development of the duty of care

In the years which immediately followed *Donoghue* v. *Stevenson* the content of the duty was generally considered to depend on the category of relationship under consideration. Judges felt bound to declare not merely that plaintiff and defendant were neighbours, but also which category of neighbour situation the parties were in, in order to determine what the defendant was required to address when exercising care.

Thus the duty which the employer owed to his employee was regarded as legally of a different order to the duty which the occupier owed to a visitor, and the nature of the occupiers' duty at that time depended on whether the visitor was an invitee or a licensee. Indeed case law between 1932 and 1960 tended to emphasise the differences between the categories of duty situations, rather than rationalise them into a general law of negligence.

In *Wilsons & Clyde Coal Co Ltd* v. *English* [1937] Lord Wright's characterisation of the employers' duty served to distinguish it from other neighbour relationships. His Lordship stated:

> The obligation is threefold, 'the provision of a competent staff of men, adequate material, and a proper system and effective supervision'.

Victims of industrial accidents could, after this decision, attach their employer with a legal responsibility for competent staff, adequate plant and equipment, and in due course instruction and supervision. On the other hand the visiting workman was disadvantaged after *London Graving Dock Co. Ltd* v. *Horton* [1951] held that a visiting workman who continued to work knowing of a risk (in that case inadequate staging on scaffolding) must be deemed to have accepted the risk, and be barred from claiming damages for injury resulting from this hazard.

The unsatisfactory state of occupiers' liability led to the Occupiers' Liability Act 1957; the distinction between invitees and licensees was abolished and statutory provision was made for situations such as had occurred in *Horton's* case.

7. The Occupiers' Liability Act 1957

The Act rationalised the duty which the occupier of premises owed to his visitors (s. 1(1)). Section 2(1) of the Act stated that the occupier owed the same duty, the ' "common duty of care" to all his visitors . . .' Section 2(2) provided:

> The common duty of care is a duty to take such care as in all the circumstances of the case is reasonable to see that the visitor will be reasonably safe in using the premises for the purposes for which he is invited or permitted by the occupier to be there.

This simplification of the occupiers' duty reduced the duty issue to a simple matter of whether the plaintiff was a lawful visitor to, and the defendant was the occupier of, the premises where the plaintiff suffered his injury. Once the plaintiff and defendant are shown to be in the category of visitor and occupier, the matter of what the occupier has to do to discharge his duty is a question of fact peculiar to the circumstances of the particular case and of no significance to the development of case law generally. Moreover, s. 1(1) makes it clear that the occupiers' duty extends to the activities being conducted on the premises (confirming *Slater* v. *Clay Cross Co Ltd* [1956]).

8. Abolition of categories?

Rationalisation of occupiers' liability encouraged a breaking down of the categories of liability and a rationalisation of the content of the duty which employers owed to their employees.

In the 1950s, after *Horton's* case, visiting workmen who suffered injury had often pleaded that they had become employees of the occupier while executing the task they had come to perform. This argument was raised after the Occupiers' Liability Act in *Savory* v. *Holland Hannen and Cubitts (Southern) Ltd* [1964]. The plaintiff was the employee of a subcontractor called to a building site to blast rock to enable the laying of foundations. The defendants were supposed to provide men to help the plaintiff, but allegedly failed to do so. The plaintiff slipped and suffered injury; he claimed that for the task in hand he had become the employee of the defendant contractor and that they accordingly owed him the duty which an employer owed to his employees. The Court of Appeal, through Diplock LJ, had no difficulty in disposing of this argument:

> . . . since the passing of the Occupiers' Liability Act 1957 . . . that is an incorrect approach to the question of negligence in a case like this. The question for the court is not whether the plaintiff was in the category of servant to the defendants *pro hac vice.* The only question is whether, in all the circumstances, the defendants used reasonable care for the safety of the plaintiff.

9. Simplification of employers' duty

The content of the employer's duty of care was considered by the House of Lords in *Qualcast (Wolverhampton) Ltd* v. *Haynes* [1959] where the plaintiff, an experienced metal moulder employed by the defendants, burnt his foot with molten metal. He was wearing ordinary boots. The county court judge found for the plaintiff, subject to 75% contributory negligence, because he considered he was bound by authority to hold that the defendants' duty included an obligation to instruct the plaintiff to wear protective clothing; the Court of Appeal upheld this decision. The House of Lords found for the defendants for, in their view, the defendants were not required to give instruction to an experienced workman. On the content of the employers' duty of care Lord Somervell commented:

> Whether a duty of reasonable care is owed by A to B is a question of law. In a special relationship such as that of employer to employee the law may go further and define the heads and scope of the duty. There are cases in your Lordships' House which have covered this ground, I would have thought by now exhaustively . . . There would seem to be little if anything that can be added to the law . . . Now that negligence cases are mostly tried without juries, the distinction between the functions of judge and jury is blurred. A judge naturally gives reasons for the conclusion formerly arrived at by a jury without reasons. It may sometimes be difficult to draw the line, but if the reasons given by a judge for arriving at the conclusion previously reached by a jury are to be treated as 'law' and citable, the precedent system will die from a surfeit of authorities.

His Lordship therefore shifted the emphasis from the legal content of the duty to the analysis of the facts of the particular situation; but he considered that the existing case law on the content of the employers' duty had become too deeply embedded to be ignored. Contemporary judicial statements nevertheless tended to emphasise that the cases merely illustrated what was essentially an unqualified duty to take reasonable care. Indeed Lord Somervell himself said in *Cavanagh* v. *Ulster Weaving Co Ltd* [1960]:

courts of first instance . . . will proceed more satisfactorily if what I have called the normal formula – that is reasonable care in all the circumstances – is applied whatever the circumstances.

10. Back to general principles

In *Home Office* v. *Dorset Yacht Co Ltd* [1970] the House of Lords had to consider whether the Home Office owed any duty to take care to prevent borstal boys from damaging the plaintiffs' property. Lord Reid took the opportunity to comment on the duty issue in negligence generally:

> . . . there has been a steady trend towards regarding the law of negligence as depending on principle so that, when a new point emerges, one should ask not whether it is covered by authority but whether recognised principles apply to it . . . . I think that the time has come when we can and should say that it ought to apply unless there is some justification or valid explanation for its exclusion. For example causing economic loss is a different matter . . .

11. Simply reasonable care?

It is difficult to ignore the cases which gave a special legal content to the employers' duty, and so distinguished it from other duty situations. It is, however, suggested that little is gained by relying on them today. Following the *Dorset Yacht* case the duty is rarely put in issue in personal injury cases; the court is primarily concerned with whether the defendant's conduct was both negligent and the cause of the injury the plaintiff has allegedly suffered. The relationship between the parties, be it occupier and visitor, employer and employee, or indeed some other relationship, will be relevant when deciding whether the defendant's conduct has shown reasonable care for the plaintiff.

BREACH OF DUTY OF CARE

12. General

A duty of care is broken by negligent conduct; whether conduct is negligent is a matter of fact established by evidence. Decisions on fact do not create precedents but judicial statements provide criteria by which situations may be evaluated. Such criteria become precedents. In the following paragraphs some of the criteria will be considered.

13. The reasonable man

The classic description of negligent conduct was laid down by Alderson B in *Blyth* v. *Birmingham Waterworks Co* (1856):

> . . . as the omission to do something which a reasonable man would do or doing something which a reasonable man would not do.

217

14. Reasonable care in all the circumstances

The criterion of reasonable care in all the circumstances, as used in the Occupiers' Liability Act, is more frequently used today than the 'reasonable man' test, but both suffer from the same limitation, namely the decision as to what is reasonable rests with the judge.

15. Objectivity

The conduct in question is evaluated objectively without reference to the special characteristics of the defendant (*Vaughan* v. *Menlove* (1837)); for example, a learner driver is expected to perform to the standard of an experienced driver (*Nettleship* v. *Weston* [1971]). When an organisation carries out an activity as part of a commercial undertaking, that organisation holds itself out as an expert and is expected to achieve the standards of an expert. In *The Lady Gwendolen* [1965] brewers transported stout from Dublin to Liverpool in their own ship. After an accident caused by poor navigation, they sought to avoid liability by pleading they were not navigators. Nevertheless Winn LJ had no hesitation in finding them liable:

> The law must apply a standard which is not relaxed to cater for their factual ignorance of all activities outside brewing: having become owners of ships, they must behave as reasonable shipowners.

16. Foresight

At the core of Lord Atkin's neighbour statement is the concept of reasonable foresight: foresight is both the basis of the duty and the criterion of the acts or omissions of the defendant. Again the test is objective, so the actual evaluation is that of the judge, with hindsight, upon careful analysis, rather than that of the defendant who often makes decisions in traumatic situations which give little opportunity for careful evaluation. It is not easy to reconcile the case law.

The defendant only has to be able to foresee that his conduct creates a risk of injury to others; it is not necessary that he should be able to foresee the actual sequence of events. In *Ogwo* v. *Taylor* (below) it was sufficient that a householder could foresee that his actions might result in a fire which would endanger firemen; it was not necessary that he should foresee the exact sequence of events.

Similarly in *Hughes* v. *Lord Advocate* [1963] post office engineers left an open manhole unattended and two children crawled under tarpaulin and then apparently knocked a lamp, which they found on the site, into the manhole. This caused an explosion which resulted in one of the children suffering severe burns. The House of Lords held that the respondents were liable for the injuries he had suffered. The lamp was a known source of danger; it was not material that the injury was caused through an unforeseeable sequence of events.

On the other hand in *Doughty* v. *Turner Manufacturing Co Ltd* [1964] a workman at the defendants' factory knocked an asbestos cover into molten liquid and a few seconds later there was an explosion and the plaintiff was injured. It was later discovered that such an explosion could take place because of a chemical reaction engendered by intense heat. The plaintiff contended that as there was a foreseeable risk of being burned by splashing there was a foreseeable risk of being burned by the molten liquid. The defendants were not liable; the actual damage suffered was not foreseeable; it was, the Court of Appeal held, of quite a different type from anything which might have been foreseen.

17. The state of the art

What is foreseeable depends largely on technical knowledge available at the time when the plaintiff was injured. Advances in technical and scientific knowledge make foreseeable today occurrences which would not have been foreseeable a few years ago. Post-accident investigations disclose the cause of that accident and enable others to learn from the experience. In *Roe* v. *Ministry of Health* [1954] the two plaintiffs entered hospital for minor surgery and left permanently paralysed. Investigation established that the ampoules of anaesthetic used had hair line cracks enabling sterilising fluid to percolate through to contaminate the anaesthetic. The Court of Appeal found that it had not been foreseeable that such an accident might occur. Lord Denning noted:

> It is easy to be wise after the event and to condemn as negligence that which was only a misadventure . . . Doctors, like the rest of us, have to learn by experience; and experience often teaches us in a hard way. Something goes wrong and shows up a weakness, and then it is put right . . . We must not look at the 1947 accident with 1954 spectacles.

His Lordship continued, however:

> Never again, it is to be hoped, will such a thing happen. . . . If the hospitals were to continue the practice after this warning, they could not complain if they were found guilty of negligence.

18. Foreseeable through experience

It may be the defendant's own experience which made the particular injury in question foreseeable. In *Stokes* v. *Guest, Keen & Nettlefold (Bolts and Nuts) Ltd* [1968] the plaintiff's late husband had been sprayed, in the course of his work, with cutting oils. He died of scrotal cancer. The deceased was the second employee of the defendants to die of this disease. Furthermore, the company employed a skin specialist who was a nationally accepted expert in skin cancer. Swanwick J considered the case law and continued:

> From these authorities I deduce the principles, that the overall test is still the conduct of the reasonable and prudent employer, taking positive thought for the safety of his workers in the light of what he knows or ought to know; . . . but where there is developing knowledge, he must keep reasonably abreast of it and not be too slow to apply it; and where he has in fact greater than average knowledge of the risks, he may be thereby obliged to take more than the average or standard precautions.

His Lordship found the employers liable.

19. Constructive knowledge

The enterprise is deemed to know what is generally known. It is not relevant that the particular defendant might not be aware of risks. Thus in *Vacwell Engineering Co Ltd* v. *British Drug House Chemicals Ltd* [1971] an explosion occurred when the defendant allowed a certain chemical to come into contact with water. The defendants were found liable for the damage caused: while they were not themselves aware of it, the risk was acknowledged in older textbooks.

20. Industrial practice

The defendants will be liable if they do not maintain the standards observed by others in like business; however, evidence that defendants are operating in the customary manner may not exonerate them. The courts may declare that the general practice is a negligent one. In *Cavanagh* v. *Ulster Weaving Co Ltd* [1960] a labourer who was carrying cement across a roof slipped and fell. An expert testified that the system adopted was 'perfectly in accord with good practice'. It was nevertheless held that the employers had been negligent: evidence as to the trade practice was not conclusive.

21. Duty to plaintiff personally

The conduct required from the defendant to discharge the duty may vary from one plaintiff to another, so that if the defendants are aware of some personal factor making a particular person specially vulnerable they may have to take special steps to protect that person. In *Paris* v. *Stepney Borough Council* [1951] a one-eyed man worked in the defendant's garage. A piece of metal flew into his good eye and caused him to become totally blind. While it was not usual for persons like him to be provided with goggles, the House of Lords had no hesitation in finding that the defendant ought to have provided eye protection to the plaintiff.

The converse also applies: if the plaintiff is a skilled person who knows the hazards of his work, it may not be necessary for the defendant to train or supervise him. It has already been noted that in *Qualcast (Wolverhampton) Ltd* v. *Haynes* [1959] the House of Lords declined to find that employers had been negligent merely because they had failed to instruct a skilled man to wear protective clothing.

Everything hinges on the facts of the case. In *Bux* v. *Slough Metals Ltd* [1974] the plaintiff had worked for many years without eye protection before a manager introduced the goggles which the then relevant eye-protection regulations required the employer to provide. Within a short time the plaintiff reverted to working without the goggles and lost his sight. The Court of Appeal found the employers were negligent in failing to instruct and persuade the plaintiff to wear the goggles. However, the plaintiff's damages were considerably reduced because of his own contributory negligence in not wearing the goggles which he was under a statutory duty to wear.

22. Cost benefit

When events show the defendant has not provided a safe system of work, whether this failure is negligence will to some extent depend on the cost of removing the hazard as opposed to the likelihood of injury being suffered and the likelihood of that injury being serious. In *Paris* an important factor was that goggles are relatively cheap, and not only is there a considerable possibility of eye injury for someone working (as was Mr Paris) under a vehicle, but eyesight is precious, particularly so for someone with only one eye. Similarly in *Roe* Lord Denning was impressed that the preventative measure (i.e. colouring the sterilising fluid) was a cheap and simple one. On the other hand an employer may not be negligent in failing to take every precaution for the safety of an employee who has to respond to an emergency itself involving serious personal injury (*Watt* v. *Hertfordshire County Council* [1954]).

23. Errors of judgment

Defendants are not liable for the consequences of errors of judgment. The distinction between errors of judgment and negligent conduct was made in *Whitehouse* v. *Jordan* [1981] while giving little guidance as to how the two types of conduct are to be distinguished. The case was of brain damage suffered at birth because a doctor incorrectly decided to attempt a forceps delivery. The House of Lords held that all that was certain was that there had been an error of judgment: it could not be said that there had been negligence, because a person might make an error of judgment while acting with care. This decision might be significant where the alleged wrongdoing is that of an employee for whose negligence the employer might be liable, but it might well be irrelevant where an employer is alleged to have a faulty system of work.

24. Employer's liability to itinerant workers

Where the defendant is an employer, the essential question will be, was the defendant operating a safe system? For the system to be safe resources (including human resources) sufficient and appropriate for the task must be put in place at the outset and retained in operation for so long as the situation requires. *McDermid* v. *Nash Dredging and Reclamation Co Ltd* [1987] is a salutory reminder of this. The plaintiff was a deckhand employed by the defendant; he had to untie hawsers attaching a tug to a dredger and, when he had finished the task, knock twice on the wheelhouse door to tell the captain it was safe to start the tug. The plaintiff was seriously injured when the captain started the tug without waiting for the signal. The House considered that the defendant employer should be liable for failure to operate a safe system of work. Lord Brandon explained:

> The provision of a safe system of work has two aspects: **(a)** the devising of such a system and **(b)** the operation of it.

McDermid was relied upon to support a recent decision of the Court of Appeal. In *Nelhams* v. *Sandells Maintenance Ltd & Gillespie (UK) Ltd* [1995], N was employed as a painter by S which was engaged by sub-contractors G for building refurbishment. All equipment was provided by the main contractors W. It was agreed that S's painters would work under the direction of G's supervisor. G's supervisor asked N to work from a ladder. N requested footing for the ladder. He was told that no-one was available. N climbed the ladder, slipped and fell. On appeal it was held that S being the employer of N remained liable for his safety while working under the instructions of G. The employer could not delegate responsibility for the safety of an employee 'lent' to another employer, though they might escape vicarious liability if damage were caused by that employee due to instructions given by the 'borrower'. However on the particular facts S were entitled to a complete indemnity from G.

25. Liability to visiting workers

The qualifications of the occupiers' duty, in the Occupiers' Liability Act 1957, s. 2(3), (4) and (5), remain of significance in personal injury litigation if the plaintiff relies on the Act. However, it has recently been suggested that if the plaintiff does not rely on the defendant having the status of occupier the ordinary principles of negligence will apply (*Revill* v. *Newbery* [1996], per Neill LJ in the Court of Appeal; the case concerned the liability of an allotment holder who shot someone apparently trying to break into his shed). These qualifications are discussed in paragraphs **26–32** below.

26. As regards special risks ordinarily incident in the calling

Section 2(3)(b) provides that:

> An occupier may expect that a person, in the exercise of his calling, will appreciate and guard against any special risks ordinarily incident to it, so far as the occupier leaves him free to do so.

Applying this rule an occupier might not, for example, be liable to a window cleaner who relied on the insecure frame of a sash window, and consequently fell to the ground. In a case on these facts, decided before the Act, the occupiers of the premises were not liable. As Lord Reid remarked:

> . . . a peculiar danger in window cleaning arises from the fact that sometimes the sash moves down unexpectedly so as to deprive the man of his hold, and the evidence shows that it is not very uncommon for this to happen and to cause a serious accident.

The case did demonstrate, however, the relationship between the occupiers' liability and the employers' liability for the House of Lords had no doubt that the employers were at fault for not providing a safe system of work – which in this instance meant ensuring the worker was provided with a safety harness (*General Cleaning Contractors Ltd* v. *Christmas* [1952]).

27. The position as regards the self-employed

If the worker is self-employed then he is obliged to take responsibility for his own safety as the Court of Appeal's decision in *Roles* v. *Nathan* [1963]) demonstrates. Two self-employed chimney sweeps were called to a central heating boiler which was smoking. When the problem continued after the initial cleaning, an expert was called in and he expressly warned the sweeps not to work in the vicinity when certain vent holes were open, particularly if the boiler were alight. The sweeps ignored this advice and were found dead one morning after the boiler had been used. In the widows' action, the Court of Appeal found the occupiers were not liable, even though there had apparently been some negligence on their part in allowing the boiler to be lit. Lord Denning expressed the opinion that *Christmas* remained good law:

> The risk of a defective window is a special risk, but it is ordinarily incident to the calling of a window cleaner, and so he must take care for himself, and not expect the householder to do so. Likewise, in the case of a chimney sweep who comes to sweep the chimneys or to seal up a sweep-hole. The householder can reasonably expect the sweep to take care of himself so far as any dangers from the flues are concerned.

28. Recent case law

A recent line of cases including a House of Lords decision in *Ogwo* v. *Taylor* [1988] (concerning liability to a fireman) have now established that the occupier owes a duty of care to workmen to avoid exposing them to unnecessary risks. Indeed the House of Lords ruling in *Ogwo* suggests that the general common law may prevail over the Act if the common law is more exacting.

In *Ogwo* v. *Taylor* [1988] a householder set fire to the loft of his house. A fireman who entered the loft to hose the fire was badly burned by the steam. His claim for damages was initially founded both on the statutory duty under s. 2 of the Act and on the common law of negligence. The Court of Appeal saw no necessity to consider s. 2 because:

> ... it is common ground that the duty of the defendant to the plaintiff at common law as the person who started the fire negligently is no lower, and may well be higher, than his duty to the plaintiff as the occupier of the premises (per Neill LJ).

The House of Lords accepted this approach and focused on the common law. In the principal speech, Lord Bridge considered *Salmon* v. *Seafarer Restaurant Ltd* [1983], a case concerning the occupier's liability to a fireman when a gas explosion followed a chip pan fire. His Lordship read, and adopted the headnote, from that case:

> The fire had been caused by the defendants' negligence and since it was foreseeable that the plaintiff would be required to attend the fire and would be at risk of the type of injuries he received from the explosion which was caused by the negligence, the defendants were liable for those injuries and damages were recoverable by the plaintiff.

Relying on this analysis the House of Lords found that the householder was liable at common law.

These later cases seem to throw doubt on whether *Nathan* was rightly decided given that there was some negligence on the part of the occupier. They also raise questions as to the relevance of the Occupiers' Liability Act 1957, s. 2(3)(b), if it is subsumed in general common law, which may exact a higher standard of care.

This suggestion is remarkable (if the defendant is sued as occupier) since s. 1(1) of the Occupiers' Liability Act 1957 provides:

'The rules enacted by the two next following sections shall have effect, in place of the rules of common law, to regulate the duty which an occupier of premises owes to his visitors . . . '

Thus the new case law can only be justified if s. 1(1) be deemed merely to abolish earlier rules of common law, or, if, as Neill LJ suggested, *supra* (relying on a statement made by the Law Commission in the special context of its *Report on Liability for Damage or Injury to Trespassers*) the rules of occupiers' liability only apply if they are crucial to the plaintiff's case.

Interestingly the Court of Appeal did not choose to follow *General Cleaning Contractors Ltd* v. *Christmas* (which was of course decided before the 1957 Act) in the case of *King* v. *Smith and Anor* [1995]. Millett LJ commented that in the 40 years since *Christmas* was decided, it had become 'well appreciated' that cleaning windows from the outside sill could be a dangerous practice. Both the employer and the occupier of the premises were held liable for the cleaner's injuries resulting from a fall from a window ledge.

29. Qualifications to the liability of the occupier

Section 2(4) places two qualifications on the liability of the occupier. It reiterates that in determining whether the occupier has discharged the duty of care to a visitor regard must be had to all the circumstances and states 'so that (for example)' two circumstances to be considered are whether the visitor has been warned of a danger, and whether the danger is due to work undertaken by an independent contractor.

30. Warnings

The occupier may discharge his duty by warning a visitor of a danger, but only if the warning is enough to enable the visitor to be reasonably safe (s. 2(4)(a)). The Court of Appeal particularly noted in *Nathan* that the chimney sweeps had been warned of the dangers of working in the fumes which built up if the sweep-hole was open. Section 2(4)(a) appears to be intended to exonerate the occupier only where the circumstances are such that once warned the visitor can avoid the danger. The provision must now be read in conjunction with the Unfair Contract Terms Act 1977, s. 2(1), which provides that an occupier of business premises (as indeed anyone else to whom business liability attaches):

. . . cannot by reference to any contract term or to a notice given to persons generally or to a particular person exclude or restrict his liability for death or personal injury resulting from negligence.

While the Occupiers' Liability Act 1984 extends liability to trespassers the provision which that Act makes for the occupier to discharge his liability by giving a warning of a risk does not appear to be restricted by the caveat of s. 2(1) of the 1977 Act.

31. Liability for independent contractors

Section 2(4)(b) states:

> Where damage is caused to a visitor by a danger due to the faulty execution of any work of construction, maintenance or repair by an independent contractor employed by the occupier, the occupier is not to be treated without more as answerable for the danger if in all the circumstances he had acted reasonably in entrusting the work to an independent contractor and had taken such steps (if any) as he reasonably ought in order to satisfy himself that the contractor was competent and that the work had been properly done.

This provision appears merely to reiterate that occupiers are not vicariously liable for the wrongdoings of independent contractors. Where a hazard has been created on the occupiers' premises by an independent contractor, the occupier will only be liable if they have been personally negligent in matters such as the selection of, or the monitoring of the work of, the contractor.

In *McTeare* v. *Dooley and Ors* [1994] a company which failed to make reasonable enquiries about a scaffolding contractor's competence was liable to a passerby injured when the negligently erected scaffolding fell from the front of the building, which the defendants occupied, to cause him injury. The High Court held that the scaffolder had recklessly disregarded public safety in the way he had erected the scaffolding but the occupier of the premises must share liability because a reasonable occupier would have made enquiries about the suitability of the scaffolder, or engaged a competent builder or surveyor to do so: in fact this occupier provided no evidence as to how scaffolder had been selected.

32. Risks willingly accepted

Section 2(5) states:

> The common duty of care does not impose on an occupier any obligation to a visitor in respect of risks willingly accepted as his by the visitor (the question whether a risk was so accepted to be decided on the same principles as in other cases in which one person owes a duty of care to another).

The issue of whether this subsection reversed the controversial House of Lords decision in *London Graving Dock Co Ltd* v. *Horton* [1951] was resolved by the Court of Appeal in *Bunker* v. *Charles Brand & Son Ltd* [1969]. In *Bunker* the defendants were the main contractors excavating a tunnel for the London Underground system; the plaintiff was an employee of a contractor called in to modify a machine in the tunnel. The plaintiff suffered injury clambering to the point at which he had to work. The appeal court found that, while the plaintiff knew of the risk he was taking, he could not be deemed to have accepted it because his obligation to his employer to carry out the work meant he was not free to refuse to take the risk.

DAMAGE

33. General

In order to succeed in an action for negligence the plaintiff must establish both that he has suffered damage and this damage was caused by the defendant. Questions may also be raised as to whether the loss was foreseeable.

34. Medical evidence

In personal injury claims the plaintiff's case largely depends on medical evidence showing that the plaintiff has suffered physical incapacity as a result of an accident or because of work conditions which have induced ill-health. This evidence will assist the judge in quantifying the damages.

35. The causation issue

The plaintiff must also satisfy the court that it was the defendant who caused the damage for which he is claiming damages. This, the causation issue, can be one of the most complex issues in the case.

A case which dramatically illustrates the causation issue is *Barnett* v. *Chelsea and Kensington Hospital Management Committee* [1968]. The plaintiff's husband visited the casualty department at the defendant hospital, complaining of vomiting. He was merely told to consult his own doctor; later in the day he died of arsenic poisoning. The widow failed in her claim against the hospital for, although they had been negligent in not treating her husband, their negligence had not caused his death. They had not administered the fatal dose of poison and, even if they had given him treatment, they could not have saved his life.

36. Plaintiff's own conduct as an influence

In *McKew* v. *Holland & Hannen & Cubitts (Scotland) Ltd* [1969] the court found it necessary to distinguish the accident which the plaintiff had suffered at the workplace from a second incident in which the plaintiff suffered further injury and found that there was no chain of causation between the first and the second injuries. The plaintiff had injured his leg at work; some days later, as he was descending a steep staircase with no handrail, his leg gave way and he fell suffering further damage. The House of Lords held that the defendants had not caused the second accident: the chain of causation had been broken by the plaintiff's unreasonable conduct in attempting the stairs with his known incapacity.

McKew demonstrates a problem which frequently arises, namely determining, in situations where the plaintiff's own conduct has undoubtedly had some influence on events, whether the injury was entirely the plaintiff's own fault or whether the plaintiff and the defendant should share responsibility. For example, in *Qualcast* their Lordships considered that the plaintiff worker was sufficiently experienced to operate safely within the system the employers had established, so the plaintiff's injury was caused entirely by his own conduct. On the other hand, in *Bux* the Court of Appeal considered that there was some negligence on the part of the defendants in operating their system of work.

37. Exoneration from liability

The courts do not normally find negligent conduct on the part of defendant employers and then exonerate them from liability for injury suffered by their employee. An exception is *McWilliams* v. *Sir William Arrol & Co Ltd* [1962]. The plaintiff was the widow of a steel erector killed when, not wearing a safety harness, he fell from where he had been working. Although the respondents were found to be in breach of statutory duty in not providing the safety equipment, they were not held liable for the death because evidence showed the deceased was not in the habit of wearing a safety harness even when it was available! The defendants' fault was not deemed to have caused the death.

38. Possibility of causation

It has been noted that where the plaintiff proves he has suffered ill-health and establishes that due to the defendants' negligence he has worked in conditions which could have caused illness of the kind of which he complains, the courts are disposed to find that the working conditions caused the illness.

39. Length of chain of causation

Some kinds of damage are not recoverable because the chain of causation between the injury and the damage suffered is too long even though there has not been, as in *McKew*, an intervening action by the plaintiff (or a third party) to break that chain.

40. Foresight and remoteness

It is often difficult to separate the duty and the damage issues: the problem can be re-formulated by asking: What is it that it is the defendant's duty to take care to prevent? The answer is that the defendant must take care not to cause injury which is foreseeable: injury will not be foreseeable if there is only a remote possibility that it will be suffered.

In *McGovern* v. *British Steel Corp.* [1986] the plaintiff was employed on a walkway on scaffolding: the walkway was bordered by toe-boards one of which got knocked out of place. The plaintiff tripped over it, but was unharmed: he then decided to put it back in place although there was no question but that it was too heavy for him to lift safely. He injured his back. The trial judge found that the accident was unforeseeable and there was no liability in negligence.

On the other hand in *Bradford* v. *Robinson Rentals Ltd* [1967] when an employee was required to make a difficult cross-country journey in a vehicle without heating, at a time when the weather forecast predicted severe cold and snow, it was foreseeable that the employee would suffer frostbite and the employers were liable when he did.

It is difficult to reconcile cases where it has been foreseeable that some injury may be caused but the actual damage suffered was not foreseeable. It is suggested that the following rationalisation (*see* **41–43**) may be made.

41. Extent of injury suffered

There is a so-called eggshell skull rule under which the defendant must take the victim as he finds him, i.e. if because of some unusual personal weakness the plaintiff suffered more severe injury than a normal person would do, the defendant must bear the cost of the injury actually suffered.

In *Smith* v. *Leech Brain & Co. Ltd* [1962] a man was, due to the negligence of his employers, splashed on the lip with molten metal; he died of cancer. In finding the employers liable to pay for the fatal injury, Parker LCJ said at:

> The test is not whether these employers could reasonably have foreseen that a burn would cause cancer and that he would die. The question is whether these employers could reasonably foresee the type of injury he suffered, namely the burn. What, in the particular case, is the amount of damage which he suffers as a result of that burn depends upon the characteristics and constitution of the victim.

Employers were similarly liable for an unforeseeably serious injury suffered in *Robinson* v. *Post Office and Another* [1974]. The plaintiff, a Post Office technician, slipped when descending an oily ladder and gashed his shin. His doctor gave him an injection which produced a very serious reaction. The doctor had not followed the correct medical procedure but the Post Office was nevertheless held responsible for the injury whose seriousness was due to the susceptibility of the plaintiff: the doctor's failure was neither the cause of the injury nor a breach in the chain of causation.

42. Unforeseeable sequence of events

It has been noted that in *Hughes* v. *Lord Advocate* [1963] their Lordships did not entertain the argument that the defendant should not be liable because the sequence of events was not foreseeable in a context when it was foreseeable that an accident could occur.

43. Unforeseeable kind of injury

In *The Wagon Mound (No.1)* [1961] the Privy Council found that a defendant should not be liable when the kind of damage suffered was not foreseeable: the case concerned damage to a wharf and a ship anchored there as a result of fire caused by oil discharged into water. In the view of the Council damage by oil was foreseeable but damage by fire was damage of a different sort and was not foreseeable. Application of this ruling creates difficulties: the argument is that oil damage is different from fire damage; however, in both instances the damage would be to property. Further it might be argued that if personal injury is foreseeable it is not relevant that the way in which that injury is brought about is not foreseeable. (But *see Doughty* v. *Turner Manufacturing Co Ltd* [1964] above.)

44. Liability for 'nervous shock'

It was noted in Chapter 13 that in recent years there has been an increase in litigation about, and a development in the law relating to, illness caused by mental stress. In the case of post traumatic stress disorder (PTSD) the House of Lords has now held, in *Page* v. *Smith* [1995], that foreseeability of physical injury is sufficient to enable a plaintiff directly involved in an accident to recover damages for nervous shock. The plaintiff was physically uninjured in the collision between the car he was driving and that negligently driven by the defendant but had been suffering from ME (a form of depression) for 20 years, and he claimed the illness became chronic and permanent as a result of the accident. The majority of their Lordships were of the opinion that where, as here, the plaintiff was the 'primary victim' a claim for PTSD might succeed even though no physical injury was suffered: however on the particular facts there was doubt as to whether the accident had caused the injury alleged.

45. Successive injuries

In *McKew* the defendant was not liable for a second accident which the plaintiff suffered through his own lack of care. Sometimes questions arise as to whether a second event terminates the defendant's liability for the first, so that the defendant is liable only for the period of time between the two events. The courts have laid down different rules according to whether the second event is another accident for which there is human responsibility, or whether it is an illness which is a natural occurrence. In *Baker* v. *Willoughby* [1970] the plaintiff suffered an injury to his leg and before his claim for damages reached trial he suffered gunshot wounds. This second accident caused such serious injury that the leg was amputated. The House of Lords rejected the contention that liability for the first injury should terminate at the time of the second accident. They held that the defendant should bear responsibility for the remainder of the plaintiff's normal life; the person responsible for the second accident would bear responsibility for depriving the plaintiff of such facility as the first accident had left.

On the other hand in *Jobling* v. *Associated Dairies Ltd* [1982] the appellant sustained a back injury when he fell at work. This accident was attributable to the defendant's fault. Three years later the plaintiff was found to be suffering from a quite unrelated disease affecting his neck. The disease rendered him incapable of work. The House of Lords held that damages awarded against the defendants should not include any sum for loss of wages for the period after the disease rendered the plaintiff unfit to work.

Progress test 14

1. What are the three factors which the plaintiff must prove in order to win a claim in negligence?

2. What is the legal content of the duty of care?

3. What is meant by the statement, 'the defendant's conduct is evaluated objectively'?

4. Is a defendant liable for 'errors of judgment'?

5. Explain how the courts take a 'cost benefit approach' to deciding whether the defendant's conduct has been negligent.

6. The defendant's conduct must have 'caused' the injury the plaintiff has suffered. Explain.

15

CIVIL LIABILITY FOR BREACH OF STATUTORY DUTY

1. Introduction

This chapter will explain the rules governing claims for damages for personal injury caused by breach of statutory duty. Where a statutory provision will support an action for breach of statutory duty, the plaintiff frequently claims both common-law negligence and breach of statutory duty. The important role played by civil litigation in interpreting the provisions of the pre-1974 safety legislation was referred to in Chapter 8, with a few examples, which should be considered in conjunction with the more detailed explanation given here.

2. Classes of statutory duties

There are two broad categories of statutory duty which will have to be considered:

(a) Duties created by Parliament primarily for enforcement in the criminal courts. The statutes which create them are properly a part of public rather than private law. For the purposes of the present chapter the duties are those in the 'relevant statutory provisions'.

(b) Duties created by Parliament solely to provide remedies for the victims of personal injury. These statutes are not part of public law since their purpose is to regulate private rights. They are statutory modifications of common law liability.

3. Distinguishing features of statutory duties

Each duty is distinct and different from any other duty, but actions founded on statutory duties do have these features in common:

(a) The duty relied on was created by Parliament not the courts. Defining the duty is therefore an exercise in statutory interpretation and every word has to be carefully considered.

(b) The duty, though originally created by Parliament, may have been interpreted by judges. Such interpretations create precedents binding in any further consideration of the issue, and of persuasive authority on the interpretation of like statutes.

(c) Liability is not necessarily liability for negligent conduct. Parliament has rarely chosen negligence as the criterion of liability: often liability is strict. Lord Wright put the matter thus in *Caswell* v. *Powell Duffryn Associated Collieries Ltd* [1940]:

> It is a common law action based on the purpose of the statute to protect the workman, and belonging to the category often described as that of cases of strict or absolute liability. At the same time it resembles actions in negligence in that the claim is based on a breach of a duty to take care for the safety of the workman.

CIVIL LIABILITY FOR BREACH OF RELEVANT STATUTORY PROVISIONS

4. General

The right to bring a civil action for damages for a workplace injury caused by breach of one of the relevant statutory provisions is governed by s. 47 of the 1974 Act. This section identifies three general classes of situation:

(a) It makes clear that there shall be no reliance in civil litigation on any of the general duties created by ss. 2–8 of the 1974 Act (s. 47(1)(a)).

(b) It confirms the then existing rights to found civil actions on certain of the earlier health and safety provisions, such as the Factories Act 1961, and regulations, such as the construction regulations, made under this legislation (s. 47(1)(b)).

(c) It creates a presumption that civil actions may be founded on duties in regulations made under the 1974 Act (s. 47(2)).

5. Intentions of Parliament

It is not known why Parliament decided that the general duties may not be relied on in civil litigation. A possible reason is that the very generality of the duties might encourage civil litigation. A second possibility is that they so closely match the tort of negligence that there would be little to be gained by relying on them. A third possibility is that the legislature was mindful that the Robens Committee had expressed reservations about the practice of using regulatory provisions as the basis of compensation actions because:

> The general psychological effect is that attention is diverted from the primary objective of accident prevention to the altogether different question of compensation for injury suffered.

6. Expansion of the range of duties

Nevertheless in the 1970s it would have been unacceptable to have removed the existing rights which were very important for ensuring compensation for the victims of industrial accidents and in s. 47(2) Parliament made a commitment to the perpetuation of the system, by creating a presumption that regulations made under the 1974 Act would carry both criminal and civil liability. Thus, while, with the passage of time, the earlier statutory provisions have been largely replaced, new regulations have created new rights; in particular the regulations introduced in January 1993 to implement the individual Directives made under the Framework Directive. Notably, however, the broad general duties in the Management of Health and Safety at Work Regulations are like the general duties in the 1974 Act itself: Regulation 15 states –

> Breach of a duty imposed by these Regulations shall not confer a right of action in any civil proceedings.

7. Judge-made rights

Today it is usual for Parliament to state expressly whether civil actions are to lie but the rights to litigate for breach of the duties contained in the pre-1974 health and safety legislation were created by judges interpreting the intention of Parliament. This earlier case law not only determined which statutory duties might be invoked in civil litigation, it also established what the plaintiff had to prove to win a claim based on such a duty. Much of the case law given below pre-dates the 1974 Act, for it was then that the framework for litigation was established.

The right to bring civil actions for breach of statutory duty lay in relation to a number of the provisions of the Factories Acts and the mining legislation and regulations made under these Acts, but not every provision of industrial safety legislation has been interpreted as giving civil rights. For example, in *Biddle* v. *Truvox Engineering Co Ltd* [1952] it was held that a person who sold or let defective factory machinery contrary to s. 17(2) of the Factories Act 1961 was not civilly liable to a workman injured by reason of the defect.

8. Significance of pre-1974 provisions

Given the phasing out of the earlier legislative duties, especially since the introduction of the six pack on 1 January 1993, the importance of the pre-1974 provisions as a basis of civil liability is declining, but for the time being some of these provisions remain of significance. Those of some significance for the immediate future include some of the provisions of the Factories Act 1961, such as s. 14 (guarding of dangerous machinery), s. 28 (safety of floors, passages and stairs), s. 29 (safe means of access and safe place of employment), and certain regulations, like the various construction regulations. Some provisions, like s. 63 of the Factories Act 1961 (removal of dust and fumes), were repealed and replaced by more up-to-date regulatory provisions even before 1993. However s. 63 has been particularly significant in claims in respect of dust-related diseases, such as pneumoconiosis, and these diseases often do not manifest themselves until many years have passed. It is possible therefore that civil claims may continue to be based on it for some years to come.

It would be tempting to believe that the value of this form of litigation is less nowadays than in earlier years because the growth of the tort of negligence has made injured workers less reliant on the statutory provisions. Indeed, although a number of regulatory codes have been brought into force since 1974 there is a dearth of case law on their interpretation in civil litigation. This does not necessarily mean they have not been successfully invoked since it is not possible to say how many cases may have been settled out of court or litigated without being reported in the law reports. Additionally many of the new regulations are concerned with control of particular substances (e.g. the Control of Lead at Work Regulations) or substances more generally (e.g. Control of Substances Hazardous to Health) where the risk is often of deterioration of health over a long period of time. Since plaintiffs can only rely on regulatory standards in relation to injury suffered after the particular regulations came into force it may yet be some time before regulations are invoked in civil actions.

9. Precedental value of earlier judicial statements

Even though the statutory duties themselves have ceased to be relevant, in some cases judicial statements made in the course of interpreting them may continue to have some precedential value. The meanings which have been given to words like 'factory', 'manual labour' and 'available' may well, following the normal rules of statutory interpretation, be of persuasive authority when these words, or expressions, are used in other similar legislation. It has been noted, when considering the ambit of the 1974 Act, that the expression 'reasonably practicable', which is used so frequently in the 1974 Act, was used in pre-1974 legislation and *dicta* on its meaning in the earlier statutes is generally accepted as indicative of its meaning in the 1974 Act itself.

Similarly, 'provided' has been subject to interpretation in earlier regulations such as those for eye protection, and created case law which may be significant in a new context. For example Regulation 4 of the Personal Protective Equipment at Work Regulations 1992 requires:

> Every employer shall ensure that suitable personal protective equipment is provided to his employees who may be exposed to a risk to their health or safety while at work except where and to the extent that such risk has been adequately controlled by other means which are equally or more effective.

It is a factual matter whether the employer is holding equipment in a place sufficiently accessible to the worker to have discharged his duties in relation to its provision. In *Finch* v. *Telegraph Construction and Maintenance Co Ltd* [1949] where goggles were, unknown to the workers, kept in the foreman's office, it was held that the duty to provide them had not been performed. In contrast in *Bux* v. *Slough Metal Co Ltd*, where the employer had made known to the workers that goggles were available in the store the duty was deemed to have been performed.

234

Para 23 of the Guidance published with the new Regulations provides:

> ... employers must do more than simply have the equipment on the premises. The employees must have the equipment readily available, or at the very least have clear instructions on where they can obtain it.

While this guidance is soundly based on case law, and good practice, so therefore valuable to employers, it does not of itself carry any legal or evidential significance in litigation.

10. Dearth of modern authorities

The relative newness of many of the regulatory provisions currently in force mean there has been little opportunity for them to be litigated. The increased use of the county courts for civil litigation means that litigation is less likely to be recorded in the law reports.

WHAT THE PLAINTIFF MUST PROVE

11. General

Given the existence of a civil right of action, either under the pre-1974 legislation or under regulations made since 1974, the task of the plaintiff is not an easy one. Indeed it has been judicially remarked, by Lord Hailsham in *F.E. Callow (Engineers) Ltd* v. *Jackson* [1971], that:

> Some of the protection to the workman which at first sight might be thought available turns out on closer scrutiny to be illusory.

The plaintiff must prove:

(a) he belongs to the class of persons whom the statute is designed to protect (**12–18**)

(b) that the defendant was the person on whom the duty was imposed (**19–21**)

(c) that the defendant was in breach of the duty (**23–25**)

(d) that the breach caused the damage (**26–27**).

12. Scope of Regulations

The plaintiff must have been working in the circumstances to which the statutory provision applies, and be of the class of persons to whom the duty is owed, when the injury was suffered. These matters were very important under the older provisions. For example, in the past much protective legislation was relevant only to factory premises and then only to persons who were employed there. The new style provisions are tightly worded but their scope may often be wider. For example Regulation 5(2) of the Provision and Use of Work Equipment Regulations 1992 states:

> In selecting work equipment, every employer shall have regard to the working conditions and to the risks to the health and safety of persons which exist in the premises or undertaking in which that work equipment is to be used and any additional risk posed by the use of that work equipment.

While this provision places a duty on employers it is not merely for the protection of employees, but for 'persons' generally. Nor is it limited to the employer's undertaking: it is owed in respect of the undertaking where the equipment is to be used. Moreover the premises need not be factory premises. It might, however, be questioned whether a field would be premises. Similarly there might be nice questions of interpretation as to the meaning of the phrase 'is to be used': would it be sufficient that the equipment 'had been used'?

It will be recalled that in a criminal prosecution brought under s. 2 of the 1974 Act it was held that an offence was committed when unsafe equipment was made available, and that this duty was not confined to the time when it was actually in use. In this instance it would seem to be relevant that the employer's alleged breach of duty would have been at a time prior to the accident.

In the absence of authority on the interpretation of more recent regulatory provisions, the following cases are given as examples of the principles of statutory interpretation.

13. 'Factory'

Section 175 of the Factories Act 1961 gives a general interpretation of the expression 'factory'. If the premises where the injury was suffered were not within the Act, or the plaintiff was not a manual labourer, the Act cannot be invoked.

In *Weston* v. *London County Council* [1941] the plaintiff was a pupil at a technical institute who was injured when operating an unguarded woodcutting machine there. The judge held that the institute was not a factory, and, moreover, the plaintiff was not employed there. Wrottesley J said:

> . . . I do not think that anyone could suggest that this institute falls within that general definition . . . , they are not occupied in a process which is incidental to any of the purposes mentioned, and it appears to me that they are there for the purposes of instruction.

On the other hand, in *J and F Stone Lighting and Radio* v. *Haygarth* [1968] (a criminal case), the House of Lords had to decide whether a room on shop premises used for the repair of radio and television sets was a place where persons were employed in manual labour and therefore within the Factories Acts. Their Lordships gave careful consideration to the expression 'manual labour', which has been used in a variety of statutory contexts. Lord Morris of Borth-y-Gest said:

> There is, I think, a clear and unbroken line of authority to the effect that in such a situation regard must be had to what is the main substantial work which a person is employed to do.

On the facts of the case, their Lordships concluded that the worker in the premises in question was engaged in manual labour and therefore the premises were a factory.

14. Plaintiff must be an employee

Normally the plaintiff must be an employee of the defendant. In *Hartley* v. *Mayoh & Co* [1954] the defendant's factory caught fire and the plaintiff's husband was electrocuted while fighting the fire during the course of his duty as a fireman. The widow's action relied on regulations made under s. 76 of the Factories Act: it was held that these regulations were for the protection of persons employed by the defendant and were not therefore intended to protect persons such as her husband.

However, whether the litigation is based on common law negligence or breach of statutory duty the courts will not allow the plaintiff and defendant to describe their relationship as contractor and self-employed worker if this is not the true nature of their relationship as the following case demonstrates. In *Lane* v. *Shire Roofing Company (Oxford) Ltd* [1995] L was a builder who traded as a one-man firm and was categorised as 'self-employed' for tax purposes. The defendant company hired L to re-roof a porch at an all-in fee of £200. The company offered equipment but L preferred his own ladder. L fell from the ladder and claimed damages from the company. On appeal the Court of Appeal held that L was really an employee, noting that in the current environment where there are more self-employed people and fewer in employment, and where there are perceived advantages in avoiding the 'employee' label, there are good policy reasons in the safety at work field to ensure that the law properly categorised workers; a court should recognise the employer/employee relationship when it existed because of the responsibilities that both the common law and statutes place on the employer. In the current case the question 'Whose business was it?' could only be answered by saying that it was the company's business not L's.

15. Exceptions

However, not all provisions of the Act protect only the employees of the defendant. For example, it is required in s. 29 of the 1961 Act that:

> There shall, so far as is reasonably practicable, be provided and maintained safe means of access to every place at which *any person* has at any time to work.

In *Whitby* v. *Burt, Boulton & Hayward Ltd and Another* [1947] the plaintiff was employed by a firm which was called in by the defendant factory occupier to repair war damage to the factory. While removing corrugated iron sheets from under a glass skylight the plaintiff fell because of a defect in timber where he was working. The court held that the plaintiff was entitled to rely on what was then s. 26 of the 1937 Act. Denning J said, bearing in mind that the provision related to every place where *any* person had to work:

> I hold, therefore, that for the safeguarding of people in factories s. 26 applies and puts the responsibility on the occupier even though the building operations are being carried out by a contractor.

The House of Lords reached the same conclusion in *Wigley* v. *British Vinegars Ltd* [1962] where the plaintiff was a visiting window cleaner. The Workplace (Health, Safety and Welfare) Regulations repealed s. 29, and it will not be replaced, since s. 2(2)(d) of the 1974 Act is deemed to cover the situation. However, general duties in the 1974 Act carry no civil liability.

16. Other parts of the premises

Similarly s. 14(1) of the Factories Act 1961 imposed the duty to guard dangerous machinery in relation to 'every person employed or working on the premises'. This provision has been held to impose a duty on an occupier in respect of an employee who was in a part of the premises where he was forbidden to go – in fact chasing a pigeon up a shaft – *Uddin* v. *Associated Portland Cement Manufacturers Ltd* [1965].

17. Which statutory provision?

Mains v. *Uniroyal Englebert Tyres Ltd* [1995] (referred to fully in Chapter 8) serves as a reminder that a plaintiff may be able to invoke more than one relevant statutory provision (in that case both ss. 14 and 29(1) of the Factories Act 1961); and one provision may impose a more stringent obligation on the employer, and therefore be more favourable to the employee, than the other.

18. Statutory interpretation

These last cases serve as a salutory reminder that in exercises of statutory interpretation it is necessary not only to look at the scope of the Act generally but also to look at the particular duty relied on in order to determine the plaintiff's rights.

19. Status of the defendant

The plaintiff must sue the person upon whom the duty is placed. The problem is to identify that person. The individual duties under the Factories Act stated the objectives to be achieved, but did not stipulate the person upon whom the responsibility for achieving them rested. In most instances this was the occupier of the premises, but there could still be disputes as to who was the occupier.

In the criminal case of *Turner* v. *Courtaulds Ltd* [1937] the company was charged, as occupier of a factory, with an offence under the electricity regulations then in force; it was alleged that they had the duty to make dead the switchboard before certain work was carried out. The failure to perform this duty caused a fatal accident. The work was being carried out by contractors and the switchboard had not been 'handed over' to the defendants. The magistrates dismissed the charge finding the defendant was not the occupier at the time of the accident. The appeal court reversed this decision holding the company was the occupier.

However, in *Rippon* v. *Port of London Authority and J Russell & Co Ltd* [1940] it was held that the person who was occupier under the Act was not necessarily the occupier for the purpose of regulations made under the Act. The first defendants were the owners of a dry dock and the second defendants were ship repairers repairing a vessel lying in the dock. The plaintiff, an employee of the second defendants, was walking down steps in the dock, when one of the steps gave way causing him to fall and sustain serious injury. It was held that the two defendants should share liability for the plaintiff's injury: the first defendants, as owners of the dry dock, remained in occupation of the premises and were liable for breaches of the relevant provisions of the Factories Act; the second defendants were occupiers for the purposes of repairing the ship and were liable for breach of relevant shipbuilding regulations.

20. The burden of the statutory duty

Similar difficulties can arise where it is controversial whether the statutory duty is imposed on the enterprise or on one of its employees, often the plaintiff himself. Thus in *Harrison* v. *National Coal Board* [1951] it was held that while duties relating to mines were imposed on the mine owner when expressed impersonally, duties relating to shotfiring were duties of the shotfirer. In a controversial House of Lords decision, *Imperial Chemical Industries Ltd* v. *Shatwell* [1965], it was held that the employers were neither personally nor vicariously liable for injuries which two shotfirers inflicted on themselves when operating in breach of regulatory duties: the duties were imposed on the men not their employer.

Most of the modern regulations impose their obligations on employers. Notable exceptions are The Control of Industrial Major Accidents Hazards Regulations, which place duties on certain 'manufacturers' and the Chemicals (Hazard Information and Packaging for Supply) Regulations 1994, which are concerned with 'suppliers'.

21. Duty rests on both plaintiff and defendant

On occasion where the duty is placed on an employer, the employer may be in breach if the regulatory provision is not observed, although the practicalities of the situation are that only the plaintiff himself could perform the duty.

In *Ginty* v. *Belmont Building Supplies Ltd* [1959] the employer was a roofing contractor subject to building regulations which required him to provide and *use* boards for work on asbestos roofs. The employer provided the necessary boards but the plaintiff worker failed to use them and fell through the roof on which he was working. It was found that the plaintiff's failure to use the boards had resulted in the defendant being (vicariously) in breach of his duty. In the event this availed the plaintiff nothing, for the plaintiff was in breach of his own duty to use the boards. Pearson J stated:

> . . . if one finds that the immediate and direct cause of the accident was some wrongful act of the man, that is not decisive. One has to inquire whether the fault of the employer under the regulations consists of, and is co-extensive with, the

239

wrongful act of the employee. If there is some fault on the part of the employer which goes beyond or is independent of the wrongful act of the employee, and was a cause of the accident, the employer has some liability.

His Lordship instanced that the employer might have failed to provide proper training or supervision; however, on the facts there was no fault of the employer which went beyond or was independent of the plaintiff's own omission.

The case may be distinguished from *Boyle* v. *Kodak Ltd* [1969] where employer and employee similarly shared regulatory duties to ensure that 'every ladder shall so far as practicable be securely fixed so that it can move neither from its top nor from its bottom points of rest'. The plaintiff employee fell, and was injured, when using a ladder which had not been lashed: it was held that the employers' duty extended to instructing and training the employee to ensure that he observed the statutory requirements. As the employers had failed to carry out this aspect of the duty, they had to accept some responsibility for the accident.

22. Defendant's standard of conduct

The standard of conduct required from the defendant in civil liability is the standard imposed by the legislature for enforcement in the criminal courts. However, the interpretation of the legislature's intentions has often been made in civil courts, and impacted back to the enforcement of the duties in the criminal courts.

23. The words of Parliament

The starting point is the words chosen by Parliament. Sometimes Parliament appears to have created strict liability, i.e. it has simply stipulated the result that has to be achieved without qualifying words. For example, s. 14(1) of the Factories Act 1961 stipulated 'Every dangerous part of any machinery . . . shall be securely fenced . . .'. Other provisions qualify that duty with concepts such as reasonable practicability; so s. 29 required 'There shall, so far as is reasonably practicable, be provided . . .' safe means of access to every place of work. The recent case of *Mains* v. *Uniroyal Tyres Ltd* [1995] has, of course, shown that s. 29 may in fact be a more onerous duty, since under s. 14 it is for the plaintiff to show that there is a foreseeable danger and under s. 29 it is for the defendant to show that it was not reasonably practicable to avoid the danger which, with hindsight, could be seen to have existed. None of the Factories Act provisions imposed absolute duties; there are some defences, and even apparently strict duties may have provisos which give scope for narrowing the definition of the duty. Thus s. 14(1) relaxed its requirement by a provision in respect of machinery which 'is in such a position or of such construction as to be as safe to every person employed or working on the premises as it would be if securely fenced'.

24. Inconsistency of judicial approach

It is difficult to extract from a study of cases any consistent approach to the task of interpreting the regulatory provisions. The judges sometimes veered towards a theory of statutory negligence, refusing to find liability unless the defendant had been at fault; on other occasions they imposed very strict liability on an apparently faultless defendant.

At the one extreme in *Brown* v. *National Coal Board* [1962], the House of Lords had to interpret s. 48 of the Mines and Quarries Act 1954 which requires the mine manager to take 'such steps . . . as may be necessary for keeping the road . . . secure'. Lord Radcliffe took the view that the manager's duty was no more than to take care, and there would be no liability in the absence of fault:

> It seems plain to me that if a manager's duty is to ask himself from time to time 'What steps are required now to keep the roadway secure?' he can only pose or answer that question in the light of the best obtainable information as to the circumstances, geophysical or otherwise, that he is to deal with and knowledge of skilled and up-to-date engineering science and practice. If he answers the question in those terms and acts accordingly, he cannot, in my view, be said to be in breach of his duty, even though there is a state of insecurity or a roof fall.

In contrast, in *John Summers & Sons Ltd* v. *Frost* [1955] the House of Lords held, in interpreting what was subsequently s. 13(1) of the Factories Act 1961, that a grindstone wheel moving at 1,450 revolutions per minute was dangerous, although the evidence showed that it would be impossible to provide a guard which would make the machine usable. The reasoning of Viscount Simonds is sufficiently interesting to warrant quoting at length:

> In particular, I think it is clear that the obligation imposed by the section to fence securely . . . is an absolute obligation. And by that, I mean that it is not to be qualified by such words as 'so far as practicable' or 'so long as it can be fenced consistently with its being used for the purposes for which it is intended' or similar words. I come to this conclusion for the following reasons . . . First, it appears to me to be an illegitimate method of interpretation of a statute, whose dominant purpose is to protect the workman, to introduce by implication words of which the effect must be to reduce that protection. Secondly, where it has been thought desirable to introduce such qualifying words, the legislature has found no difficulty in doing so . . . Thirdly, it was decided as long ago as 1919 . . . that the obligation . . . was absolute and that, if the result of a machine being securely fenced was that it would not remain commercially practicable or mechanically possible, that did not affect the obligation: the statute would, in effect, prohibit its use . . . Fourthly, the provision to s. 14(1) affords a strong indication that the substantive part of it imposes an absolute obligation: for, unless its effect is absolutely to prevent the operator from coming into contact with a dangerous part of the machine, there would be little meaning in the provision of an alternative which has just that effect. Fifthly, the absolute obligation imposed by s. 14(1) is subject to the regulation-making power of the Minister . . .

One way in which the courts have interpreted the strict liability of fencing provisions such as s. 14(1) has been to read in a proviso that the defendant will only be liable if it is 'reasonably foreseeable' that the machine is dangerous if unfenced. In *Hindle* v. *Birtwhistle* [1897] it was held that because it was reasonably foreseeable that a shuttle might fly out of a loom, either as a result of careless handling or impurity in the material, the machine ought to be fenced. However, case law on reasonable foresight in relation to fencing provisions has by no means always been invoked to the advantage of the worker.

In *Burns* v. *Joseph Terry & Sons Ltd* [1950] a machine was guarded by a rail about four feet above the floor, but parts above this rail were only partially guarded. Above the machinery was a shelf. The plaintiff climbed a ladder to empty the shelf and got his hand caught in the machinery. In a claim for breach of s. 13(1) (fencing of transmission machinery) the Court of Appeal found that the defendant was not liable because the machinery was fenced against reasonably foreseeable dangers.

25. Duty to do what is 'practicable'

The view that an element of fault ought properly to be present in defendants before they are made liable for breach of duties is reflected in the interpretation of duties in which the defendants are required to do what is 'practicable'. The courts have considered that what is practicable must be judged by the state of technical and, where relevant, medical knowledge at the time when the defendant is alleged to be in breach of duty. Thus in *Richards* v. *Highway Ironfounders (West Bromwich) Ltd* [1955] the Court of Appeal found that the defendants were not in breach of their duty under the first limb of s. 47(1) of the Factories Act 1937, although they had failed to take all practicable, or any, measures to protect the plaintiff against the inhalation of dust and had failed to provide appliances, although the nature of the process made it practicable so to do. The Court of Appeal so held because at the time in question it was not known that the dust created by the process in which the plaintiff was working was injurious. They were liable under the second limb of s. 47(1), which required them to take protective precautions whenever dust was in substantial quantities!

A similar interpretation was placed on the first limb of s. 47(1) of the 1937 Act by the Court of Appeal in *Adsett* v. *K and L Steelfounders & Engineers Ltd* [1953], in that instance in relation to the state of technical knowledge. The defendants having failed to provide a satisfactory dust extraction system until some time after the plaintiff had first been at risk, Singleton LJ commented:

> I realise that . . . the question is whether they had taken all practicable measures, but it must be remembered that, until the defendants discovered the system of installing an extractor under the grid, there was no such system in existence. Can it then be said that the system which they discovered was practicable long before such discovery? . . . it would appear to be hard on the defendants if, in those circumstances, they were made liable for not discovering sooner something which, for the benefit of the community, they discovered in 1941 . . .

26. Cause of the injury

The plaintiff will not succeed in his claim unless he has suffered an injury caused by the risk the provision was intended to control. The problem of causation was especially evident in relation to the fencing provisions of the Factories Act. In *British Railways Board* v. *Liptrot* [1969] it was held that since the fencing requirements only related to dangerous parts of a machine it could not be relied on by a plaintiff who had suffered injury because the machine as a whole was unsafe. In *Eaves* v. *Morris Motors Ltd* [1961] it was held that fencing required for a part of machinery did not help a plaintiff where injury had been caused by a workpiece moving under power and held in the machine by a chuck, nor did it include injury caused by materials in the machinery. In *Sparrow* v. *Fairey Aviation Co Ltd* [1964] it was held that the worker is not protected if what comes into contact with the dangerous part of a machine is a handtool used by the worker, as distinct from the worker's body or clothing. And in *Nicholls* v. *Austin (Leyton) Ltd* [1946] it was held that the provisions did not protect the worker from materials, such as pieces of work, thrown out from the machine.

27. Controversial interpretations

Most controversial of all, in *Carroll* v. *Andrew Barclay & Sons Ltd* [1948] the House of Lords held that the fencing provisions were intended to protect the worker from getting into the machine, not to protect the worker from injury by pieces of flying material ejected from the machine: so in this case s. 13 did not provide a remedy where an accident was caused by the breaking of a belt. Further, in *Close* v. *Steel Company of Wales Ltd* [1962] the plaintiff could not recover damages for breach of s. 14(1) in respect of injury suffered when the bit of an electric drilling machine shattered and entered his left eye. While bits frequently shattered, there was no evidence of such an accident having happened before because the pieces were generally light and did not fly out with force. The House accepted the proposition that 'the fence is intended to keep the worker out, not to keep the machine or its product in' and did not think that this interpretation should be modified in cases where it was foreseeable that workers might be injured by materials, parts of the machine or workpieces, ejected from the machine.

DEFENCES TO BREACH OF DUTY

28. General

The defendant may be able to plead a defence, either one of the general defences to civil liability, or a defence made available by the statutory provision itself in the context of criminal liability, provided this has been allowed by the legislation in question (s. 47(3) of the 1974 Act).

29. In civil actions

Special defences available in criminal proceedings may therefore not be readily available in civil actions. For example, the Chemicals (Hazard Information and

Packaging) Regulations 1994 give a person injured by breach of these regulations a right to sue (regulation 16(1)(b)), while in criminal proceedings only the defendant has the defence that he took 'all reasonable precautions and exercised all due diligence' to avoid the commission of the offence (regulation 16(4)). (Section 47(3) of the 1974 Act would seem to mean that the defence would not be available in civil litigation, since the regulations did not state that it would be so available.)

30. Defence of 'due diligence'

A number of the new regulations allow the defendant in criminal proceedings to avoid liability where it is established 'due diligence' has been exercised, but the use of this defence is by no means universal. Many of the post-1974 regulations have been pitched at the level of what is reasonably practicable, which is a defence available to the employer, against criminal liability (s. 40) and might historically have been invoked in civil liability (*Nimmo* v. *Alexander Cowan & Sons Ltd* [1968]). It may be, however, that s. 47(3) has denied the employer of this defence to civil liability under regulations made subsequent to the 1974 Act. The regulations to implement individual Directives made under the Framework Directive are apparently of strict liability. They usually require an employer 'to ensure'. For example Regulation 5(1) of the Provision and Use of Work Equipment Regulations 1992 provides that:

> Every employer shall ensure that work equipment is so constructed or adapted as to be suitable for the purpose for which it is used or provided.

However Regulation 5(4) provides:

> In this regulation 'suitable' means suitable in any respect which it is reasonably foreseeable will affect the health or safety of any person.

An employer might therefore plead, by way of defence, that what had occurred was not reasonably foreseeable.

Some of the new regulations also incorporate the concept of reasonable practicability. For example, Regulation 9(3) of the Workplace (Health, Safety and Welfare) Regulations 1992 provides:

> So far as is reasonably practicable, waste materials shall not be allowed to accumulate in a workplace except in suitable receptacles.

Regulation 3 of the Management of Health and Safety at Work Regulations 1992 imposes a strict duty on employers to carry out a risk assessment for the purpose of identifying the measures which must be taken to comply with the requirements of the 'relevant statutory provisions'; many of these provisions require the employer to do what is reasonably practicable to achieve health and safety in the circumstances to which they apply.

STATUTORY MODIFICATION OF THE COMMON LAW

31. General

Parliament has, upon occasion, made statutory provision for situations where judge-made case law has failed to cater adequately for accident compensation. The two areas relevant to this work where the legislature has intervened are occupiers' liability and consumer protection. The statutory modification of occupiers' liability has been discussed.

32. The Consumer Protection Act 1987

The Consumer Protection Act 1987 must now be considered. Part I of that Act, passed to enable UK law to comply with an EC Directive on product liability, imposes strict liability for unsafe goods. It was intended to make an alternative and better provision than the tort of negligence for those who suffered injury as a result of defective goods: by releasing them from the burden of proving that the goods were defective because of the defendant's negligent conduct.

33. Who is protected?

The legislation enables any person to sue in tort in respect of death or personal injury or any loss of or damage to any private property (s. 5). A worker injured in the workplace, though not normally considered to be in the category of 'consumer', might nevertheless be able to bring an action under the Act.

34. Who is liable?

The Act places liability upon producers (s. 2). A producer is a person who has manufactured a product or, in the case of a substance which has not been manufactured, but has been won or abstracted, the person who won or abstracted it, or the person who carried out an industrial process in respect of it (for example, in relation to agricultural produce) (s. 1(2)). The Act does not apply to the producer of game or agricultural products which have not been subject to an industrial process at the time they were supplied (s. 2(4)). The producer of a product in which components or raw materials are comprised is not necessarily liable for faults in the components (s. 1(3)): the Act intends liability to lie with the producer of the unsafe part. Liability may be imposed on any person who holds himself out as being the producer of the product, for example by putting his name on the product, or on any person who has imported the product into the EC. The Act recognises that the plaintiff may have difficulty in identifying the producer of the defective product so the plaintiff may in appropriate circumstances look to the supplier or others in the chain of distribution. The supplier may be left bearing liability if unable to identify other persons, such as the producer, who ought more properly to bear the responsibility.

35. What is a product?

For the purposes of the Act product means any goods or electricity, and includes anything that forms part of, or is a component of, another product. The general interpretation section (s. 45) states that goods includes substances, growing crops and things comprised in land by virtue of being attached to it and any ship, aircraft or vehicle.

36. When are goods defective?

Section 3 provides that a product will be deemed to be defective if: 'the safety of the product is not such as persons generally are entitled to expect'.

In determining what persons might be entitled to expect, circumstances which are to be taken into account include the manner in which, and purposes for which, the product has been marketed (s. 3(2)(a)); what might reasonably be expected to be done with or in relation to the product (s. 3(2)(b)); and the time when the product was supplied by its producer (s. 3(2)(c)). It might well be, therefore, that a producer would not be liable for injury caused if products intended for domestic use were subjected to the same use as 'heavy duty' models normally supplied to industrial users. This would suggest that if an employer acquired domestic equipment for use at the workplace, any subsequent injury suffered by a person employed at that workplace would be attributed to the employer's negligence rather than to the statutory liability of the producer of the goods. If the equipment had been brought to the workplace by the worker himself, as might be the case in respect of certain relatively small handtools, the employer might still be negligent in permitting the worker to do this.

37. Defences

Section 4 of the Act provides the following defences to the producer of defective goods:

(a) that the defect is attributable to compliance with any requirement imposed by or under any enactment or with any Community obligation; . . .

This defence is quite narrow. It does not mean that if goods comply with relevant regulatory standards they cannot be the subject of liability under this Act. The paragraph only provides a defence where the regulatory standard is the cause of the defect. For example, if the product were manufactured in compliance with relevant electrical standards, the producer would not be liable if damage were suffered because these standards proved inappropriate. If, however, the injury was suffered because the plastic casing housing the product was inadequate the producer would not be able to rely on his compliance with the electricity regulations to exempt him from liability.

The following defences all relate to circumstances in which the goods came into use and are fairly self-explanatory:

(b) that the person proceeded against did not at any time supply the product to another; or

(c) that the following conditions are satisfied, that is to say –

(i) that the only supply of the product to another by the person proceeded against was otherwise than in the course of a business of that person's; and

(*ii*) that [the defendant was not the producer or if he were he did not act with a view to a profit]; or

(d) that the defect did not exist in the product at the [time when the defendant supplied it].

The so-called 'state of the art' defence is more controversial:

(e) that the state of scientific and technical knowledge at the relevant time was not such that a producer of products of the same description as the product in question might be expected to have discovered the defect if it had existed in his products while they were under his control.

This defence enables the producer to establish that the defect was not generally appreciated within the industry at the time at which the particular unsafe product was put on the market. The defence is very relevant to chemical substances and, as far as the consumer market is concerned, is of especial value to the pharmaceutical industry. If the defendant successfully raises this defence the plaintiff is thrust back on the law of negligence to establish that the defendant was at fault in not being aware of the risk. It is not unknown for judges to declare an industry negligent, but the task of the plaintiff to achieve such a ruling must inevitably be a hard one. The producer of a component of a product may raise the defence that the defect was not in the component but was attributable to the design of the end product or to compliance by the defendant producer with instructions given by the producer of the subsequent product (s. 4(1)(f)).

38. Application of the Act

Part I of the Act applies to products put into circulation after 1 March 1988 and liability may be attached to the producer for up to ten years after the product has been put into circulation, though clearly the longer the product has been in circulation the more probable that the producer will be able to establish that the defect was not there when the product was put into circulation.

The liability described above is completely independent of criminal liability: Part II of the 1987 Act deals separately with criminal liability.

Section 41 of the Act provides (in language, and with purpose, not dissimilar to that used in s. 47(2) of the 1974 Act):

(1) An obligation imposed by safety regulations shall be a duty owed to any person who may be affected by a contravention of the obligation and, subject to any provision to the contrary in the regulations and to the defences and other incidents applying to actions for breach of statutory duty, a contravention of any such obligation shall be actionable accordingly.

Thus under the 1987 Act as under the 1974 Act regulations whose primary sanctions are criminal may also be the basis of civil liability.

39. Relationship with other statutory provisions

The Employer's Liability (Defective Equipment) Act 1969 enables the injured employee to sue his employer, rather than the manufacturer of any defective equipment which had caused him injury in the course of his employment. The employee might consider the 1969 Act provides more valuable rights than the 1987 Act. Apart, however, from the fact that the two pieces of legislation are not necessarily coterminous in relation to workplace accidents (e.g. the terms 'product' and 'defective equipment' might not bear the same meaning), the plaintiff under the 1969 Act cannot succeed unless he can show that the manufacturer of the defective product had been negligent, whereas under the 1987 Act liability is strict.

It would appear that there is a considerable similarity between articles and substances to which s. 6 of the 1974 Act relates and the products to which the 1987 Act relates, but there is no civil action for any person who suffers personal injury as a result of a breach of s. 6 of the 1974 Act. On the other hand, the 'state of the art' defence might be less significant at the workplace than in the general market, bearing in mind the duties which s. 6 of the 1974 Act imposes on manufacturers and suppliers (and others) of articles and substances for use at the workplace, to carry out research and testing before they are put into use, and the duties which the Control of Substances Hazardous to Health Regulations impose on employers in relation to substances used at the workplace.

40. Likely future developments

This chapter has had to rely on interpretation of statutory provisions, of considerable age: indeed many of them, while containing words like 'provide' which are to be found in current regulations, are themselves actually or virtually obsolete. The future of this kind of civil liability can only be a matter of speculation; but the following matters may be noted:

(a) In future, liability will be capable of arising only under Regulations made under the 1974 Act: there will be no question of liability under primary legislation – except under Part I of the Consumer Protection Act 1987.

(b) The nature of the post-1974 regulations is different from that of the statutory provisions which gave rise to many of the precedents cited in this chapter. The new Regulations lay down systems rather than standards. This might in itself give rise to a rather broader approach to the interpretation of the provisions.

(c) Civil litigation is less likely to be reported than it was twenty or thirty years ago when many of the precedents were created. This is because:
    (i) many cases are settled out of court
    (ii) much more litigation is in the county courts nowadays and therefore not reported

(*iii*) reporting is itself rather more selective: cases which do not include important points of law are not widely reported.

(d) There is a subtle change in the judicial approach to statutory interpretation, especially where the provision to be interpreted is one which is intended, as is likely to be the case in respect of occupational health and safety, to implement European Directives. The judges look less to the wording of the provision and more to its intention.

(e) The development of the tort of negligence makes it less necessary for litigants to rely on statutory provisions.

(f) The changed nature of work risks: the Factories Acts were largely concerned with the hazards faced by those engaged in heavy industry. A higher proportion of workplace injury nowadays is concerned with ill-health rather than accidents. It will, however, be interesting to monitor whether the Manual Handling Operations Regulations 1992 result in civil litigation, given that in the introduction to their publication on these Regulations the Health and Safety Executive state that more than a quarter of the accidents reported each year are associated with manual handling.

(g) Judges may be less willing to create liability for breach of statutory duty where the statute is silent on the matter. For example in *Richardson* v. *Pitt-Stanley and Others* (1994) the Court of Appeal had to consider whether a director of a company which had failed to insure against liability to its employees, as required by the Employers' Liability (Compulsory Insurance) Act 1969, could be made personally liable to pay damages to an employee who had suffered injury in the course of employment. Section 5 of the Act provided for a criminal penalty. While criminal liability rested primarily on the employer s. 5 provided that

> where an offence under this section committed by a corporation has been committed with the consent or connivance of, or facilitated by any neglect on the part of, any director, manager, secretary or other officer of the corporation he, as well as the corporation, shall be deemed to be guilty of that offence . . .

On the facts of the case the director could be held criminally liable for the company's failure to comply with the Act but in the view of the majority of their Lordships this did not entitle them to impose civil liability upon him. In the view of Russell LJ it would be anomalous if the directors were to bear civil liability while the company of which they were directors was subject to no such liability.

Progress test 15

1. What provision does the Health and Safety at Work Act make for civil liability for breach of statutory duty?

2. What must a plaintiff prove to succeed in an action for breach of statutory duty?

3. To what extent is 'foresight' relevant to breach of statutory duty?

4. What defences are there to actions for breach of statutory duty?

5. How does the Consumer Protection Act fundamentally alter common law liability?

6. Has the plaintiff necessarily lost a product liability claim if the defendant successfully pleads the state of the art defence?

16

GENERAL DEFENCES TO CIVIL LIABILITY

1. Introduction

In strict theory a defendant does not have to plead a defence until the plaintiff has established the defendants' liability. There are two general defences to civil liability:

(a) *volenti non fit injuria*; and
(b) contributory negligence.

These defences have in common that the defendant alleges that the plaintiff's conduct has been such as to affect the defendant's liability.

VOLENTI NON FIT INJURIA

2. The plaintiff was *volens* of the risk

The defence of *volenti non fit injuria*, which translates loosely as assumption of risk, rarely succeeds in employment situations. In *Smith* v. *Baker* [1891] the House of Lords distinguished knowledge (*sciens*) from acceptance (*volens*) and found that, although a plaintiff might know of a risk, he might not have accepted it. If he had no power to remove the risk, his only way of avoiding it would have been to terminate his employment. A similar decision was reached in *Bunker* v. *Charles Brand & Son Ltd* [1969], a case brought by a visiting worker against the occupier of premises. Following these two cases there have been very few cases where the courts have found that a plaintiff worker accepted the risk which led to his injury. Where the defence succeeds it completely releases the defendant from liability.

3. Plaintiff at fault

Where the plaintiff worker has been at fault difficult questions can arise as to whether or not the fault has been so great as to make the plaintiff rather than the employer responsible for his injury. Thus in *Qualcast (Wolverhampton) Ltd*

v. *Haynes* [1959] an experienced employee who failed to use protective equipment was unable to attach any liability to his employers for the injury which he suffered as a result of his conduct. It was not a case of the employee accepting the employers' negligence: the fault was entirely that of the employee.

The situation is less clear where two workers have created a risk when working together and as a result of their conduct one or both of them is injured. In this case, while the employer is perhaps faultless, he might be made vicariously liable for the negligence of the one worker which caused injury to the other. This factual situation has been before the House of Lords on at least two occasions.

In *Stapley* v. *Gypsum Mines Ltd* [1953] the employers had instructed the deceased (Stapley) and another employee (Dale) to bring down the roof of part of the gypsum mine to make the working place safe. The workers could not achieve this but the deceased continued to work in the area and was killed when the roof fell. It was argued for the employers that the accident was the result of the negligence of the worker and they should not bear any liability. The House of Lords, on a careful consideration of the facts, found that Dale's negligence, in failing to take proper steps to bring the roof down, had to some extent caused the accident and for Dale's negligence the employers were vicariously liable.

Their Lordships came to a different conclusion in *Imperial Chemical Industries Ltd* v. *Shatwell* [1965]. George and James Shatwell were two shotfirers who, in disregard of both their employers' instructions and statutory duties imposed on them personally, created a risk which resulted in personal injury to them both. In George's action against the employers it was held that they were not vicariously liable; *Stapley*'s case was considered to be an authority only on the matter of causation, the defence of *volenti* not being considered. Their Lordships found that on the facts the brothers had been *volens* of the risk they were creating. The plaintiff had fully appreciated the risk the brothers were taking; moreover, the statutory duty which had been broken was one which was placed on the plaintiff employee personally. So the employers were not liable.

4. Rescue situations

The defence rarely succeeds where the plaintiff has gone outside the scope of his employment in order to assist in an emergency situation, or to carry out a rescue. In rescue cases, however, the defendant will be the person whose negligence caused the danger, and this may not be the employer of the plaintiff. So in *Haynes* v. *Harwood* [1935] the defendant's horse was negligently left where it might cause injury to children. A child threw a stone and the horse bolted. The plaintiff policeman managed to stop the horse but was seriously injured. It was held that the defence that the policeman was *volens* of the risk could not be raised by the defendant.

CONTRIBUTORY NEGLIGENCE

5. General

Contributory negligence is a defence which the defendant may raise: it is not for the court to raise the issue even though the evidence may suggest the plaintiff was partly to blame (*Fookes* v. *Slaytor* [1979]). At common law proof of the plaintiff's negligence was a complete defence and the plaintiff was left remediless. The Law Reform (Contributory Negligence) Act 1945 now governs the situation and it provides for the apportionment of liability between plaintiff and defendant in cases of contributory negligence by the plaintiff. Section 1(1) provides that the damages recoverable:

> . . . shall be reduced to such extent as the court thinks just and equitable having regard to the claimant's share in the responsibility for the damage . . .

Section 1(2) requires the court to find and record the total damages which would have been recoverable if the claimant had not been at fault. In practice the plaintiff's damages are reduced by a percentage comparable to the degree of fault which the court finds in the plaintiff.

6. 'Negligence' and 'fault'

The title of the Act refers to 'negligence', but s. 1(1) uses the word 'fault' and states that damages shall be apportioned:

> Where any person suffers damage as the result partly of his own fault and partly of the fault of any other person or persons . . .

Section 4 states:

> 'Fault' means negligence, breach of statutory duty or other act or omission which gives rise to a liability in tort or would, apart from this Act, give rise to the defence of contributory negligence.

7. Interpretation of 'fault'

It has also been held that fault applies both to conduct causing the accident and to conduct affecting the severity of the injury. This interpretation has arisen from a number of road accident cases concerning the wearing of seat-belts (e.g. *Froom* v. *Butcher* [1975]) and crash helmets (*O'Connell* v. *Jackson* [1972]); in these cases wearing the protective equipment would not have avoided the collision but it would have made the consequences of the collision less severe. While this approach does not appear to have been expressly adopted in industrial accident cases it has in a sense been acknowledged: in *Bux* v. *Slough Metals Ltd* [1974], for example, where the plaintiff suffered eye injury when not wearing goggles, it was not suggested that goggles would have prevented the plaintiff being splashed with molten liquid – they would, however, have protected the plaintiff from serious injury. Although the argument was not presented in this way, the plaintiff's contributory negligence in not wearing available goggles did result in his damages being reduced.

8. Availability of the defence

Section 4 makes it clear that the defence is available in both common-law negligence and breach of statutory duty claims. The fault of the plaintiff is more likely to be negligence, though there are, as has been noted, occasions (e.g. *Ginty* v. *Belmont Building Supplies Ltd* [1959]) where plaintiff and defendant are both in breach of statutory duty. In such cases the plaintiff's damage may be reduced. In some less frequent cases the defendant may sometimes escape all liability if his duty is no more than coterminous with the duty which the plaintiff has broken (as in *Ginty*).

9. Plaintiff's standard of care

Where the defendant argues that the plaintiff's conduct has been negligent a question then arises as to the standard of care the plaintiff ought to exercise. Should his conduct be judged by the same standard as is applied to the conduct of the defendant? In road accident cases, where both plaintiff and defendant are drivers, it is clear that the conduct should be to the same standard in each case. It is not certain that this is so where the plaintiff is an employee and the defendant is his employer: it was not the view expressed by the House of Lords in *Caswell* v. *Powell Duffryn Associated Collieries Ltd* [1940]. In this case the plaintiff was the mother of a miner who was killed in the defendants' mine by reason of the defendants' breach of their statutory duty to fence machinery. Lord Atkin put forward this argument:

> The argument is that safety obligations are placed upon employers for the purpose of protecting not only workmen who are careful but also those who are careless: and that the object of the legislature is defeated if the right to sue for injuries caused by the breach of the safety regulations is denied to the careless workman for whose benefit amongst others the legislation was specially enacted.

While Lord Porter did not go so far as this, he did suggest that the standard of care expected of the worker might not be the high standard expected of persons in other circumstances. He said:

> The skill gained by a worker may enable him to take risks and do acts which in an unskilled man would be negligence, and on the other hand the fatiguing repetition of the same work may make a man incapable of the same care, and therefore not guilty of negligence, in doing or failing to do an act which a man less fatigued would do or leave undone . . .

10. Regard to all the circumstances

Neither of their Lordships was making a statement of general application to all industrial accident cases: their statements were made in the context of, and would seem to have no relevance beyond, breach of statutory duty cases.

254

Moreover, it must be borne in mind that they were made at a time when contributory negligence completely defeated a claim for damages. Now that this is no longer so it is arguably better for the court to apply a common standard of care but take into account the argument of Lord Porter when apportioning damages. That the Act should have this effect was argued by Denning LJ in *Davies* v. *Swan Motor Co (Swansea) Ltd* [1949]:

> The legal effect of the Act of 1945 is simple enough. If the plaintiff's negligence was one of the causes of his damage, he is no longer defeated altogether. He gets reduced damages. The practical effect of the Act is, however, wider than its legal effect. Previously, to mitigate the harshness of the doctrine of contributory negligence, the courts in practice sought to select, from a number of competing causes, which was *the* cause – the effective or predominant cause – of the damage and to reject the rest. Now the courts have regard to all the causes and apportion the damages accordingly.

There is evidence that this is what in fact happens. For example, in *Laszczyk* v. *National Coal Board* [1954], while the plaintiff was held to be contributorily negligent, being in breach of a statutory duty binding on himself, the court noted that he was at the time acting under instructions from his superior, and his damages were reduced by a mere 5%.

Progress test 16

1. What are the principal defences to common law liability?

2. Why did the defence of assumption of risk succeed in *ICI* v. *Shatwell*?

3. What statute governs the defence of contributory negligence?

4. How does the statute define 'fault'?

Part Four

SYSTEMS AND PROCEDURES AT THE WORKPLACE

17

SAFE SYSTEMS AT THE WORKPLACE

1. Introduction

The previous chapters have been concerned with the rules of law created by Parliament and judges in relation to the prevention and compensation of personal injury. The remainder of this book will consider procedures and systems which the law, or good management practice, require for the achievement of safe workplaces.

2. The importance of systems

The law places emphasis on systems. The common law of negligence expects organisations to operate to safe systems. The 1974 Act, in its general duties, demands a systematic approach to safety: regulations after 1974, such as the Control of Substances Hazardous to Health Regulations 1988 (re-issued in 1994), also require employers systematically to assess situations and then respond in systematic ways. This approach was taken much further in the British response – i.e. the Six Pack – to recent European Directives. Indeed the need for a systematic approach is now so deeply embedded into regulatory provisions that it is clear that no organisation can discharge its safety obligations without a complete systematic review of its operation. Whatever particular regulations, such as the Manual Handling Operations Regulations 1992, may require for particular tasks or situations, the risk assessment requirement of Regulation 3 of the Management of Health and Safety at Work Regulations 1992 clearly demands a thorough review of the whole of the organisation's undertaking, by the employer, or the self-employed person, as the case may be.

Regulation 3 states that this risk assessment is:

> for the purpose of identifying the measures he needs to take to comply with the requirements and prohibitions imposed upon him by or under the relevant statutory provisions.

The introduction of the Six Pack substantially reduces the number of situations in which the organisation is, by virtue of specific regulations, required to take a systematic approach to risks.

However, in its *Review of Health and Safety Regulation* [1994] the HSC identified that there was still 'clearly a case for bringing together the risk assessment . . . provisions of modern legislation.' They then identified eight sets of regulations making a requirement for some risk assessment.

THE SAFETY POLICY

3. General duty

It was noted when considering employers' general duties to their employees that s. 2(3) of the 1974 Act requires employers to prepare and, as often as appropriate, revise a safety policy and to bring this policy to the notice of all of their employees. The general requirements of s. 2(3) are now supplemented by Regulation 4 of the Management of Health and Safety at Work Regulations which requires:

(1) Every employer shall make and give effect to such arrangements as are appropriate, having regard to the nature of his activities and the size of his undertaking, for the effective planning, organisation, control, monitoring and review of the preventive and protective measures.

(2) Where the employer employs five or more employees, he shall record the arrangements referred to in paragraph (1).

It should be noted, however, that the employer is not required by 4(2) to record the arrangements in writing: possibly, for example, the information could be stored on computer. There is in Regulation 8 a requirement to provide the information to employees.

4. Content of the safety policy

Section 2(3) makes three specific requirements of an employer in respect of the safety policy:

(a) a general statement of policy (5–7)

(b) the organisation for safety (8–12)

(c) the arrangements for carrying out the policy (13–14).

The essence of a safety policy is that it has to be tailor-made for an organisation by that organisation. Nevertheless the following comments may be made.

5. Statement of policy

What is required is a general statement of intent. The language and apparent philosophy of s. 2(3) may seem a little dated in the 1990s, in the context of corporate planning, because it does not ask that the employer have a safety plan for progression over time: it merely requires that the employer make a statement of commitment to safety. In practice many organisations have produced a single side of paper, doing little more than stating that the employer intends to comply with the Act, and often going on to say that they expect all employees and other persons to comply with the duties which the Act imposes on them. This brief statement usually bears the signature of a senior member of management as further indication that the senior managers of the organisation are committed to the policy.

6. Safety policy and the corporate plan

The corporate plan will undoubtedly have set out the company's aims and objectives, probably for a five-year period, indicating the goals the organisation intends to achieve in terms of development of markets, expansion of turnover, reduction of production costs and so on. Arguably a safe organisation ought at least to cross-reference its safety policy, and other safety arrangements, to its corporate plan. The suggestion that safety be built into the corporate plan is the more pertinent bearing in mind that since s. 79 of the Companies Act 1967 there has been a possibility that regulations might impose a requirement that the public company's annual report to shareholders include a statement on the company's safety performance in the year under review. While regulations do not appear to have been made, the power to do so is repeated in s. 235, and Schedule 7, Part IV of the Companies Act 1985.

Moreover, now that so many organisations include environmental protection as one of their corporate objectives it will, at least, be anomalous if improvement of workplace safety is not a corporate objective.

7. Impact of policy on workforce

Section 2(3) of the 1974 Act apparently perceived the safety policy as an organ-isational commitment to employees and required the employer to bring the policy to the attention of the employees. Experience suggests that the policy statement makes little impact on employees. Whether this is important may be questioned provided employees have been trained to operate the safe systems which it envisages for their particular work. Interestingly, the recording require-ment under Regulation 4(2) of the Management of Health and Safety at Work Regulations 1992 is more explicitly a management tool. As has been noted, while Regulation 4 does not require the employer to provide employees with a record of the arrangements made for health and safety, the requirement to inform employees is in Regulation 8.

8. Safety organisation

The second requirement of s. 2(3) is that the employer set out his organisation for safety. Formerly it was perceived that the safety policy ought to have appended to it a list of the personnel with safety responsibilities from senior management down, and the chain of communication between these persons and this information might be expressed in, or at least supplemented by, a chart.

Such charts are less likely to be appropriate in current organisational structures where responsibilities are often devolved to divisions or departments. In this environment it is, however, all the more important to set out clearly the extent to which local managers are intended to budget for, adopt and enforce safety matters. It has, for example, become customary to expect risk assessment to be undertaken by management at a local level, certainly in relation to matters within the span of their management responsibility.

The provision of information in the policy should reiterate the terms of individual contracts of employment and also serve as a source of information to the workforce who will need to know both their own responsibilities and the managers to whom they should communicate matters related to safety.

It is misguided to avoid spelling out individual roles because 'safety is everyone's business.' Each individual needs to be aware of personal responsibilities and how these relate to the responsibilities of other persons within the organisation.

Even in today's streamlined organisational systems it must remain good practice to indicate a senior manager – probably at board level (perhaps the person who signed the policy statement) – to take ultimate responsibility for safety within the organisation.

9. Requirement for 'competent' persons

It may well be that the organisation will have appointed a safety officer/adviser/manager with responsibilities confined to safety. While this person should be identified in the safety policy, it will be misguided to believe that such an appointee, who may be a relatively junior manager, can have total responsibility for safety.

The appointment of 'competent' persons to assist the employer in undertaking the measures he needs to take, to comply with the requirements and prohibitions imposed upon him by statutory provisions, in compliance with Regulation 6 of the Management of Health and Safety at Work Regulations 1992, will necessitate the identification of persons, either within the organisation, or without, with special safety responsibilities; it may be logical to name these persons in the safety policy. But it will rarely be appropriate to expect the safety officer to accept full responsibility unless such officer is both very highly qualified and appointed to the highest level of management within the organisation, having both resources and authority to demand money be spent and action taken when necessary.

10. Safety representatives

While safety representatives may be mentioned in publications describing the system within the organisation it should be remembered that they are not persons with management responsibilities for safety. The names of safety representatives might be given to enable employees to know the persons with whom safety issues may be discussed. However, including the names of employee safety representatives is going beyond what s. 2(3) envisages and employers may consider it preferable to encourage employees to communicate on safety issues directly with management rather than to management through safety representatives. Indeed, given the duty which Regulation 12 of the Management of Health and Safety at Work Regulations 1992 places on employees to notify their employer or 'any other employee of that employer with specific responsibility for the health and safety of his fellow employees' it may be positively misleading to name safety representatives in the safety policy, since it is unlikely (though not impossible) that the employer's system will authorise safety representatives to act as the employer's agent for the receipt of such information.

Employers will no doubt have a view on the kind of role they would like safety representatives to perform, but at a time when the whole concept of worker participation is controversial it is not wise to be categorical about the systems of good practice which employers should encourage.

11. Effect of producing a safety policy

The process of producing a safety policy may cause organisations to look critically at their organisational structure generally and discover weaknesses that are of significance to matters other than safety.

12. Safety arrangements

Management, preferably through specialist safety personnel, should since 1974 have become aware of the desirability of considering the various tasks which have to be performed in the course of the organisation's ordinary activities, having regard to the situations which do or might occur, identifying where there are hazards and laying down routine procedures for dealing with them. Many organisations have dealt with these matters by annexing to, rather than writing into, their safety policy, codes of practice setting out routines and procedures for dealing with hazardous situations. Risk assessment should refine this process.

13. Matters to be addressed

Safety arrangements must ensure that all relevant Regulations are complied with. In practice it is likely to be necessary to have systems for ensuring that:

(a) Only authorised personnel are on the premises, and for ensuring visitors are instructed about, or protected from, hazards both for their own safety and for the safety of others.

(b) Adequate arrangements have been made to enable persons and vehicles to pass safely through the property, including members of the public where the public are lawful visitors to the premises (see Regulation 17 of the Workplace (Health, Safety and Welfare) Regulations 1992).

(c) Purchasing procedures are such that products introduced into the workplace are free from hazard, or, if this is not possible, risks are identified and controlled.

Particular regard should be had to the Control of Substances Hazardous to Health Regulations 1994 and the Chemicals (Hazard Information and Packaging for Supply) Regulations 1994.

(d) Suitable personnel are selected and personnel are properly trained for the functions they have to perform (the Six Pack continually emphasises the need for training).

(e) Personnel are provided with and trained to use whatever protective equipment is necessary for their work (see Personal Protective Equipment at Work Regulations 1992).

(f) Appropriate plant and equipment is selected, properly used and properly maintained (see Provision and Use of Work Equipment Regulations 1992).

(g) Visiting workers are properly informed as to the hazards and procedures of the site, and detailed arrangements are made to ensure they can work safely and do not endanger others by their work (see Regulation 10 of the Management of Health and Safety at Work Regulations 1992).

(h) Maintenance and other similar work is not undertaken without granting a 'permit to work', and once such a permit has been granted its terms are followed by the worker to whom it is granted, and it is observed by other workers (see, more generally, Regulation 7 of the Management of Health and Safety at Work Regulations 1992).

(i) Where major construction works are being undertaken there must be a system which meets the requirements of the Construction (Design and Management) Regulations 1994. (See also the Construction (Health Safety and Welfare) Regulations 1996.)

(j) There are proper emergency procedures to contend with fire and other catastrophes, ensuring, through practice drill, persons recognise the signal to evacuate the premises and know how to proceed when that signal is given (see Regulation 7 of the Management of Health and Safety at Work Regulations 1992).

(k) There is access for emergency services.

(l) There are proper systems for damage control, including, where appropriate, firefighting teams (see Fire Precautions Act 1971 and regulations made under it) and, in all cases, first-aid provision (see Health and Safety (First-Aid) Regulations 1981).

(m) Full consideration is given to the safety of the neighbourhood, including the control of routine emissions from the premises, the control of vehicular traffic, and the protection of the neighbouring community in the event of catastrophes. In those installations which fall under the relevant sections of the Control of Industrial Major Accidents Hazards Regulation 1984 these matters will need to be addressed in a safety case.

(n) Arrangements have been made to comply with the Control of Substances Hazardous to Health Regulations 1994 where it is not possible to avoid the use of hazardous substances.

(o) Proper arrangements are made for safety representatives to carry out their functions.

(p) There is a system for evaluating, and if necessary, acting on relevant information received from safety representatives or other persons (NB. Regulation 12 of the Management of Health and Safety at Work Regulations 1992).

(q) There are systems for keeping the safety policy under review and for the allocation of funds for routine updating and renewal of plant and equipment, for routine training of personnel and for responding to emergencies.

This list is inevitably somewhat general and may not include all the matters to which a particular organisation needs to pay attention. The matters which have to be addressed, and the way in which arrangements are made to deal with these matters, must vary from organisation to organisation and be tailor-made to suit the operation.

14. Preparation process

The safety policy must be in writing and brought to the attention of all employees. It must be updated whenever necessary. While it is not a legal requirement that the policy be drawn up and revised by management in discussion with employees, to involve employees in the exercise is certainly in the spirit of consultation between management and employees which is an important feature of the 1974 Act. More specifically, where there are safety representatives, appointed under the Safety Representatives and Safety Committees Regulations 1977, consultation with safety representatives about changing the safety policy would be within the ambit of Regulation 4A of those Regulations. Now that further regulations have been introduced to provide for safety representatives in other than unionised workplaces employers will need to consult with such representatives on these matters.

Nevertheless the production and content of the policy is ultimately management's responsibility.

15. Employee involvement

Involving employees in drawing up a policy is one way of alerting employees to the existence and content of the policy. At the very least, however, every employee ought to receive a personal copy of the published policy if the employer is to feel confident that he has discharged the duty to bring the policy to the attention of each employee.

16. Significance of policy

Drawing up a policy should cause an organisation to look critically at its provision for safety. The inspectorate has found the safety policy a useful starting point when conducting a workplace inspection. They will expect the policy and practice to coincide. To satisfy the inspectorate the policy must not merely be a piece of paper whose contents bear no relation to the realities of the workplace.

17. Updating of policy

Given the rapid economic changes which have occurred in recent years, resulting in changed workplace structures both in terms of technology and manpower, there may be many workplaces where a policy which was satisfactory when drawn up is well overdue for updating if it is to be meaningful.

THE IMPORTANCE OF RESOURCE MANAGEMENT

18. General

The 1974 Act differs fundamentally from earlier safety legislation in the emphasis which it places on the role of human behaviour in achieving safe systems. The outline account given above of the requirements of a safety policy serve to stress that this is so. The identification of hazards and of systems for their control, and the carrying out of the systems selected, all require careful selection, training and monitoring of personnel as indeed many of the new regulatory provisions stipulate. The duty which the Act places on employers to do all that is reasonably practicable to ensure safety at the workplace will not be achieved unless the employer has accepted the close relationship between safe systems and personnel and contracts management.

19. Legal enforcement of duties

While employers may note that the Act places complementary duties on both contractors and individual employees, those duties, like the employers' own duties, bear criminal sanctions and are enforced only by the inspectorate. Employers must utilise management systems to establish and maintain safety arrangements. In so far as employers can invoke the law it will be in contract rather than under the 1974 Act itself.

20. Safety arrangements

The following account will consider first the arrangements which an organisation should make to ensure that its own employees operate safely and secondly the arrangements which should be made by appropriate managers within the organisation to ensure that other organisations with which it deals have a similar concern for safety.

THE ORGANISATION AND ITS EMPLOYEES

21. General

Safety arrangements should be considered when identifying the specifications for jobs within the organisation; such consideration should largely determine the training needed for persons appointed to, or already on, the staff. In turn, safety performance in relation to these arrangements should both form a part of ongoing staff appraisal, and bear a significant relationship to disciplinary procedures. Throughout the process, from selection to dismissal, the contract of employment will be a material consideration.

22. Selection

When selecting individuals who are qualified and competent to fulfil employment roles safety requirements should be taken into account. Job specifications should be related to safety arrangements.

23. Qualifications required

There are currently relatively few cases in which the law dictates that employment roles with safety responsibilities must be given only to persons with specific qualifications, but this may change. Lead bodies are identifying the subject matter for courses to lead to National Vocational Qualifications. Many of these courses are likely to include some safety training. The Occupational Health and Safety Lead Body has produced the check list of competencies which will need to be demonstrated for NVQs levels 3 and 4 in Occupational Health and Safety Practice, and training courses may in future relate to these and aim to provide the background technical and academic information required for these NVQs for safety management. It may be some time before the law stipulates the vocational qualifications needed for particular jobs, but the time may soon come when whether a person has such qualifications is taken into account when considering whether they are competent for particular employment roles.

24. Competence

In some cases possession of a recognised qualification may be a necessary prerequisite for appointment; in other cases lack of qualification may create a presumption against suitability for a task. In all cases, however, competence will be something distinct from qualification. Paper qualification indicates only training for the task; competence indicates ability to perform the task. Full competence is likely to come only after experience of doing the work in question. Employers need to look for evidence of the employment record of the candidate, unless they are offering only a junior post. It is precisely this combination of knowledge and experience which NVQs seek.

25. The employment contract

The successful applicant will receive a contract of employment. While the law does not require this to be in writing it does require that an employee (whether part time or full time) be given, not later than two months after the beginning of employment, a written statement as evidence of certain of the terms and conditions of the employment. This document need not be the contract of employment, but the systematic employer may prefer to incorporate the material required by the statute (s. 1 of the Employment Rights Act 1996), into a full written contract indicating within it, or by reference to other documents, not only the matters required by the Act, but also terms and conditions which relate to job performance. The matters of relevance to safety include the title of the job, the nature of the task to be performed; the training, if any, that will be provided; the system of appraisal of performance; the length of any probation period, and disciplinary rules and procedures.

26. Importance of the contract of employment

The contract is vitally important because its provisions are the yardstick by which to measure whether or not the employee's work is at a satisfactory standard. Any existing employee who is re-deployed into different work should be provided with a new contractual document to reflect the new terms and conditions of employment.

27. Training

(a) *Induction*: it has for many years been customary to provide induction training for persons newly appointed to a workforce. The cost benefit of prolonged induction programmes may be doubted, since the amount of information that a person new to the organisation can absorb is probably limited. Induction is therefore best kept down to the minimum needed to ensure that the newcomer has a very broad understanding of the organisation but a sufficient knowledge of safety procedures.

(b) *Start of job*: many of the new regulations contained in the six pack specifically require the employer to provide training to workers before they begin to use plant or equipment. The employer will therefore be well advised to ensure that the new employee, or the long-standing employee placed in a new work situation, is conversant with the particular plant and equipment, including any personal protective equipment, before starting the job. This training should be provided even where the worker has been selected on the basis of being already trained for the situation.

(c) *On-going training*: following an induction training, the employee should be given a fuller training, over time, relating to the task for which the contract has been given. In the case of jobs with any management responsibilities, this training should cover not only the safety requirements of the job, but also the appropriate rudiments of human resource management, focusing on how to achieve performance by others and what to do if the required performance is not achieved.

28. Ongoing appraisal

When the initial training period is over the employee's performance should be monitored in the context of technical advances. The employee may be expected to be willing to adjust to evolutionary changes in workplace practices, such as the introduction of new plant and equipment or new methods of management, though the employer almost certainly will need to provide training for this (*Cresswell* v. *Board of Inland Revenue* [1984]).

29. Unsatisfactory performance

An employee's unsatisfactory performance of the contract, in relation to safety, or indeed other matters, may amount to breach of contract, warranting termination of the contract at common law, or enabling the employer to dismiss the employee fairly under the Employment Rights Act 1996. However, before dismissing an employee the employer should take care to ensure that the evidence of unsatisfactory performance is sufficient to warrant termination of the contract.

30. Termination of contract at common law

An employer may terminate the contract of an employee who has not two years' continuous full-time employment without risk of a complaint being made to an industrial tribunal by the employee who has been unfairly dismissed. In the case of such short-term employees, the employer need only have regard to the terms of the contract of the worker concerned, when considering whether terminating the contract could possibly lead to common-law liability for breach of contract.

If the contract has made adequate provision for a probationary period and appraisal of the employee within that period, and the performance of the worker has in fact been properly monitored in that period, there may be clear grounds for the employer to terminate the contract in the probationary period, without notice and without fear of litigation. To this must be added the important exception that an employee does not require any period of continuous employment to qualify to complain about discrimination or dismissal as a result of relevant activities or representations to the employer concerning health and safety at the workplace (Employment Rights Act 1996, s. 44 and s. 100).

31. Implied contractual terms

It has been held that there is, in addition to express contractual terms, an implied contractual term that the employee will work with the employers to make the employers' operation a viable business concern. This gives employers some scope to adopt rules and systems of work additional to those which are expressly made contractual terms, but on the other hand does not entitle the employee to follow these working rules slavishly to the detriment of the sensible operation of the business. Thus, in *Secretary of State for Employment* v. *ASLEF* [1972], where railway workers, operating a work to rule, insisted on meticulously following the employers' safety rules in such a way as to disrupt the normal train timetable, Roskill LJ said:

> It was not suggested that strictly speaking this (i.e. the rule book) formed part of the contract of employment as such. But every employer is entitled within the terms and the scope of the relevant contract of employment to give instructions to his employees and every employee is correspondingly bound to accept instructions properly and lawfully so given. The rule book seems to me to constitute instructions given by the employer to the employee in accordance with that general legal right.

On the other hand it has always been an implied contractual duty of the employers to take reasonable care for the safety of employees and since *Johnstone* v. *Bloomsbury Health Authority* [1991] it may well be arguable that such a term extends to protecting the employee against undue mental stress and that in the interests of public policy particular contractual terms as to hours of employment cannot override this implied term.

32. Dismissal in everyone's best interests

In cases where there is not clear evidence of breach of an express contractual term, the employer may consider that it is in everyone's best interests to terminate the contract with notice, or immediately with wages in lieu of notice. In either case the notice should be the contractual notice period, as set out in the contract, or, failing that, at least the minimum set out in s. 86 of the Employment Rights Act, i.e. one week if the employee has been employed over one month but under two years. (An employee with over two years' service might nevertheless complain of unfair dismissal (**34**).)

33. Continuous service

It should not be forgotten, however, that if the employee has long service with the employer or an associated employer, then, although the unsatisfactory work is in the context of a new work role, for which a new contract has been given, the new contract is likely to be, for statutory purposes, continuous with other employment within the organisation, so that the employee enjoys the benefit of the unfair dismissal provisions of the Employment Rights Act. Moreover, dismissal for incapacity (other than ill-health) will not be 'fair' if the employee has not been trained by the employer for the job.

34. Unfair dismissal

The Employment Rights Act 1996, s. 94, gives an employee with the requisite continuous employment a right not to be unfairly dismissed. If the employee can satisfy an industrial tribunal that he has been dismissed there is a presumption that the dismissal was unfair. The employer can only rebut this by satisfying the tribunal that the reason (or at least the principal reason) for the dismissal was one which the statute permits, and the employer must have acted reasonably in treating that reason as a sufficient reason for dismissal (s. 98).

The reasons most likely to be relevant to unsafe conduct are those set out in paragraphs (a) and (b) of s. 98(2), namely:

(a) related to the capability or qualifications of the employee for performing work of the kind which he was employed by the employer to do; or
(b) related to the conduct of the employee.

35. Employee's incapacity to perform the task

Any inherent incapacity of the employee to do the task required by the contract of employment ought normally to have become apparent and led to dismissal well before the end of the two years' of continuous service which must have elapsed before the employee would have the right to complain to an industrial tribunal. This provision is therefore most relevant where the employee has become incapable, often through deterioration in health, after the appointment, or if the employer has promoted the employee to a level at which that employee is unable to perform satisfactorily. However the Disability Discrimination Act 1995 may, after January 1997, require employers to give more consideration than formerly as to whether they are able to provide employment for persons who have, or who suffer during employment, disabilities. Subject to regulations made under the Act the employers will have to ensure that they do not unjustifiably discriminate against the disabled.

36. Offer of alternative employment

In cases under paragraph (a) where the problem is of the employee's capacity to do the work, the dismissal is unlikely to be fair unless the employer has properly discussed with the employee the possibilities of alternative employment within the organisation (e.g. *Spencer* v. *Paragon Wallpapers Ltd* [1977]).

37. Employee's misconduct

Paragraph (b) is in effect concerned with misconduct: unsafe conduct will fall within the general ambit of misconduct. Such conduct may disregard express safety rules, e.g. smoking in a 'No smoking' area; or conduct which though not expressly prescribed is clearly unsafe, e.g. a pilot bringing an aeroplane in to make a bad landing (*Alidair Ltd* v. *Taylor* [1978]).

38. Requirement for proper investigation

A dismissal will not normally be fair unless the employer has conducted a proper investigation to find out to the best of his ability the full circumstances of the case, and this investigation should include giving a hearing to the employee whose employment is at stake. Indeed it has fairly recently been reasserted by the House of Lords that even if the employer has a good reason for dismissal, that dismissal may be rendered unfair if the employer dismisses without following appropriate procedures (*Polkey* v. *AE Dayton Services Ltd* [1987]). In the case of a relatively minor safety lapse (e.g. smoking in an area where there is no special danger of fire or explosion assuming that there is not a no-smoking policy in force; see *Dryden* v. *Greater Glasgow Health Board* [1992]) dismissal for a first offence would not be likely to be fair. The employer would be expected to follow the warnings procedure in that employer's disciplinary code. In the case of a major lapse (as was deemed to be the situation in the *Alidair* case) a single instance of unsafe behaviour might warrant dismissal, provided that the employer had conducted a proper enquiry and was satisfied that the facts were indeed that the employee's conduct had been extremely unsafe.

39. Dismissal and the terms of the employment contract

Whether the employer is entitled to dismiss an employee for either incapacity or misconduct is largely, but not entirely, a matter of evaluating the employee's behaviour in the context of the terms of the contract. The employer's conduct in dismissing would hardly be reasonable if the employee's failure were in the context of the employer having asked the employee to do something that the employee's contract had not required, or if the employer had failed to provide training for the task. Moreover, safety rules, like any other disciplinary rules, must be clearly made known to employees and systematically enforced. It would not be fair to dismiss an employee for failing to observe a safety rule which had fallen into abeyance, even though enquiry established that there was clear evidence of the particular employee's unsafe conduct.

40. Employer's unsafe conduct

The employer should bear in mind that there have been successful complaints of unfair dismissal made by an employee who has been required to work in unsafe or unhealthy conditions. The employee will allege that there has been a constructive dismissal within the Employment Rights Act 1996, s. 95(1)(c) which covers the situation where:

> The employee terminates that contract, with, or without notice, in circumstances such that he is entitled to terminate it without notice by reason of the employer's conduct.

In order to succeed the employee must establish that the employer's conduct amounted to a breach of the contract (*Western Excavating (EEC) Ltd* v. *Sharp* [1978]); it has been held that failure to investigate a complaint about unsatisfactory safety equipment did entitle an employee to succeed in a claim for unfair dismissal (*BAC* v. *Austin* [1978]). This case law is now strengthened by the new statutory protection given to those who suffer discrimination or dismissal as a result of their responses to unsafe working conditions (see Employment Rights Act 1996 ss. 44 and 100; but see *Baddley* v. *Mehta* at p. 181).

SAFETY AND COMMERCIAL CONTRACTS

41. General

There are two major classes of commercial contracts in relation to which an organisation should certainly ensure that adequate provision has been made for safety. They are (a) contracts for the supply of articles and substances, and (b) contracts for the performance of work.

42. Supply of articles and substances

Section 6 of the 1974 Act imposes on suppliers of articles and substances a duty to ensure that they are, so far as is reasonably practicable, safe at all times when they are being used etc. by persons at work, and there are also duties both in s. 2 of the Act and in regulations (e.g. the Control of Substances Hazardous to Health Regulations) on employers to ensure that articles and substances at the workplace are safe for those employed there. Employers, therefore, through their contracts department, their safety manager and relevant line managers, need to ensure that the supplier has complied with his s. 6 duties, and that the goods supplied under the contract do conform with the contractual specification both in respect of an initial consignment and, equally importantly, in subsequent consignments. Those responsible for taking delivery of articles and substances both at the warehouse and the individual workstations should be alerted to the need for vigilance on this matter.

It hardly needs to be said that the supplier of the articles and substances must for their part ensure that the goods supplied are both in accordance with their contractual commitments and in compliance with s. 6 of the 1974 Act bearing in mind that the supplier must give priority to honouring the duty in s. 6.

43. Contracts for the performance of work

In earlier chapters discussion of the two important criminal cases of *R* v. *Swan Hunter (Shipbuilders) Ltd* and *Mailer* v. *Austin Rover Group plc* stressed the importance of safe systems when two organisations contract for one to provide labour for the performance of services for the other. The cases demonstrate the ways in which ss. 3 and 4 require the head contractor, and the other employer of labour, to liaise to ensure that neither workforce is endangered by the ways in which the respective undertakings are conducted, separately or in relation to each other, and also to ensure that visiting workers operate on premises which are safe for the purposes for which they have come on to those premises.

44. Selection of the undertaking

When entering into contracts for the performance of services, as when making contracts of employment, great care should be taken in the selection of the undertaking with whom the contract to undertake the work is made. In particular it should be borne in mind that a low tender for the work may mean (though this is not inevitably the case) that safety has not been costed. Thus it may be advisable to check the safety record of the organisation before making a contract with them.

45. Specification of work systems

In the situations under discussion, the systems under which the work is to be undertaken should be spelled out at the tender stage, or at the very latest in the contractual documents. The occupier of premises contracting for another workforce than his own to come on to, and work on, his premises should stipulate the system in which the work is to be done, both for the protection of his own workers and for the protection of his visitors, and possibly third parties: the work might create neighbourhood risks – as where, for example, construction work is being carried out near a highway.

Both the *Mailer* and *Swan Hunter* cases and the later cases on s. 3, particularly *Octel*, demonstrate that contractual arrangements that merely set out a plan of work are not on their own sufficient to ensure that safe systems will be operated. In *Mailer*, for example, it had been stipulated that the head contractor's paint thinners should not be used; they were used and this was at least one of the reasons for the catastrophe. In *Swan Hunter* the visiting workforce was not even given the blue book explaining how to weld in confined spaces. It may be doubted, however, whether merely supplying the instruction book as a contractual document would have ensured that the work was carried out in accordance with the system in the book.

Since these cases were decided Regulation 10 of the Management of Health and Safety at Work Regulations 1992 and the Construction (Design and Management) Regulations have further emphasised the need to ensure that visiting workers are properly instructed both for their own safety and the safety of others.

46. Provision of safety training

Safe systems in these cases require that the framework is set out in the contract, but it may be necessary to go further and provide the visiting workers with induction training to ensure that they operate safely within the environment in which they have to work: it may not be sufficient for an organisation merely to convey its safety rules and system to another employer. It may be necessary to communicate with the visiting workers directly and in some instances actually provide the training necessary to operate the system documented in the contract papers.

The need to communicate with workers personally about the systems they must operate when visiting a workplace was made clear in the official report of the Piper Alpha disaster. The report disclosed that a very high proportion of the workforce consisted of subcontractors' workers who were not familiar with the Piper Alpha installation and had not been introduced to the emergency procedures for that installation. Many of the victims probably were not familiar with the layout of the installation or the muster points, and may not have been familiar with the arrangements for abandoning the installation.

47. Performance monitoring

Initial training is unlikely to be sufficient; it is likely to be necessary to monitor the performance of the visiting workforce to ensure that the contractual system is complied with; both *Octel* and the *British Steel* case demonstrate this. Indeed it may be desirable to write into the contract both a stipulation that subcontractors' workers attend an induction programme on the safety systems needed and a power for the head contractor to monitor the safety performance in the currency of the contract.

48. Failure to observe safety requirements

Failure to observe safety requirements would then clearly be a breach of contract and entitle the head contractor to take steps to remedy the situation. What steps are appropriate will depend on the severity of the situation. In some instances it may be appropriate to require a particular worker to stop work and leave the site; in other situations it may be necessary to stop the whole operation. In the worst situations the conduct of the subcontractors may be so unsatisfactory as to justify requiring them to leave the work unfinished. Similarly the subcontractor should monitor the safety provision made by the head contractor and stop the work if conditions are unsafe. While for both contracting parties there is less room for dispute if the contract has spelt out what each expects from the other, and there is evidence that the express arrangements have not been honoured, there can be no doubt that, provided there is evidence of unsafe conduct, the party suffering from it would be entitled to treat the matter as a breach of the contract and respond accordingly, even if the contract itself were silent on the matter.

49. Requirements under the Framework Directive

Regulations to implement the Framework Directive may require that a person be nominated to be in overall control in circumstances where two workforces work in close proximity in addition to the requirements which the Construction (Design and Management) Regulations 1994 impose for large-scale operations.

50. Effects of commercial considerations

Commercial considerations will obviously militate against anything which delays work in progress; this in itself should be a good incentive to arrange a proper system in the first place, bearing in mind that nothing is more likely to cause disruption than an accident!

SAFE SYSTEMS AND SAFETY REPRESENTATIVES

51. General

The code of practice which accompanies the Safety Representatives and Safety Committees Regulations 1977 advises safety representatives that in performance of their functions they should keep themselves informed of their employers' health and safety policy and the organisation and arrangements for fulfilling that policy.

52. Inspection and consultation

Periodical inspections carried out by safety representatives may identify weaknesses in safety arrangements. Consultation between representatives and their constituents may also identify matters of concern.

An organisation which is safety conscious will wish to use the safety representative system to positive advantage in monitoring its safety performance: it should also be advantageous to management to use the committee as an organ for positive consultation where management is proposing to change operational systems in ways which may impact on safety.

Regulation 4A of the Safety Representatives and Safety Committees Regulations 1977 now imposes a duty on employers, who have safety representatives in compliance with that statutory system, to consult with such representatives before introducing changes in the safety regime at the workplace. In the Health and Safety (Consultation with Employees) Regulations 1996 for other than union-appointed representatives Regulation 3 replicates Regulation 4A.

Progress test 17

1. What matters should a safety policy contain?

2. What responsibilities has an employer to train employees?

3. In what circumstances may an employer fairly dismiss an employee for unsafe conduct?

4. In what ways may an organisation effectively ensure safe systems between itself and other organisations?

5. How can safety representatives help an organisation to achieve safe systems?

18

PROCEDURES AFTER AN ACCIDENT

1. Introduction

This chapter is concerned with the steps which an employer is required by law to take, and the systems which should be in place, in order to deal with an accident or dangerous occurrence. It will go beyond the strict legal requirements and discuss steps which good management practice suggests should be taken. It will not be concerned with installations to which the Control of Industrial Major Accident Hazards Regulations 1984 apply; these regulations were discussed in Chapter 10.

2. Emergency procedures

In order to ensure optimum damage control, emergency procedures must be kept in place and individuals must be trained to respond to emergency. The systems needed will vary from one workplace to another, to take into account such factors as the nature of both the workplace and the activity, and the personnel on site.

The matters which will be considered here are:

(a) prevention of injury

(b) provision of medical treatment

(c) reporting of the accident

(d) investigation of the causes of the accident.

PREVENTION OF INJURY

3. Procedures for imminent danger

The immediate response to serious and imminent danger must be to remove from the danger area all persons who might otherwise be placed at unnecessary risk. Regulation 7(1) of the Management of Health and Safety at Work Regulations 1992 now requires every employer to establish procedures to be followed in the event of serious and imminent danger to persons at work in his undertaking. Regulation 7(2) requires that the employer's procedures shall, so far as is practicable, require persons at work who are exposed to serious and imminent danger to be informed of the nature of the hazard and of the steps taken or to be taken to protect them from it. These persons must be enabled to stop work and immediately proceed to a place of safety and be prevented from resuming work in any situation where there is still a serious and imminent danger.

Regulation 7(1) also requires the employer to appoint competent persons to implement evacuation procedures, while at the same time enabling all persons if necessary to take 'appropriate steps in the absence of guidance or instruction and in the light of their knowledge and the technical means at their disposal' to stop work and proceed to a place of safety.

It will be noted that the employer's duty is not limited just to the protection of his employees: it does not, however, under Regulation 7, extend to members of the public. The catastrophic disaster on the Piper Alpha offshore installation demonstrated vividly the need for an organisation to train visiting workers as well as its own employees in emergency procedures: the vast majority of the victims of the explosions and fire on Piper Alpha were not employees of the operator of the installation and they were lamentably unaware of the layout of the installation and of its emergency procedures (the Management of Health and Safety at Work Regulations brought into effect after the Piper Alpha disaster do apply to offshore installations in the North Sea).

There are many workplaces, such as retail shops, educational establishments, hospitals and residential homes where the employer's emergency procedures will have to give consideration (very often priority) to the safety of the public.

It is implied in Regulation 7 that the systems set up to comply with the Regulations must be rehearsed from time to time: without testing the system and training of the employees concerned the employer could not have confidence in the effectiveness of the system.

The emergency procedures should include, and are usually required by law to include, emergency warning systems and identified escape routes (see for example the Fire Precautions Act). There will also need to be mustering points where a roll call can be taken: these should be at an appropriate distance from the danger and accessible without exposure to hazard, e.g. without crossing a major highway or other danger zone.

The most common hazard with which all emergency procedures will need to relate is fire, but there may be other foreseeable dangers, such as terrorist bombing, which procedures will need to cover.

4. Dealing with accident victims

In some accident situations, where the communal risk is minimal, evacuation is not needed and the primary concern is to deal with accident victims; for example, a worker might have received injury to a limb or suffered electric shock. If such an accident has occurred there may be an instinctive reaction to rescue the victim, without stopping to consider whether such intervention might lead to further personal injury. Emergency procedures need therefore to stress the importance of carrying out appropriate shut-down procedures, such as switching off a machine, or cutting off a power supply, before carrying out rescue.

PROVISION OF MEDICAL TREATMENT

5. First-aid

The accident victim must receive medical treatment speedily. Circumstances may require that the emergency ambulance service is called, with a view to hospitalisation of the victim, but first-aid should be immediately available. The Health and Safety (First-Aid) Regulations 1981 interpret first-aid as:

(a) in cases where a person will need help from a medical practitioner or nurse, treatment for the purpose of preserving life and minimising the consequences of injury and illness until such help is obtained; and

(b) treatment of minor injuries which would otherwise receive no treatment or which do not need treatment by a medical practitioner or nurse.

6. Provision of first-aid equipment

Regulation 3 requires employers to ensure that there is available such equipment and facilities as are adequate and appropriate in the circumstances for enabling first-aid to be rendered to their employees if they are injured or become ill at work. The requirements of the regulations apply to every workplace, unless a special exemption has been granted (Regulation 6), or the situation is within one of the categories identified in Regulation 7 (diving operations, merchant shipping and certain mines). The exempted situations are dealt with in other special regulations. It is also the duty of self-employed persons to provide, or ensure that there is provided, such equipment, if any, as is adequate and appropriate to enable them to render first-aid to themselves.

7. Availability of qualified first-aiders

Regulation 3 also requires employers to ensure that there are sufficient suitably qualified persons available to render necessary first-aid to their employees. Persons nominated 'first-aiders' must normally have been properly trained; that is they must at least have had the training, and obtained the qualifications, the Health and Safety Executive has approved. Exceptionally, there may, however, be circumstances in which it is sufficient to appoint an untrained person to take charge of the situation and the equipment. This will be the case only where either the absence of the first-aider is temporary, or the nature of the undertaking, the size of the workforce, or the location of the establishment (i.e. proximity to other sources of medical assistance, such as a hospital) make this minimal provision acceptable. The code of practice which accompanies the regulations makes it clear that it is unlikely to be sufficient to have only minimal provision for the time that a regular first-aider is on holiday.

8. Information to employees

Employers must inform their employees of the arrangements for the provision of first-aid, including the location of equipment, facilities and personnel.

9. General application

These regulations replace many older regulatory codes which previously related to specific workplaces or activities, such as factories or offices. Unlike some earlier regulations, they do not stipulate the exact number of qualified first-aiders needed at any workplace, or the exact equipment to be provided. They leave it ultimately to the employer to decide what is 'adequate and appropriate in the circumstances': the code of practice gives some guidance on these issues.

REPORTING OF ACCIDENTS

10. General

The revised accident reporting regulations, the Reporting of Injuries, Diseases and Dangerous Occurrences Regulations 1995, came into force on 1 April 1996; these regulations replace the 1985 regulations of the same name and four other sets of regulations. The new regulations were prompted by perceived shortcomings in the earlier version and incorporate changes recommended by recent judicial and public inquiries (including the Fennel inquiry into the Kings Cross fire, the Hidden inquiry into the Clapham rail crash and the Cullen inquiry into the Piper Alpha disaster). There are also changes intended to improve the flow of information about patterns of occupational accidents, and to provide a better idea of the incidence of accidents to members of the public, particularly in relation to sports activities. The new requirement is to report injuries to the public, which arise out of or in connection with work, where a member of the public has to be removed from the scene of the accident under medical care. HSC expect that the requirement to report public injuries will mean that an additional 15,000 injuries a year will be reported.

11. Application of the regulations

The new regulations apply to almost all work activities, covering not only accidents causing personal injury (including fatalities and 'conditions'), but work-related diseases and certain dangerous occurrences (i.e. incidents in which no-one was injured). Not only are the provisions of the regulations detailed and complex but they are supplemented by a number of detailed schedules. The regulations do not apply to the armed forces, civil aviation or the situations governed by the Ionising Radiations Regulations 1985.

12. Duty to report

The regulations impose the obligation to report upon 'the responsible person'. Regulation 2 interprets 'responsible person'. Where, as will normally be the case, the victim is 'an employee at work', the responsible person is the victim's employer. In the case of the victim being a 'trainee' the duty is on the 'trainer'. In other cases the obligation falls on 'the person for the time being having control of the premises . . . at which the accident . . .' or dangerous occurrence or disease occurred. The occupier's obligation only arises, however, if the occupier is carrying on a trade or business at the premises. In effect the occupier's obligation is in relation to injuries involving the self-employed and members of the public. Employers remain liable to report accidents suffered by their employees, even though these occurred when they were undertaking work at premises where the employer was not the occupier. Finally there are some special situations, such as mines, where the obligation is placed on the manager, and quarries where it falls on the owner.

13. Specific injuries or dangerous occurrences

Regulation 3(1) imposes an obligation to report specified injuries or dangerous occurrences. In effect the specified situations represent the more serious situations including major injury suffered as a result of physical violence. In these situations the responsible person must forthwith notify the enforcing authority thereof by the quickest practicable means; and within 10 days send a report thereof to the enforcing authority on a form approved for the purposes of this Regulation.

In practice reporting to the Health and Safety Executive (or the relevant local authority) will initially be by telephone and then, within the week, on form F2508.

14. Exemptions from notification

The notification requirements do not apply to injury suffered by patients undergoing treatment in a hospital or surgery, work-related road transport injuries or injuries suffered in road construction or maintenance; or in building operations on a building adjacent to or over a road (Regulation 10).

15. Injuries to be notified at once

Regulation 3(2) specifies the injuries and conditions to which the reporting procedure applies. Those to be notified forthwith are:

- fracture other than to fingers, thumbs or toes
- amputation
- dislocation of the shoulder, hip, knee or spine
- loss of sight (temporary or permanent)
- chemical or hot metal burn to the eye or any penetrating injury to the eye

- injury resulting from an electric shock or electrical burn leading to unconsciousness or requiring resuscitation or admittance to hospital for more than 24 hours
- any other injury: leading to hypothermia, heat-induced illness or unconsciousness; or requiring resuscitation; or requiring admittance to hospital for more than 24 hours
- unconsciousness caused by asphyxia or exposure to harmful substances or biological agents
- acute illness requiring medical treatment where there is reason to believe that this resulted from exposure to a biological agent or its toxins or infected material.

16. To be notified within seven days

Those to be reported within seven days are any accident which has resulted in over three days' consecutive incapacity for work (Regulation 3(3)).

17. Death of an employee

If an employee dies as a result of a reportable accident within a year of the accident occurring, the employer has to inform the enforcing authority, in writing, as soon as he learns of the death, whether or not the accident was reported (Regulation 4).

18. Specified diseased to be reported

There is a duty to report cases of certain specified diseases. Schedule 2 lists the diseases and the work activities for which they are reportable. The duty to report only rests on an employer, and then only if a doctor has notified the employer in writing that the employee or trainee has been diagnosed as suffering from a relevant disease. A self-employed person has a similar duty to report.

Reportable diseases include:

- certain poisonings
- some skin diseases such as occupational dermatitis, skin cancer, chrome ulcer, oil folliculitis/acne
- lung diseases including occupational asthma, farmer's lung, pneumoconiosis, asbestosis, mesothelioma
- infections such as: leptospirosis, hepatitis, tuberculosis, anthrax, legionellosis and tetanus
- other conditions such as: occupational cancer; certain musculoskeletal disorders, decompression illness and hand-arm vibration syndrome.

19. Keeping records

Regulation 7 requires the responsible person to record any event which has had to be reported, and keep this record for at least three years from the date when it was made. The record has to contain the information required by Schedule 3 of the regulations. This is, in the case of a reportable accident or occurrence:

    (a) Date and time of accident or dangerous occurrence.
    (b) The following particulars of the person affected:
        (*i*) full name;
        (*ii*) occupation;
        (*iii*) nature of injury or condition.
    (c) Place where the accident or dangerous occurrence happened.
    (d) A brief description of the circumstances.
    (e) The date on which the event was first reported to the relevant enforcing authority and the method by which the event was reported.

There are similar requirements for reportable diseases.

20. Dangerous occurrences

Schedule 1 lists the dangerous occurrences which have to be reported, even though there has been no personal injury or notifiable disease resulting from the occurrence. The Schedule is in four parts: the first is general; the remaining parts relate only to mines, quarries and railways. Part I specifies dangerous occurrences in relation to:

1. Collapse, overturning or failure of load-bearing parts of lifts and lifting equipment.
2. Explosion, collapse or bursting of any closed vessel or associated pipework.
3. Failure of any freight container in any of its load-bearing parts.
4. Plant or equipment coming into contact with overhead power lines.
5. Electrical short circuit or overload causing fire or explosion.
6. Any unintentional explosion, misfire, failure of demolition to cause the intended collapse, projection of material beyond a site boundary, injury caused by an explosion.
7. Accidental release of a biological agent likely to cause severe human illness.
8. Failure of industrial radiography or irradiation equipment to de-energise or return to its safe position after the intended exposure period.
9. Malfunction of breathing apparatus while in use or during testing immediately before use.
10. Failure or endangering of diving equipment, the trapping of a diver, an explosion near a diver, or an uncontrolled ascent.
11. Collapse or partial collapse of a scaffold over five metres high, or erected near water where there could be a risk of drowning after a fall.
12. Unintended collision of a train with any vehicle.
13. Dangerous occurrences at a well (other than a water well).
14. Dangerous occurrence at a pipeline.

15. Failure of any load-bearing fairground equipment, or derailment or unintended collision of cars or trains.
16. A road tanker carrying a dangerous substance overturns, suffers serious damage, catches fire or the substance is released.
17. A dangerous substance conveyed by road is involved in a fire or released.

The following dangerous occurrences are reportable except in relation to off-shore workplaces:

18. Unintended collapse of: any building or structure under construction, alteration or demolition where over five tonnes of material falls; a wall or floor in a place of work; any falsework.
19. Explosion or fire causing suspension of normal work for over 24 hours.
20. Sudden, uncontrolled release in a building of: 100 kg or more of flammable liquid; 10 kg of flammable liquid above its boiling point; 10 kg or more of flammable gas; or 500 kg of these substances if the release is in the open air.
21. Accidental release of any substance which may damage health.

Additional categories of dangerous occurrences apply to mines, quarries, relevant transport systems (railways etc.) and offshore workplaces.

21. Site of occurrence

When an accident or occurrence has to be reported to the enforcing authority the site of the occurrence should not be disturbed until after the relevant inspectors have either visited and completed their enquiry at the site, or indicated that they do not intend to visit. Nevertheless immediate steps should be taken to isolate the danger, e.g. cut off the power supply, or fence off the area where the accident occurred. Any victim will, of course, have been removed as quickly as possible, but it may be appropriate to mark out, perhaps with chalk, the position and circumstances in which the accident left the victim.

22. Additional reports

In addition to reporting to the enforcing authority good management, and perhaps contractual obligations, suggest the following reports should be made with considerable speed to the following:

(a) *The personnel department*. Applicable only where the victim is an employee.

(b) *Next of kin*. In the case of an employee, the personnel department's records may include the name and address of a person the victim has stated should be notified in case of accident – this may not, of course, be next of kin! It would be good practice to keep such information on record and to act on it rather than to search for the person whom the law would classify as next of kin. It will be a matter of company policy to decide whether communication with relatives should be through the personnel department or managers more closely associated with the victims.

(c) *Notify head office.* If the accident has occurred at a branch or when working away from the employers' premises this may be expedient. This is a matter which should be addressed when formulating company policy: it may be sufficient to inform the personnel department.

(d) *The organisation's insurance company.* How this report is to be made will no doubt be dictated by the insurance company concerned.

(e) *The employer of the victim.* This will only be applicable where the victim was the employee of another organisation than the occupier of the site where the accident occurred.

(f) *The safety representative.* The Safety Representatives and Safety Committees Regulations 1977 give union safety representatives a qualified right to inspect where there has been a notifiable accident or dangerous occurrence or a notifiable disease (*see* Chapter 12). There is no obligation on an employer to notify relevant safety representatives of their rights, but it is suggested that it would be good management practice to cooperate with safety representatives in such circumstances.

(g) *The nominated person in mines.* The regulations give to persons nominated by the trade union under the Mines and Quarries Act the right to receive notice of fatal accidents, major accidents or dangerous occurrences.

CARRYING OUT AN INVESTIGATION

23. Management investigation

Quite independently of any investigation which the inspectorate, safety representatives or the insurance company may conduct, management should conduct an inquiry with the objectives of identifying the causes of the occurrence and preventing such an event occurring again. The inquiry will almost certainly include:

(a) interviewing personnel, at both management and junior level, including, but not confined to, taking statements from witnesses

(b) inspecting the site

(c) inspecting plant and equipment, and testing substances.

This inquiry may also extend to taking advice from experts not in the employment of the firm.

In *Waugh* v. *British Railways Board* [1980] the House of Lords held that certain accident reports might be called in evidence in any subsequent litigation. In that case a victim's widow sued for damages, alleging that the defendant employers had negligently caused her husband's death. She sought disclosure of a report prepared by the defendants, partly for the purposes of establishing the cause of the accident and partly for the purpose of preparing for litigation.

Their Lordships dismissed the defendants' claim that the report was a privileged document, holding that the primary purpose of making the report was not related to litigation.

24. Disclosure of management investigation's results

It seems certain, therefore, that the majority of reports made as a result of in-house investigation following an accident would not be privileged. Nevertheless in the interests of identifying the cause of the mishap and introducing better workplace systems, such reports should be made. It is suggested that a well-managed organisation should not be unduly perturbed by the implications of this case.

Such investigations should result at least in reports to both the safety committee and to management.

CONCLUSION

25. Overview

Setting up and maintaining safe systems should keep to a minimum the occasions in which accidents and ill-health result from poor working conditions. Unfortunately hazards are all too often only recognised with hindsight, after the event. It is only small consolation that wisdom comes with hindsight and leads to improvements for the future.

Wisdom comes from experience at national as well as organisational level, as a result of rapidly expanding technical knowledge. This, and the desire of the European Community for harmonisation of occupational health and safety laws, makes it likely that before long further EC occupational health and safety Directives will be adopted and in due course reflected in the law of the UK. However, it seems equally likely that for the foreseeable future any amendments to the detail of the law will take place within the framework set out in these pages.

It is to be hoped that with the development of safety awareness, readers of this book will not have to put into effect the procedures set out in its final chapter. But it would nevertheless be unwise, and for the most part contrary to legal requirements, not to have the procedures in place to meet the eventuality of a systems breakdown leading to personal injury.

Progress test 18

1. What measures should an organisation take to ensure 'damage control' after an accident has occurred, and in what order should it take them?

2. What are the principal provisions of the Reporting of Accidents and Dangerous Occurrences Regulations?

3. On whom does the obligation to report normally fall?

4. What information has to be reported?

5. What information must be entered in the accident book?

6. What are the provisions of the First-Aid Regulations?

7. Why should an organisation take particular care to ensure that its accident reports are thorough and accurate?

INDEX

Accidents
    competent persons, 278
    Control of Industrial Major Accidents
        Hazards Regulations 1984, 148–9,
        277
    emergencies, 277–8
    fire precautions, 278
    first-aid, 279–80
    information, 280
    investigations, 285–6
    Management of Health and Safety at Work
        Regulations 1992, 277
    medical treatment, 279–80
    offshore installations, 278
    prevention, 277–9
    procedure, 277–87
    reporting, 280–5
    safety cases, 148–9
    victims, 278–9
Acts of Parliament *see* Legislation
Agriculture, 47
Appeals, 18, 19, 165–6
Appraisals, 269
Armed services, 46
Asbestos, 149

Best practicable means, 68
Breach of statutory duty, 231–50
    causation, 242
    civil actions for, 31–2, 34–5, 109
    codes of conduct, 32
    common law modifications, 245–9
    consumer protection, 245–9
    contributory negligence, 254, 255
    damages, 32, 202, 210, 232
    defences to breach of duty, 243–4, 246–8
    defendants, 238, 239–40
    definition, 231–2
    directors, 249
    due diligence, 244
    employees, 237–8
    equipment, 235–6
    exceptions, 237–8
    expansion of range of duties, 233
    'factories', 236–7
    guidance, 235

Health and Safety at Work etc Act 1974,
    66
    inconsistency, 241–2
    interpretation, 110
    machinery, 238
    Management of Health and Safety at Work
        Regulations 1992, 244
    negligence, 232, 234
    occupiers' liability, 238–9
    precedent, 234–5
    product safety, 59, 245–9
    proof, 235–43
    'reasonably practicable', 240, 242, 244
    safety of premises, 96
    self-employed, 237
    standard of care, 66, 240
    standards, 234
    statutory interpretation, 238
    strict liability, 22, 240, 241

Case law, 9–11
Causation, 226, 227, 242–3
Charter of Fundamental Social Rights of
    Workers 1989, 13–14
Chemicals (Hazard Information and
    Packaging) Regulations, 152–3
Civil law, 14–15 *see also* Compensation,
    Damages
    breach of statutory duty, 31–2, 34–5, 109
    compensation, 15
    courts, 17–18
    liability, 21, 109–10, 141, 193–201
        exclusion of, 137
Codes of practice, 141
    approval, 159
    breach of, 159
    breach of statutory duty, 32
    Control of Substances Hazardous to Health
        Regulations 1988, 152
    directives, 51
    employers' duties, 74
    Health and Safety at Work etc Act 1974,
        49–50, 51, 157–9,
    Management of Health and Safety at Work
        Regulations 1992, 128–30
    notices, 159